PRAISE PAGE

"This magnificent book provides not only a thoughtful view of modern American history, but deep insight into a vital question: why does the United States feel such a drive to intervene in so many countries so far from our own shores? With vivid storytelling and magisterial knowledge, Angulo takes us on a century-long journey from the Spanish-American War to the War on Terror. Along the way, he uncovers themes that shape both our approach to the world and our national psyche."
—Stephen Kinzer, author of *Overthrow: America's Century of Regime Change From Hawaii to Iraq*

"*Empire and Education* is the first comprehensive account of America's educational occupations abroad. It is a series of compelling narratives of the US governments' successive efforts to remake other nation's educational systems in its own image and interests. Angulo shows how American educational debates were exported into foreign territories but then distorted by the power and interests driving the occupations. Beautifully written and unfailingly insightful, this book is the place to go to get a broad overview of US history as an imperial power as well as an introduction to individual educational occupations from Puerto Rico to Iraq."
—Julie Reuben, professor, Harvard Graduate School of Education

"Angulo hits hard at the imperialist designs of the United States, in places such as the Philippines, Japan, Germany, Puerto Rico, Afghanistan, and elsewhere. He shows how education operates as an integral part of the imperialist effort. Readers should pay attention to, and heed, this compelling analysis."
—Wayne J. Urban, Paul W. Bryant Professor of Education, The University of Alabama, Tuscaloosa

"History of education is sometimes—mistakenly—seen as a narrow subject, whereas, of necessity, education policies are always intimately connected with the social and political world. A. J. Angulo's investigation of American imperialist ambition pays close attention to concomitant self-serving transformations of indigenous education systems.

This is a shocking story that should be essential reading for historians and government alike."
—Pam Hirsch, Faculty of Education,
University of Cambridge

"While the history of the American empire is doubtless a story of greed and power, it's also one of American textbooks, civics lessons, and schoolmarms in foreign lands. Angulo deftly weaves these two stories together into a compelling, erudite, and much-needed history of imperialism and education abroad. Read, enjoy, and learn. I did."
—Julian Go, associate professor of
Sociology, Boston University

"This book is by far the most original and comprehensive treatment of the complex nature of education as a tool of American foreign policy. Angulo's writing is crisp, and his arguments are powerful."
—Thomas G. Dyer, University Professor Emeritus,
University of Georgia

"Angulo has written a provocative and timely cautionary tale. In this highly readable account, he takes a hard look at how greed has trumped goodwill far too many times when the United States has gone to war and become an occupying power—with consequences that should concern us all."
—Lisa Jarvinen, assistant professor of American Studies,
La Salle University

"[Angulo] expands the record, reorders it, and breaks new ground. Strictly speaking, *Empire and Education* is not a hole-filling revisionist work. This story has never been told in exactly the same way . . . I see *Empire and Education* as a significant contribution to US history that reorients standard treatments of education, shifting it from the wings to center stage. Along the way, it expands and deepens the history of education as a crucial specialization. There is nothing like it on the market."
—Donald Warren, professor emeritus,
Indiana University

"A. J. Angulo has gone where no historian has ventured before. *Empire and Education*'s sophisticated and complex interpretation of American education as a global hegemonic force places American education within the geopolitics of world events. Simply groundbreaking."
—Derrick P. Alridge, professor,
University of Virginia

PREVIOUS PUBLICATIONS

William Barton Rogers and the Idea of MIT (Baltimore, MD: 2009).

    Nominated for the 2010 Linda Eisenmann Prize for Distinguished Scholarship
    Winner of the 2009 Richard Slatten Prize for Excellence in Virginia Biography
    Winner of the 2009 History of Education Society Outstanding Book Award

Empire and Education

Empire and Education

A History of Greed and Goodwill from the War of 1898 to the War on Terror

A. J. Angulo

EMPIRE AND EDUCATION
Copyright © A. J. Angulo, 2012.

All rights reserved.

First published in 2012 by
PALGRAVE MACMILLAN®
in the United States—a division of St. Martin's Press LLC,
175 Fifth Avenue, New York, NY 10010.

Where this book is distributed in the UK, Europe and the rest of the world, this is by Palgrave Macmillan, a division of Macmillan Publishers Limited, registered in England, company number 785998, of Houndmills, Basingstoke, Hampshire RG21 6XS.

Palgrave Macmillan is the global academic imprint of the above companies and has companies and representatives throughout the world.

Palgrave® and Macmillan® are registered trademarks in the United States, the United Kingdom, Europe and other countries.

ISBN: 978–1–137–02451–0 (Hc)
ISBN: 978–1–137–02452–7 (Pb)

Library of Congress Cataloging-in-Publication Data

Angulo, A. J.
   Empire and education : a history of greed and goodwill from the War of 1898 to the War on Terror / A.J. Angulo.
     p. cm.
   ISBN 978-1-137-02451-0—
   ISBN 978-1-137-02452-7
    1. United States—Foreign relations—20th century. 2. United States—Foreign economic relations—20th century. 3. United States—History, Military—20th century. 4. Business and politics—United States—History—20th century. 5. Democratization—Government policy—United States. 6. Democracy—Government policy—United States. 7. Educational assistance, American—History—20th century. I. Title.

E744.A66 2012
327.73009′04—dc23   2012010453

A catalogue record of the book is available from the British Library.

Design by Newgen Imaging Systems (P) Ltd., Chennai, India.

First edition: August 2012

To William F. Mills

Contents

List of Figures		xi
Preface		xiii
One	After the *Maine*	1
Two	Benevolent Education	19
Three	Culture and Citizenship	33
Four	Hampton Creole	51
Five	By Executive Order	67
Six	Greatest Generation	87
Seven	Zero Hour	99
Eight	In Perpetuity	113
Nine	Private Matter	125
Ten	Complex Problem	137
Acknowledgments		143
Notes		145
Bibliography		169
Index		179

Figures

4.1 US military occupation government budget allocations (in Gourdes), 1928–1929   57

4.2 Haitian student population distribution, 1928–1929   57

Preface

Two years after the dust had settled from the War of 1898, Henry Cabot Lodge picked up his pen and wrote a letter to his colleague, William Howard Taft, that identified the major impulse for going to war with Spain. Lodge at the time was a rising senator from Massachusetts and one of the most vocal advocates of American expansion abroad. Taft had already been sent to lead one of the colonial "possessions" recently acquired from the Spanish empire. "It has been my firm belief," Lodge argued about Cuba, Puerto Rico, and especially the Philippines, that these US acquisitions "would not only become an important market to us for our finished goods but what is still more important would furnish a large opportunity for the investment of surplus capital."[1]

What Lodge didn't know at the time was that he'd not only put his finger on why the United States fought in Asia for a conflict that began in the Caribbean, but also on what would become the central problem of the American century. This problem shaped the course and character of American interventions abroad from the War of 1898 to the War on Terror.[2]

Lodge explained it this way. The overaccumulation of wealth in the hands of a few distorted market realities. As economic titans moved their concentrated wealth almost in unison from one investment to another, they created "needless competition" that drove up prices for otherwise average investments. American investors, industrialists, and Wall Street bankers began to clamor for new ways to make a profit and this, in part, fueled the drive to create an American empire abroad, or as he put it, "a new field for American enterprise and capital." These new fields not only provided a crucial outlet for selling US goods, but also provided valuable natural resources and material that investors sought to exploit. Other factors certainly played a role. Newspapers of the era, looking to sell copies and also turn a profit, created heroes and villains, painting simple portraits of individuals deserving praise or wrath. The stories stirred public sentiment and generated pressure on President William McKinley to do something about a series of islands in the Pacific that he admitted not being able to find on a map "within two thousand miles." The military, too, wanted to expand their horizons as much as those wanting new places to invest. Securing bases in the Caribbean and the Pacific meant securing safe harbors for US naval forces, such as the Great White Fleet, that wanted to flex their muscles to the world. Even a slight sense of inferiority—when compared with the British, Dutch, French, and Spanish Empires—contributed to the desire to expand. Some, like Lodge, believed that the only way to be taken seriously on the world's stage was to have an empire too.[3]

To justify the inevitable human cost to acquire this "new field," expansionists like Lodge needed a humanitarian rationale and many turned to the idea of exporting American education and democracy. The two—education and democracy—had been joined together in the American psyche since Thomas Jefferson fretted about the lack of public education in the United States and warned that "if a nation expects to be ignorant and free... it expects what never was and never will be." Warnings of this kind led to the establishment of the first systems of public education in early to mid-nineteenth-century New England. Self-governance, came the refrain, required an educated citizenry. Schools began to represent one of the critical pillars of the republic. After the Civil War, two kinds of educational ideals began to flourish: one centered on literacy, civics, liberal arts, and preparation for living in a democracy and another centered on technical, industrial, and agricultural training to prepare for making a living. Many viewed the two as mutually exclusive and even the most prominent advocate for industrial education, Booker T. Washington, suggested that only after learning technical skills or a trade should African Americans begin to worry themselves about what it means to live in a democratic society. Washington's counterpart, W. E. B. DuBois, rejected the industrial education argument and demanded immediate political equality and access to education that would fully emancipate African Americans and prevent the potential of a second slavery. By the time the United States flirted with the idea of acquiring an empire of its own, industrialization had transformed just about everything in the country, including schools and ideas about education. Schools expanded in size and grew in number. As enrollments skyrocketed due to urbanization, immigration, and population explosion, school leaders turned to the factory model as the solution to their problems. They began to see themselves as chief executive officers and managers of factories that produced learning and who faced constant demands to increase production. Through subdividing labor using grade-levels and centralizing decision-making through school boards, schools attempted to meet the demands of the progressive era. Many resisted this trend. Those who did, like John Dewey, believed that schools had lost sight of the need to prepare students for participating in a democracy. He and others argued that a factory model of education prepared students to do little more than accept factory work-life.[4]

Between Lodge and Dewey, there existed a wide spectrum of interests and values that resurface throughout the story of *Empire and Education*. It's as much a story of greed and wealth as it is of teachers, schools, and democracy. It's a story that contains scoundrels and crooks as well as the high-minded and those with high hopes. It's a story that involves familiar names, colorful personalities, and obscure US figures who impacted the lives of others abroad in the name of citizens back home. It's ultimately a story that spans 110 years of American efforts to extract wealth and promote democracy abroad.

During this period, the United States had a hand in a variety of coups, revolutions, and regime changes. Officials from the White House and State Department as well as representatives from corporations and conglomerates signed off on actions against democratically elected leaders around the world. Theodore Roosevelt, for instance, fomented an independence revolution in Panama against Colombia to negotiate a better canal agreement with a newer, weaker state in 1903. When he wondered about the legality of his actions, Roosevelt's counsel jested that "you have shown that you were accused of seduction, and you have conclusively proved you were guilty of rape." Around the same time, lumber and mining companies leaned on the United States to do something about Nicaragua's President Jose Zelaya who fought them over violations of the country's tax and labor policies. Taft sent the Navy, Zelaya resigned, and a corporation-friendly regime was installed by 1910. Honduran president Miguel Davila met a similar fate when he tried to tame American banana interests in his country and was replaced in 1912. This brash form of "big stick," gunboat, and dollar diplomacy began to fade with the creation and expansion of the CIA, after which regime changes became ever more sophisticated, as in Iran, Guatemala, Chile, and elsewhere. These stealthy operations were implemented for a variety of political, economic, and ideological reasons and fill the pages of a well-established body of literature.[5]

This book will not explore any of these episodes of American adventurism abroad. Rather, the focus of this book is on one particular type of intervention: the explicit US occupation of a foreign country. Unlike other kinds of interventions, the occupations selected for this book translated—in real and practical terms—into complete control over a foreign population and its government. Unlike shadowy, covert operations, explicit US occupations, in almost all cases, decided and openly published new laws and regulations for a foreign land and its people. The open, public, transparent quality of these US takeovers allows for an exploration of the economic and educational policies that characterized the occupations of Cuba, the Philippines, Puerto Rico, Haiti, the Dominican Republic, Japan, Germany, Afghanistan, and Iraq. The policies tell us whose interests won out and whose were ignored or dismissed. They also tell us much about whether the US occupations served to spread democracy around the world or to spread an American empire or to accomplish some combination of the two.

At the heart of these occupations stood two progressive ideals born during the time of the War of 1898 and, in one form or another, carried right through to the War on Terror: humanitarian progressivism and efficiency-oriented progressivism. Humanitarian progressivism at home gave rise to movements that sought to improve the quality of life for all, but particularly for poor, immigrant, and working-class families. Out of humanitarian progressivism came settlement houses, temperance movements, women's rights and suffrage movements, labor rights, child labor laws, compulsory and democratic education, antiracketeering laws, trust-busting, and antimonopoly laws, among many other movements and legal initiatives. Efficiency progressives had an entirely different goal. They sought to increase productivity, wealth extraction, exploitation of human and natural resources, and, of course, profits. They sought to externalize costs for doing business through tax and labor policies that favored their interests, political contributions to protect their investments, and government subsidies that gave them a marketplace advantage. They also produced an army of efficiency experts who traveled across the country using time management studies that tracked the movements and behaviors of factory workers to squeeze as much productivity out of labor as possible.[6]

The two kinds of progressives clashed at home as the closing of the western frontier meant that the seemingly unlimited natural resources of the American west had reached its natural boundary with the Pacific shoreline. Efficiency experts seeking to maximize profits collided with a new reality that eliminated child labor from the factories and thwarted the trend toward consolidation, monopolization, or what we now call "too big to fail." In short, humanitarian progressives working to clean up life at home inspired efficiency progressives to move their operations abroad and seek ways to extract wealth, productivity, and resources beyond US borders where these new laws didn't apply.

The dual character of American progressivism can be seen in the US occupations abroad from Cuba to Iraq. In each case, the humanitarian element came first as the catalyst for mobilizing the American public to support these interventions in the affairs and lives of people in other parts of the world. People were moved by stories of cruelty, injustice, and inhumanity and created positive associations with the idea of spreading the American way of life abroad and teaching others about the merits of American-style democracy and education. They were also moved by the desire to end humanitarian crises and rebuild nations in the western democratic image. But then came the hard part: keeping informed about the US occupations that resulted from these calls to humanitarian duty. US occupations established in response to these calls were rarely monitored or tracked as carefully by the American public as the original rationale for intervening in the first place. Corporate and industrial representatives, as seen throughout the twentieth century, often moved in to extract wealth and advantage when the flag-waving turned to other crises or injustices. These representatives typically held beliefs and interests that conflicted with the aims and desires of those working toward socially beneficial ends. And what remained, as the limelight turned elsewhere, was a struggle between strains of humanitarian and efficiency progressivism that Americans left in their wake.

This book is about that struggle and how it played out in terms of the economic and educational policies the United States has implemented beyond its own borders. It's the story of *Empire and Education* and it begins with a fistfight in Cuba.

Chapter One
After the *Maine*

The fight didn't last long. By all accounts, in fact, it was a single punch that finished it. Alexis Frye had decked the quartermaster of the USS *Sedgwick*, crystallizing Frye's reputation as both a hero and a villain.[1]

For obvious reasons, Frye had a reputation as a hero with Cuban teachers, and with all of Cuba for that matter, because of the stands he'd taken as superintendent of schools during the first US occupation of the island. He wasn't like the other occupation officials, although he started out sharing many of their views, particularly at the outset of the War of 1898. By the summer of 1900, however, his views had changed and he was on the *Sedgwick* because he had dreamed up and turned into reality a plan to take more than twelve hundred Cuban teachers to Harvard. Frye had a simple request of Quartermaster J. W. McHarg—he wanted the seaman to assign cabins to the Cuban ladies. Many were tired, seasick, and wanted some privacy, not to mention relief from the scalding sun of early July. McHarg ignored them, or so it appeared to Frye. For months, Frye had gone over every detail of this historic trip and he'd be damned if this would ruin its first day. Now red-faced and angry, he repeated his request; the quartermaster continued to busy himself with other matters, at which point Frye started assigning rooms himself. McHarg found out, tried to stop what Frye was doing, and they got into an argument. The argument quickly turned into a scuffle, and it ended in the most improbable way with Frye, an author and former geography teacher, punching out the seaman on the ship's deck. Frye completed the room assignments and instantly become a hero to the several hundred teachers aboard the *Sedgwick*. The knockout symbolized that he truly had their best interest at heart and would do whatever it took to make sure they were well served. To the rest of Cuba, the punch was probably cathartic. Freud, who was working on his theories of psychoanalysis at the time, might have said that the great frustrations of the Cuban people, pent up and repressed as they were under the weight of US occupation, found a release through this blow. What we know for sure is that Frye could do little wrong in the eyes of Cubans after the *Sedgwick* incident.[2]

To occupation officials, on the other hand, Frye was a villain, a traitor even. The person in command of the occupation at the time, General Leonard Wood, accused Frye of "the most intense radicalism" and called him "a very desirable man to get rid of." The situation only got hotter for Frye when Wood and others discovered that he'd raised the Cuban flag on the US naval ships during their voyage and that he'd translated the Cuban anthem into English, replacing one line that read "Dread no longer the government of Spain" with "Dread no longer the foreign oppressor." This was too much for Wood. Frye's views about the occupation, he thought, stoked the flames of Cuban nationalism. What Wood wanted was pacification and, ultimately, US annexation of the island.[3]

The differences between Frye and Wood, simple as they may seem, mirrored larger forces at work in the long history of US interest in Cuba, the conflicting ideas about its occupation, and the political maneuverings having to do with the island's future. Although Frye's entrance came midway through the story of America's takeover of Cuba from 1898 to 1902, his efforts with the country's education system made public very real tensions that existed within the occupation government. Wood himself suggested in reference to support for Cuban schools that "in no better way can the people of the United States show their interest in the building up of Cuba." Frye agreed, but had different ideas about how to do this. This trip and summer session at Harvard was, to his mind, not a gift "from nation to nation, but from teacher to teacher." Whatever the differences that stood between Frye and Wood, they both came to the conclusion that education had become a centerpiece in the US occupation of Cuba.[4]

* * *

Long before the arrival of Frye, Wood, and the rest of the US military government, Cuba had caught the attention of American political and commercial interests. President James Polk in the late 1840s considered prying the island from Spanish control and bringing it into the Union as a slave state. Industrialists viewed the island as indispensible for US economic development as trade between the two rapidly increased during the second half of the nineteenth century. While attempts at territorial annexation had failed, an "annexation of trade" emerged with Cuba (and much of Latin America) through reciprocity treaties. This occurred largely after the so-called Ten Years' War from 1868 to 1878 that Cuban independence fighters waged against the Spanish colonial government. Economic interest in Cuba sharply increased as the Spanish grip over the colony began to weaken and the price of sugar declined in the 1880s. Presidents Harrison and Cleveland pushed for "open door" policies to allow for greater US expansion of American capital into Cuba and the rest of Latin America. McKinley's Tariff of 1890 continued the trend, creating a climate conducive to US investment in Cuban manufacturing and sugar plantations.[5]

The turning point that made the idea of invading and occupying Cuba more plausible came with Madrid's appointment of General Valeriano Weyler to the seat of power in Havana. As governor of the colony beginning in 1896, his charge was unambiguous: pacify the natives. American newspapers of the era facilitated invasion talk with sensational stories about the brutality of Weyler's crackdown. Known as "the Butcher," Weyler became the villain that helped mobilize the United States to action.[6]

The Weyler campaign inspired a great surge of activity by US economic and military expansionists. In the year of the US invasion, New England papers began to clamor about how "war will help...productive industry" and that "any amount spent freeing Cuba would return an extraordinary profit." Massachusetts senator Henry Cabot Lodge also longed for a piece of Cuba. Lodge considered the island "a necessity" because he believed the United States needed "at least one strong naval station" in the "West Indies." Along with these discussions about the profitability of a Cuban land grab was also a reference to the need to help Cubans defend themselves against the Spanish troops. The rhetoric implying the need for action against Spain had built up enormous pressure in America, especially in New York and Washington, DC. But the culminating explosion occurred at sea. When the USS *Maine*, stationed at the time in a Cuban harbor, exploded, taking with it the lives of 266 marines, the path to war had already been paved.

Spain was quickly blamed, attacked, defeated, and ultimately relieved of three colonial possessions: the Philippines, Cuba, and Puerto Rico. Later, investigators found that the *Maine*'s own powder had caused the ship's destruction.[7]

Then came the military occupation. The United States installed an occupation government in Havana that placed a mix of American officials and Cuban nationals in cabinet-level positions. Cabinet posts held by nationals were in many cases in name only. Actual power resided in the hands of the US military governor and his advisors. The single obstacle to their complete control of the island was the Teller Amendment passed before the invasion and occupation. According to the amendment, the United States wanted a free and independent Cuba and the removal of Spanish forces and influence. In intervening in Cuba, America "disclaims any disposition or intention to exercise sovereignty, jurisdiction, or control over said Island except for the pacification thereof, and asserts its determination, when that is accomplished, to leave the government and control of the Island to its people." This smoothed out resistance from anti-imperialists who warned against turning the island into a US colony and secured the necessary support for US intervention. To expansionists and annexationists, the Teller Amendment was foolhardy. It stood in the way of long-term political, economic, and military involvement in Cuba. These were the limitations placed on a military government that immediately exercised sovereignty, jurisdiction, and control over the island and that eventually turned to questions about how to handle education under US rule.[8]

* * *

Little happened with Cuban schools and higher education under the first military governor, General John Brooke. His priorities centered on consolidating power and dealing with immediate social and political problems. He faced hunger, illness, unemployment, and uprisings. He responded with relief programs, pacification of the army, sanitation of cities and ports, and infrastructure projects for rebuilding roads, buildings, and communication. Brooke grouped the Department of Justice and Public Instruction together and assigned a Cuban attorney, Jose Antonio Gonzales Lanuza, as its secretary. During this period, the Cuban educational system languished. Brooke decided to close the normal schools, deny teachers back pay owed before the invasion, and ignore months-long delays in payments to teachers under the occupation. Not surprisingly, these moves fueled animosity toward the US occupation among the very people who would influence the next generation of Cubans. The process, to them, was probably as significant as the result. The Cuban people had no say in any of these unilateral decisions, and no democratic process was used.[9]

As Brooke ignored systemic problems in Cuban education, other commanders on the ground couldn't avoid the fallout. General William Ludlow in Havana reported that of the city's twenty-five thousand children, a mere four thousand or five thousand are "at present receiving instruction even in the most elementary sense." The vast majority were on the streets, "going without instruction and discipline." He estimated that the occupation needed to more than double the number of schools and teachers in the capital alone. General Leonard Wood, who at the time served as regional governor of Santiago, complained that "no such thing as a free school, in the American meaning, exists or has existed in Cuba." Wood was convinced that he had a better plan for running not just Santiago, but all of Cuba. As McKinley's friend and former physician, he would soon get his chance.[10]

In the meantime, under Brooke's tenure as US military governor, Secretary Lanuza began to work on comprehensive school reform. A finished version of his proposal appeared in October 1899. It called for universal, free, and compulsory education; schools were to integrate, become secular, and remove Spanish history from their curriculum. If schools added anything to the curriculum, the law encouraged practical and agricultural courses. Textbooks could also be selected at the local level with approval from occupation officials. Schools would receive funding from the occupation government, but power to appoint teachers, board members, and school inspections would be left to local communities. This was the first school reform proposal created by and for Cubans. Lanuza sent the law to the military governor hoping for immediate action. Brooke yawned. He shelved the law and moved on to other matters.[11]

Brooke's inactivity on the Cuban education front couldn't have been missed by Washington officials like William T. Harris. As US commissioner of education, equivalent to today's US secretary of education, Harris had big plans for Cuba, mostly to Americanize the Cuban people and bring about aggressive changes to their school system. He believed that "great powers" and higher forms of civilization, like the United States, had a duty to help those "not fully ripe for self-government." To this end, he argued for the creation of a new system of education to be established by US military governments abroad. The most important position in this new system was that of the superintendent of schools, who would be charged with regular inspections of schools and governing the educational institutions of foreign populations. Harris wanted this new superintendent to take an army of American teachers to Cuba to organize English lessons in the schools and thereby help to bring about "civilization" to the island. Harris's ambitious vision, while unevenly reaching the military governments in a position to govern these schools, nevertheless represented a sentiment among many State and War Department officials. They believed more needed to be done in education, and fast. The key figure in circumventing the difficulties and expediting these kinds of plans was Secretary of War Elihu Root.[12]

It's unclear if Harris and Root ever met, but Root, who in essence took charge of Washington's colonial policies, most likely read an address Harris made to the American Educational Association called "An Educational Policy for Our New Possessions." It was time, Harris believed, to accept the fact that America had essentially become an empire with possessions. The goal now was to ask, What should we do with them? Harris's answer was simple: "[E]mancipate them from tribal forms and usages and train them into productive industry." Root sent instructions to the colonies that reflected these convictions—an empire must teach its subjects to be loyal, productive workers in agriculture and industry.[13]

Just as Brooke was bringing his governorship to a close and Harris and Root were preparing American colonial policy, Alexis Everett Frye decided he wanted to fight in the Philippines. The problem was that he didn't exactly have combat experience. He had been a schoolteacher in Massachusetts, an assistant to educational reformer Francis W. Parker in Illinois, a superintendent of schools in California, and author of the most successful school geography textbooks in America. Frye had gone back to Harvard to finish a course of studies by the time the War of 1898 broke out. Moved by the idea of war and conquest, he wrote to Root, offering to serve as a soldier "till our [US] flag floats in peace over the islands." Harvard's president Charles W. Eliot knew Frye well and discouraged the Philippine adventure: Why not go to Cuba? And better yet, why not go as director or superintendent of schools?[14]

* * *

Frye arrived in Cuba in mid-October 1899. Root had seen his references from Eliot and others, as did Brooke. They liked what they saw and sent him as soon as they could.[15]

Brooke hired Frye as an educational consultant. The idea was that Frye would shore up the governor's lack of knowledge about educational policy and practices. He would also represent Brooke in meetings with Secretary Lanuza. By the last days of October Frye had met with Brooke, Lanuza, and Cuban newspaper reporters, and had reviewed Lanuza's school reform. On October 28, Brooke called Frye to his office and told him he had twenty-four hours to write an entirely new school law. Pressure had built up to where Brooke felt the need to approve something the very next day and didn't want to sign Lanuza's proposal. Frye worked through the night and handed Brooke an entirely new law the next day. Brooke approved and, with the stroke of a pen, decreed the first wholesale, American-style educational reform on Cuban soil.[16]

There was little chance that this was going to go over well with the public. Taking just a few hours to plan the fate of Cuba's children and their future, by someone who'd been in the country just a matter of days, had the potential to create blowback. Cuban educational reformers were already closely watching developments coming from the military occupation. They had challenged the occupation's decision to close down the normal schools, deny teacher back pay, and ignore complaints about delays in their current pay. What's more, reformers had decried the selection of Lanuza, a former attorney, as head of public instruction. Such Cuban papers as *Escuela Moderna* (*Modern School*) chided that "to organize and direct the primary schools, to advise and instruct the teachers we only need lawyers who cannot find work in other places." Others, like *La Lucha (The Struggle)*, claimed that the Frye law existed because of Lanuza's "incompetence." Had there been a Cuban educator as secretary who knew about education, Frye might not have been allowed so much power and control over educational reform. Still others, like Cuban educational reformer Carlos de la Torre, described the law as "filled with deficiencies and contradictions." Few celebrated the school law designed and decreed by the United States.[17]

Making matters worse, Cubans discovered that Frye had received a new assignment as superintendent of schools. *La Lucha, La Discusion,* and others opened fire on the decision. They loathed the idea of an "American pedagogue who will impose his criteria and his educational policy on teachers and students alike." It was nothing short of "handing Cuba's destiny over to the American government." They also declared education an internal matter, not one for foreign governments and occupation generals to decide. Echoing parts of the Teller Amendment, they wondered what mandates concerning schools, textbooks, and instructor qualifications had to do "with the maintenance of public order." Cubans felt a serious encroachment on their right to self-determination and considered education a sensitive cultural and perhaps even sacred matter. Frye posed a threat—not only to their ambitions for autonomy and independence, but also to their sense of dignity. That Frye, who'd never visited Cuba before, could have the authority to reconstruct the nature and character of the nation's schools system was nothing short of "humiliating and distressing." Putting him directly in charge of schools as superintendent with an annual salary of $4400 also didn't help, especially considering that most Cuban teachers received a mere $50 per month.[18]

Frye felt the heat. He thought about how to respond and came up with the idea that he would give his salary away to charity. His best-selling geography series made him "a man of independent means," as Eliot put it. He didn't need the money, so he decided to work for nothing. Frye, however, had misread the Cuban people. What they wanted more than anything was a right to determine their own future. They wanted autonomy. Thank you for the charitable thought, said one observer, but it would be better to "carry the philanthropy to the extreme of leaving his place to any one of the several Cubans who would act with the same competency as he." It appalled another observer to have foreigners "ignorant of our language, our customs, our history, and way of life" in charge of their children's daily lessons.[19]

Frye made a few more missteps before the tide began to change. He took firm control over textbook selection and placed his own *Geografia Elemental* (translation of *Elements of Geography*) on the order list. That alone didn't raise eyebrows. But two other matters did: the fact that his was the most expensive book on the list, sometimes twice as expensive as the others, and that the order for his books was the second most expensive textbook purchase made by the occupation. The idea of profiting from a military occupation had the potential to sour relations, so he decided to donate his share of royalties. This too missed the mark, though, much like the row over his salary. What Cubans wanted was to write their own textbooks, ones that would "respond better to the ideas that have been inculcated in our children." What's more, the textbook problem paled in comparison to Frye's decision to make English compulsory "in all schools as soon as possible." His law had established a higher pay scale for teachers who could teach English and required all teachers to take instruction in the language, among other teacher-training subjects, over the summer. "In no nation in the world," cried the *Escuela Moderna*, "was the teacher forced to teach a language other than that of his country's." According to Frye's law, they have to if they wanted to continue teaching.[20]

As the occupation's popularity reached new lows, the Cuban people felt increasingly alienated. The occupation had turned a blind eye to the collective demands of the people, especially when it came to education. They mostly wanted an elimination of English requirements in their schools, reintroduction of civics in the curriculum, an increase in teacher salaries, curbing of the superintendent's centralized power, and the removal of Frye from his post. By most measures, Frye appeared to be on his way out. The policies he'd promoted and the approaches that he'd taken had failed to win public approval.[21]

By the time General Wood took over as military governor of Cuba in January 1900, Frye had turned a corner. He had hired two Cuban associate superintendents. Bringing them into his office reduced some of the tension created by Frye's educational reform and began to thaw the icy relations the office had with occupation critic Arturo Diaz of the *Escuela Moderna*. Frye also decentralized educational power and handed the reigns to local governments. He gave local school boards greater autonomy than expected over matters of teacher appointments and requirements. And, most startling to critics, he made a complete reversal over making English the official language of the curriculum. He now believed that the United States had no right to impose its language on Cuba. In a nod to his new outlook, he left the matter of English in summer teacher-training programs up to local school boards. His policy retained special privileges for English teachers and those who learned to teach English, but he dropped the subject from teacher exams and certification.[22]

The real success for Frye came with the "Teacher's Manual" he prepared for the Cuban school system. Teachers got the impression early on that the manual would be a rule book of how the US occupation planned to control and dominate the system. They had learned under Spanish rule that the manuals produced by a colonial power directed them to what could and could not be taught. They understood manuals as another form of subjugation. When Frye's publication finally came out, the education community lit up. The manual made clear, from the start, that teachers would have "absolute freedom for every teacher to use his own method of teaching." This marked the beginning of freedom of teaching and freedom of thought in a country with a history of political, intellectual, and theological repression. It also marked the most important turning point in Frye's role as superintendent of schools in Cuba. Former critics from the *Escuela Moderna* became staunch Frye allies. They announced that they not only approved of the manual, but also agreed to help "disseminate his book throughout the nation."[23]

Frye continued to win allies with a massive wave of school openings from January to June 1900. He began with 635 elementary schools and by summer the number had risen to 3,313. Enrollments shot up sevenfold during the same period. The occupation government hired over three thousand teachers and while the quality of these hires proved to be uneven, the rapid growth and serious effort invested in education created a radically different climate for both occupation officials and Cuban citizens. It generated excitement and hope for the future. It provided a reason for Cubans to believe that the occupation wasn't going to be permanent. Cuban education was seen as the launching pad for Cuban independence.[24]

* * *

General Wood hardly appreciated playing second fiddle, and Frye had begun to overshadow him. The military governor's first move was to slow Frye down. When Frye resisted, Wood tried to isolate him within the occupation. And when Frye took Cuban teachers to Harvard, the governor locked him out. Their battle over Cuban education posed one of the major internal conflicts of the occupation.

Wood attempted to slow Frye down by putting a halt to the wave of school openings. When Frye began this campaign in 1900, his office had an $80,000 budget. With the new schools, that amount increased to over $230,000, representing 12 percent of the overall Cuban tax receipts managed by the American occupation. Despite the popularity of the campaign among Cubans, Wood ordered all of Cuba's provincial governors—who were all US military officers—to stop opening schools. The decree came without warning and took Frye by surprise. Cubans protested the abrupt shift in policy and Wood responded with the following concession: Schools that had already begun construction may finish. All other projected schools would have to wait.[25]

Frye, who'd been left out of the loop, gave Wood an irresistible opening to further isolate the superintendent. He complained to the military governor that he felt overworked by the twofold duties of the superintendent's job: to manage and to design the school system. Managing the system involved all of the financial, inspection, and supervision duties related to school organization. It required Frye's presence everywhere across Cuba and took time away from designing a lasting educational plan with new curricula, teacher-training programs, and laws to assure continued support for these efforts. He asked Wood to divide these duties, to relieve him of finances and supervision, and to allow him to devote his time to design matters. Wood agreed to this request and spoke of creating a Chief Inspector's Office. What Frye didn't see coming was that Wood had designs for using this new office to push him out of Cuba. The new position, called the commissioner of public schools, stripped the superintendent's office of its power. The occupation transferred the last vestiges of Frye's authority to a board of superintendents, composed of six provincial administrators over which he would have no control. The new office was being designed with the explicit intent of making Frye's position obsolete. Wood secured authority over Cuban schools by planning the appointment of a low-ranking officer—First Lieutenant Matthew Hanna—to the position of commissioner.[26]

Frye continued unaware of the machinations occurring behind closed doors. He had been consumed with school openings and with sketching out plans for creating summer programs for teacher training. Of all the projects on his desk, the one that drew most of his attention was the prospect of taking a group of Cuban teachers to Harvard.[27]

The idea of a giving Cuban teachers a summer session in Cambridge began when Ernest L. Conant, a legal advisor to the occupation, suggested sending twenty or so Cubans to Harvard. Frye followed up on the idea and contacted both Wood and Harvard's president Eliot with a plan of sending 500–1,000 teachers. Frye wanted these teachers to "breathe the atmosphere of the greatest school in America" and bring back ideas about education, democracy, and citizenship intended to have a lasting impact on the Cuban people. The most pressing problem was raising the funds necessary for the trip. The cost was likely to run in the tens of thousands of dollars and Wood had no interest in diverting funds from the occupation budget. Frye understood this and designed a plan with Eliot to raise the money. During a meeting in Cambridge, they became even more ambitious. They set their sights at raising $70,000 to bring 1,450 teachers. At no other point in American history had such a project—that combined education and foreign relations—been considered, much less attempted. Newspapers across the country announced the start of the "subscription" to help fund the project. As Eliot had anticipated, funds came pouring in and even exceeded the target amount. The plan had worked and was set in motion.[28]

Excitement for the Harvard summer session spread across both countries. It provided an almost unheard of opportunity for greater mutual understanding, the improvement of relations between the United States and Cuba, and for the improvement of Cuban schools. Nevertheless, not all Cubans were happy with this plan.

Some Cubans objected on cultural grounds, others raised political questions. The cultural concerns had to do with the honor of Cuba's young female teachers. To many Cuban traditionalists, the idea of sending a daughter abroad without supervision was unthinkable. It went against the grain of the country's social and cultural mores. Frye responded by adding designated chaperones and a few physicians to the list of voyagers. With this move, the cultural objections quickly dissolved. The political ones, however, were trickier. Nationalists were highly sensitive to the occupation's Americanization efforts. They did not want to become part of the United States and saw the excursion as "another shrewd movement on the part of the American officials to Americanize the teachers, and thus Cuba." These nationalists wanted independence for their country, autonomy to decide how to spend their tax revenues, and an end to the occupation. Trips to Harvard, from what they could tell, were a political distraction. Frye lessened opposition by describing the trip as a gift between teachers, rather than nations, and promising to open three normal schools in the near future. Teacher training would remain in Cuba; the trip was a one-time opportunity, not an ongoing Americanization effort.[29]

Having largely muted his critics, Frye moved forward with the plan. A total of 1,397 teachers signed up. All seemed to be going according to plan until Governor Wood stepped in and made a unilateral decision about teacher pay. Wood decided to stop making salary payments to those teachers who had signed up for Frye's summer trip. His stated reasoning was that they might not receive their payments in time and, therefore, would be better served if they were paid when they arrived at port, ready to travel to the United States. Frye objected and probably believed Wood had a more malicious intent. Instead of approaching the military governor directly, he contacted President Eliot with a desperate plea to help him with the situation. As Frye understood it, Wood's decision was sure to cause many who had enrolled to drop out because of a lack of funds necessary just to get to port. Eliot contacted Root about the matter; and Root then contacted Wood. The governor responded to Root's concerns by dismissing the problem and criticizing Frye as a man of "very little executive ability." The payment plan remained in place and over 120 teachers failed to make it to port. Those who dropped out were largely from the most rural and destitute areas, a population Frye and Eliot most wanted on board. Those who could afford the trip made their way to the transport ships with chaperones and physicians in tow.[30]

Aside from the *Sedgwick* incident, the voyage was uneventful, although their arrival in Cambridge created a stir. Newspapers reported on the exotic beauty of the young Cubans. Some were interviewed, others romantically pursued, still others proposed to, and a last portion invited to join American families (or their help staff), permanently. Almost all attended receptions, dances, and parties.[31]

The actual classes at Harvard began on July 5, 1900. Most of their time was spent on English—two daily lessons, including classes on Saturday. Other courses involved geography, history of the United States, history of Spanish colonies, educational administration, library studies, psychology, and a handful of field trips to historic sites relevant to the American revolution near Bunker Hill, Concord, Lexington. Through it all, the Boston-Cambridge papers described the Cuban teachers as grateful, but cautious. They were grateful to have the opportunity to visit the United States and impressed by what they saw. They appreciated the opportunity to study at Harvard and visit sites relevant to American history. At the same time, they were cautious in their response to the political objectives of being taught English and American history and being taken to revolutionary war sites. Recognizing that they represented Cubans back home, they wanted the American public to know that Cubans wanted independence, autonomy, and self-determination more than anything else. They wanted a "Cuba Libre," said one teacher to a reporter, and wanted to "know more definitely when the control of our dear Island will become our own." By the end of August, it was time for their return. Along the way, they visited schools, libraries, and universities in New York, the Liberty Bell in Philadelphia, and President William McKinley in Washington, DC.[32]

* * *

During Frye's absence, Wood had turned Cuba's political and educational system inside out. The governor had scheduled a constitutional assembly for later in the year. At this assembly, he mandated that Cuban leaders draft a new constitution that included the following stipulation: "That the government consents that the United States may exercise the right to intervene" militarily on the island, among other restrictions to its sovereignty and economic interactions with other countries. Wood and many others in the occupation understood that their time in Cuba was coming to a close, but they continued to have annexationist feelings. They were constrained by the Teller Amendment and what they wanted was a new amendment that would give them indirect control over Cuban affairs. Secretary of War Elihu Root shared the same view and responded by writing a proposal granting the United States an open-ended right to intervene directly and indirectly in Cuban affairs. It became known as the Platt Amendment and gave renewed hope to American expansionists. Platt was ultimately signed by Cuban leaders under threat of continued occupation if they failed to capitulate.[33]

Wood also tossed out Frye's educational reform law and decreed a new one created by his first lieutenant Matthew Hanna. The goal was to centralize power in the hands of a commissioner of education, appointed at Wood's discretion, and to eliminate Frye's Office of Superintendent. To Frye's mind, the move was tyrannical, unjust, and emblematic of the entire military occupation. "Any nation that tried to trample upon human liberty," he told a Cuban reporter after his return, "was a tyrant." Cuba, he continued, should defend "against all foreign powers, no matter which in coming years might presume acts of tyranny." The message, coming from one of the most popular Americans in Cuba, was a thinly veiled, but powerful critique of the US military government. Wood became incensed. Seeing Frye's statements as an attack on the authority of the occupation, he called Frye a subversive and a radical, and he decided "to make it too hot for Frye to stay here any longer." By isolating Frye and further eroding his power as a voice for Cuban education, Wood succeeded. Frye submitted his resignation in January 1901.[34]

Despite his rocky start in Cuba, he had gained the trust of many Cubans. *La Discusion*, once a Frye critic, now mourned the loss and saw Wood's hand in Frye's departure: "The only American tree that shadowed [Wood] had fallen." With Frye gone, so too went his promises and priorities. He had promised that the trip to Harvard was a temporary gesture between teachers, not nations. He considered it a priority to reopen normal schools in Cuba to increase the number and quality of Cuban teachers. By these promises and priorities, he made clear that teacher training would and should be in the hands of Cubans.[35]

Lieutenant Hanna, Wood's appointed voice on education-related matters, abandoned the objectives established during Frye's tenure. When the Cuban board of superintendents voted to create a Havana teacher-training institute, Hanna blocked this and similar efforts across the country. When considering what to do about training new Cuban teachers, he decided to send them to US normal schools. Hanna sent sixty female teachers to New Platz Normal School in New York and had plans to send fifty male students to state normal schools in Connecticut. Some interpreted this use of the Cuban treasury as a way to have Cubans pay for their own Americanization. Hanna also increased the number of students studying English from four thousand to fourteen thousand in 1902. He believed injecting more English into the minds of Cuba's young would "do wonders for Cuba."[36]

What's more, Wood and Hanna introduced more practical studies in the Cuban educational system and launched Americanization programs. With the Platt Amendment and a related "reciprocity treaty," Wood predicted that US corporations would "transfer their industries to Cuba, and the island would, under the impetus of new capital and energy, not only be developed, but gradually become Americanized, and we shall have in time one of the richest and most desirable possessions in the world." While Wood shared this vision with Root, Hanna was busy establishing a manual training program that was required of every male starting with kindergarten and continuing on through the rest of their schooling. Hanna imported American teachers to help facilitate the expansion of his industrial education project. For direct Americanization projects, he received aid from such expansionist organizations as the American Patriotic League. Through Hanna's office, the League created the City School Program designed to "cultivate American principles into the heats and minds of Americans, native or adopted." This Americanization project took the form of citizenship training that taught children about American-style civic engagement and political rights. When Harvard's Eliot learned of the program, his response was that "things American ought not to be forced on the Cubans... it was not advisable to teach the American civil government to foreigners." By the end of the occupation, Wood had mandated and Hanna had facilitated the establishment of City School Programs across the Cuban island.[37]

The Wood-Hanna educational policies eclipsed Frye's previous school reform efforts. They amounted to a rejection of Cuban-based teacher training, an increase in demands for English in the curriculum, an expansion of industrial training beginning with Cuba's youngest students, and an effort to use education as a means to Americanize the Cuban people.

* * *

As Frye's efforts faded, so too did his pattern of educational reform that proved to be an exception rather than the rule. More common was the Wood-Hanna approach to the "natives" that centered on opening a country to American business, teaching its people how to be industrious workers, and Americanizing them while troops still controlled the ground. Cubans, however, had a longing that couldn't be suppressed, a longing that sustained them in long and bloody conflicts with the Spanish. It was a longing that made them suspicious about the American invasion and occupation of Cuba. It was a desire to be free, independent, and autonomous from any empire or foreign control. The Teller Amendment stated that they would finally get their day, but the Platt Amendment dashed these hopes.

The physical occupation of Cuba lasted from 1898 to 1902 and resumed briefly from 1906 to 1909. From then on, intervention took on a more subtle, indirect form. The US government rewarded Cuban administrations that supported American corporate interests, but punished those that failed to fall in line. Cuban frustrations with American meddling in Cuban affairs ended with the radical revolution of the 1950s. Radical revolutionaries drew on the long history of economic penetration and the weak to nonexistent building of democratic institutions, such as education, in their rise to power. That's what Fidel Castro meant at the start of the Cuban revolution that "it will not be like 1898, when the Americans came and made themselves masters of the country."[38]

Empire trumped education during the first occupation of Cuba, leaving a weak state open to winds of foreign intervention, and fanning the flames of revolt and revolution. But this episode, in terms of length and influence, pales by comparison with a multidecade occupation just getting started nine thousand miles away.[39]

Chapter Two
Benevolent Education

When President William McKinley decided to take the War of 1898 to the Philippines, he did so without much to go on. He relied on insights derived from prayer, claiming that he had received "light and guidance" on what to do with that seven thousand island archipelago. But all this light created some crucial blind spots. He wanted to "Christianize" the Filipinos, without having much grasp of how Spain had already beat him to this. Spanish colonization of the islands, now almost three and a half centuries old by the time McKinley sent warships to the region, had brought with it the founding of nearly a thousand Catholic churches. He also wanted to "educate the Filipinos and uplift them," suggesting there was a great, untapped opportunity to do so. But the Spanish had beat him to this too, having already established over twelve thousand public and private primary, secondary, and postsecondary institutions of education. McKinley, in short, imagined the colony populated with savages in need of civilization and, by all accounts, his conception was woefully misguided. For many, it wasn't at all clear what those islands in the Pacific had to do with Cuba or the sinking of the USS *Maine*. What the general public needed to know, as far as the administration was concerned, was that the United States was at war with Spain and some of its colonies too.[1]

All this talk of uplift for Filipinos, however, receded into the background when McKinley brought the message to the American business community. He had a different line for them when it came to this new adventure. McKinley spoke of the "commercial opportunity, to which American statesmanship cannot be indifferent" when discussing intervention in the Philippines. The islands could serve as a commercial means and end. As a means to an end, the great benefit of getting involved over there was because of its proximity to China.

Those islands stood right next door to China's massive markets and could serve as a vital staging ground for American trade. As an end in and of itself, the islands represented a bonanza of natural resources. American commercial, industrial, and agricultural businesses stood to benefit from those resources ripe for development.[2]

For the Filipinos, this "opportunity" resulted in a bloody military campaign that ended with the creation of a US military government in December 1898. American officials took over the central government and began to decide how the island's taxes would be spent, what legislation should be passed, and what projects deserved highest priority. The military governor held executive power and final decision-making authority until 1901 when an American-run civilian government was established. Whether military or civilian, US occupation officials controlled the island's destiny for decades. Nowhere was this more true than in the case of education.[3]

* * *

William Howard Taft (later, US president) and W. Cameron Forbes served as two of the most influential governors in the early history of the US occupation of the Philippines. During both administrations, education took a backseat to American commercial interests, although the education officials they appointed sometimes bucked this trend. Taft and Forbes had much in common, so it's hardly surprising that they approached their rule over the Philippines in much the same way. Before sailing to the Pacific islands, Taft had established a reputation for favoring big business interests as an appellate court judge. His later career crystallized this reputation with decisions, such as *Truax v. Corrigan*, that decisively benefited corporations at the expense of organized labor. Before he had seen a single Filipino, he believed the islanders needed help governing themselves and claimed that US occupation and American businesses could provide that help. When he assumed his role as occupation governor, he claimed that the Filipinos needed 50–100 years of US occupation and tutelage "before they shall ever realize what Anglo Saxon liberty is." To his mind, it would be best to "declare the future intention of the United States to hold the islands indefinitely." Forbes came from a prominent business family that had amassed fortunes in commerce, railroads, and the Bell Telephone Company. As governor of the Philippines after Taft, Forbes made commercial interests his top priority. He chose to "build roads first and schools afterwards" in the interest of attracting American capital and business to the islands. The schools he had in mind would serve those same commercial interests. "We want men taught to work with their hands," he explained, and therefore "we want to see agricultural schools and arts and trades schools in greater abundance."[4]

The US occupation took its first step toward reforming and restructuring Filipino education when it organized the Department of Public Instruction in March 1900. Captain Albert Todd was put in charge of the new department, where he spent $100,000 on readers, texts, and US flags for schools across the archipelago during his five months in the newly created office. Todd, an officer of the sixth artillery unit, had no background in educational administration and questioned the value of his own work with this new assignment. "[M]uch that is now being done, following largely after the old Spanish system," he reflected, "is of small intrinsic utility, and is chiefly valuable as it shows the good will of our government in establishing or continuing schools for the natives." He put US soldiers, who were trained for combat, in classrooms throughout the country to teach English in part to deal with the many practical concerns having to do with overcrowded schools, inadequate facilities, limited courses of study, lack of supplies, the military goal of pacification of insurgents, and the long-range goal of compulsory education. Just as important, Todd faced value-laden questions that resurfaced under subsequent public instruction officials, questions that had to do with what teachers would teach and what students would learn. Would education serve the purpose of self-governance, citizenry, and democracy or would it satisfy commercial interests of utility and productivity? He left these larger questions for others to answer.[5]

Todd probably felt relieved when his short-lived administration of the country's school system came to an end with the arrival of Fred Atkinson in July 1900. Atkinson's name came up during a conversation between Charles W. Eliot and William H. Taft on a train ride from Washington to Boston. Taft wanted someone who knew something about education to take charge of schools in the Philippines and asked Eliot for a recommendation. Eliot suggested Atkinson, who had by that time graduated from Harvard, received a doctorate from the University of Leipzig, and served as a principal of a high school in Springfield, Massachusetts. As a secondary school administrator, he understood the role of superintendents and state-level offices like the secretary of education, but he'd never served in those positions. He was a secondary school principal. After a brief interview, Taft hired him on the spot as the Philippines's new general superintendent of public instruction.[6]

Before meeting a single Filipino, Atkinson formulated a plan for what these "natives" needed in terms of education, schooling, and training. He produced a program of reform that answered the value-based questions that dogged his predecessor and turned that program into a piece of legislation drafted shortly after taking over the position. The US occupation approved and passed his proposal in January 1901.[7]

Atkinson's proposal, also known as Act 74, centralized the system of education, changed the language of instruction, and put compulsory education at the top of his department's priorities. Centralization allowed Atkinson to secure control over the system by appointing division superintendents and setting employment and institutional policies. Under Atkinson, division leaders had the power to hire and fire local Filipino teachers. Beyond that, these division superintendents followed Atkinson's lead, which included the founding, creation, and maintenance of normal, agricultural, and trade schools. Centralization also empowered Atkinson to change the language of instruction. Spanish was the language of the laws of the land and of public education before the American occupation. He considered it "too expensive" to hire Spanish-speaking teachers and decided it would be more efficient for the occupation to simply change the official language. Atkinson's reform also provided for a strict separation of church and state. No religious instruction was allowed during school hours, but a compromise with religious leaders was made to allow such instruction after school hours on specified days of the week. The only part of the proposal that the occupation government tossed out was a section on compulsory education. Atkinson had pushed for mandatory schooling, arguing that it should be "obligatory for all children between the ages of 6 and 12 years old." The occupation government denied this request because of a general lack of facilities. The ones they had were "entirely inadequate to provide for the children of school age, if such a provision was enforced." Otherwise, Act 74 sailed through the approval process.[8]

With the initial reform process underway, Atkinson made the most well-known (some might say, notorious) decision of his tenure: the recruitment of approximately one thousand American teachers to the Philippines. This was a reversal of an earlier position he'd taken before his arrival. According to one observer, "Mr. Atkinson does not expect to fill the school with [imported] English-speaking teachers. He hopes and intends to employ natives." During his first year, Atkinson changed his mind and began the largest campaign of this sort in US history. Since the greatest number of them—over five hundred—traveled on the USS *Thomas*, the whole lot became known as the Thomasites.[9]

As a group, the Thomasites were paid well above (e.g., double) most of their American counterparts back home. But their qualifications generally left much to be desired. Dozens had only a high school diploma; over one hundred had no teaching experience at all; another hundred had only a year or two of teaching under their belt. As such, their motivations for making the journey to the Philippines raised questions and eyebrows. Critics called the Thomasites nothing more than "carpet-baggers [who] come to exploit the country in their small way." Some Thomasites, like Blaine F. Moore, lived up to the stereotype. Blaine talked openly about being drawn to the Philippines for potential adventure and mining opportunities and having little interest in being "shut up with a lot of little brown kids" that he described as "wriggling, squirming, talking, barbarians" and "brown half-savages." Despite his views about the Filipino people and what he viewed as the futility of the "benevolent" enterprise of education in the Philippines, Blaine later rose through the ranks to become a provincial superintendent of schools.[10]

Under Atkinson, these teachers witnessed four major reforms of the curriculum during his two years as general superintendent of schools. In each case, he attempted to Americanize the Filipino course of study. Nevertheless, the two most notable efforts—Atkinson's first and last—were completely different from one another. His first curricular reform drew almost exclusively from his own personal experiences as a principal in the Massachusetts public school system. It's what he knew. Atkinson created a program spanning four years and including reading, language, spelling, math, geography, nature study, drawing, sewing, physical training, hygiene, music, writing, rhetoricals, and history. For many of these areas, he mandated the use of specific texts and these texts quickly kicked up unwelcome attention. Some critics called out the texts for being devoid of Filipino context and for teaching students about "the world's great men...Such men as Washington, Lincoln, [and] McKinley." They also made references to characters (e.g., Jack Frost) and foods (e.g., strawberries) that had no significance to Filipino children. By the end of his term, Atkinson became sympathetic to these criticism and called for contextually sensitive textbooks. But by that time, he'd already moved on to his last educational reform effort that centered on practical education. The two kinds that he pushed in the Philippines were manual and vocational instruction. He advocated offering manual training as early as elementary school with a focus on boxes, toy boats, kites, leather, and weaving. Vocational training took its place in the secondary school curriculum and focused on carpentry and metal work. "Education in the Philippines must be along industrial lines," Atkinson wrote to Booker T. Washington, the famed promoter of industrial education in the United States, "and any and all suggestions from you and your work will be invaluable." Washington invited Atkinson to visit the Tuskegee and Hampton Institutes. Atkinson accepted, toured the schools for a month, and returned to the Philippines an evangelist for industrial education. To the occupation government, he argued for a wholesale expansion of practical education. Atkinson believed that "there should be established throughout the Philippine Islands schools of agriculture. It will be necessary to send to our agricultural colleges for instructors... These instructors should follow the plan of work of Hampton and Tuskegee." This push for industrial education caught the attention of Governor Taft, but it failed to gain momentum in terms of school foundings. By 1902, there was only one trade school, with 149 students, in the entire archipelago.[11]

Atkinson's appointment as general superintendent of schools from 1900 to 1902 was a disappointment to the occupation government. Education officials described him as disorganized and unsuited for administration. He fell behind on teacher salaries and paid them in Mexican currency rather than dollars. He attracted attention because of extended leaves of absence spent vacationing in Japan and Hong Kong. When he requested a raise, Governor Taft replied that he should "think of anything but salary... He lacks, it seems to me, in force." Another occupation official noted that Atkinson had not read the interests of the Filipinos properly. The industrial education gambit fell flat because the "people have been accustomed under their earlier instruction to regard education as a means of putting themselves in positions where manual labor is not required." All of this set the stage for Atkinson's firing in fall 1902.[12]

David Barrows, Atkinson's replacement, came with an entirely different background and perspective. Barrows was an academic. He had received his doctorate in anthropology from the University of Chicago and had specialized in Native American tribes in southern California. He'd taught at normal schools and state universities and received his first appointment abroad as Manila's superintendent of schools under Atkinson's direction. He had a more nuanced understanding of the Filipino people and their educational needs and potential.[13]

Barrows's primary concern was with the role of education in the establishment of a democratic society. His understanding was that the masses of uneducated Filipinos were at the mercy of the elites. He called for dealing with the "ignorance and poverty of the race" through a system of "universal primary instruction for the Filipinos of all classes and every community." He recognized the potentially exploitative practices of the Filipino elites, the US occupation government, and the American commercial interests, and viewed education as way to address the problem. Unlike Atkinson, Barrows understood American industrial and agricultural corporations as a threat to Filipino democracy.[14] These promoters and speculators, he claimed, are anxious to create

> a great body of unskilled labor, dependent for living upon its daily wage, willing to work in great gangs, submissive to the rough handling of the "boss," and ready to leave home and family and go anywhere in the islands and to labor at day wages under conditions of hours and methods of labor set by their foreign employers.[15]

To his mind, "the character of a government must be measured by the protection it affords the weak." Barrows understood this as the central tension between the interests of capital and the establishment of an educational system for a democratic society.[16]

To tackle this problem, Barrows made some immediate changes to the Filipino educational system. He revised the course of study, emphasizing skills necessary for defense against exploitation. The curriculum was simplified to center on reading, writing, and math. "Two years of instruction in arithmetic given to every child," he suggested, "will in a generation destroy that repellent peonage or bonded indebtedness that prevails throughout this country." Barrows's curriculum aimed at destroying the tenant farming and virtual enslavement of the Filipino peasants because of their lack of mathematics. He added civics as a formal subject area and encouraged civics role-playing in clubs and mock institutions. Physical exercises centered on sports and health, with only minimal attention to industrial or agricultural skills training.[17]

Barrows met with resistance from the US occupation government. The governor at the time, US attorney James Smith, wanted to move in exactly the opposite direction, stating that "the facilities for securing a practical education will be enlarged and extended as far as the financial resources of the Government will permit." Other occupation officials like W. Morgan Shuster, a career civil servant, and W. Cameron Forbes, then serving as secretary of commerce and police, also wanted more practical education. When Barrows returned to the United States for a short visit in 1906, these occupation officials leaned on the acting director of education, Gilbert Brink, to implement a new primary course of study that centered on practical skills training, undoing much of the work Barrows had completed over the previous four years. Brink recited the party line on this, adding that elementary school students "should have acquired a fair knowledge of some simple trade or handicraft." The message was clear: Barrows stood in the minority in wanting education for a democratic society. What the occupation wanted was training that would serve the interests of American investors and speculators. When Barrows came back from the United States, he discovered the changes that had been made and expressed disgust. "To those who advocate 'practical instruction,'" he said to occupation leaders, "I reply that the most practical thing obtainable for men is a civilized community, and their most desirable acquisition is literacy." Although disappointed with what the occupation had done in his absence, not all was lost. He could still point to some of his own accomplishments, such as the threefold increase in the number of teachers he'd put in the classroom and the doubling of average daily student attendance. But he identified significant challenges that remained, ones that had been further complicated by the shift back to practical instruction. The low rates of completion bothered him. Filipino schoolchildren tended to finish an average of a year and a half in school. School funding, moreover, never achieved a secure footing and faced frequent threats and crises. Barrows described municipal revenues and expenditures as "barely more than half sufficient" for the task at hand.[18]

Who was to blame? Barrows directed his venom toward the occupation, by then called the Philippine Commission. They'd shown tepid support for his initiatives. They had never stood behind the idea of education as serving the needs of a democratic society. The American-run government, he stated, "has persistently neglected to provide anything approximating an adequate system of primary school finance... I have encountered the greatest ignorance, indifference and inability to see the necessity of this matter on the part of the Commission throughout the time that I have had to go to it for funds." What the occupation wanted, argued Barrows, was a robust program of road-building, port-building, and other public works projects that ultimately came at the expense of education. W. Cameron Forbes, still serving in Commerce and Police, ran political circles around Barrows when it came to funding. Forbes managed to move funds away from Barrows's division, both surprising the school leader and forcing the elimination of several intermediate schools. This maneuvering on Forbes's part signaled the upper hand given to commercial interests at the expense of public schools. When it appeared that Forbes was going to be selected the next governor of the Philippines, Barrows headed for the exit and resigned.[19]

Governor Forbes was probably delighted to see Barrows go. For the next several years, Forbes and his handpicked director of education, Frank R. White, set to work in undoing Barrows's reforms. They had made clear that they wanted Filipinos taught to "work with their hands" and could hardly wait for the proliferation of agriculture and trade schools. Forbes also directly privileged the construction of "roads first" and "schools afterwards." It was clear there was no room for the likes of Barrows in this administration.[20]

Forbes and White had a different goal in wanting to build up the elite class of Filipino society. This very much reflected where Forbes placed his hopes for the future of the Philippines. He argued that the occupation needed to "devote our first money toward increasing the wealth of the people." By "people" he meant the monied Filipinos who owned property, large sugar or tobacco plantations, and satisfying their interests through subsidies and internal improvements that aided their particular commercial ventures. By "our first money," Forbes meant the Filipino tax receipts and how the US occupation planned to spend their taxes without a democratic process that would have involved the Filipinos themselves. White repeated the position in terms of education when he linked the functions of his office to the interests of domestic and foreign capital. He pressed for a complete overhaul of the nation's school system along industrial education lines because, as he described it, it was of "inestimable commercial importance." The task before them was in convincing the Filipinos that they should accept the latest educational reform.[21]

Much like those who came before him, White's first move as chief education official in the Philippines was to call for an overhaul of the curriculum. Reform-weary Filipinos saw a dramatic increase in manual and vocational instruction in primary schools. White mandated that the ratio of academic to industrial schoolwork, as represented in contact hours, would be as follows: first grade, 4.5:1; second grade, 5:2; third grade, 5:1.3; and fourth grade, 5:1.5. By 1913, White proudly remarked that "every school in the Philippines, except the 37 offering secondary instruction, gives industrial work in one form or another." The reform produced a system that devoted less time to English and arithmetic and more emphasis on "character training" as well as cleanliness, conduct, and industrious education. What's more, White (and Forbes) abandoned the goal of universal education. With this no longer a goal or even a priority, White could state without controversy that the "number of teachers employed must necessarily be diminished." He could also report on declining student numbers without penalty. During White's tenure, schools dropped almost one hundred thousand students from their rosters (610,493 in 1910 to 529,655 the following year) during a single year. His policies led to the closing of almost 800 primary schools.[22]

White continued to slash education operations, shocking even Forbes when the reports came out. White decided to close one thousand barrio schools that served the rural poor and offered primary education. He did so to pay for an increase in intermediate schools that served a largely elite segment of the Filipino population, and completed this move while Forbes was away. When the governor returned, White received an earful. Forbes called for a special treasury request to open one thousand primary schools to accommodate one hundred thousand more children. This cavalier back and forth that impacted the lives of Filipino children did not impress reporters covering the reform policies. Domestic reports criticized the US occupation officials for living on huge salaries while "half a million children of school age, that is, half of all Filipino children, are deprived of education" With little improvement in terms of retention and promotion of students, these reports had plenty of evidence to support their claims. They could point to the occupation's own figures that, in 1912–1913, less than half of first graders made it to the second grade.[23]

After a decade of educational reforms, an investigation into the status of Filipino education was conducted. The Monroe Commission, as it was dubbed, tested thirty-two thousand students with four years in the US-occupied educational system. Columbia professor Paul Monroe, leading the commission, found that these students read at the level of an average American second-grade student. The report faulted the overemphasis on industrial work in primary schools for the failures they found in Filipino education.[24]

Others viewed the overemphasis on industrial skills training as symptomatic of a larger problem: the influence of capital in an occupied country. The trend toward industrial and vocational education mirrored the way American officials treated such issues as land, tariff, and transport policy. Each area reveals the way in which capital received consistent, sweetheart deals while the disadvantaged saw wild fluctuations in their educational and economic condition.[25]

Of the seventy-three million Philippine acres, only five million were privately owned. American corporations wanted the publicly held lands "upon proper terms." The occupation tried to give twenty-five thousand acres to every American company that applied for the development of precious metals, coal, and timber in the country, but the US Congress set the limit at twenty-five hundred acres. To circumvent the limit, American officials managed to secure four hundred thousand acres through the occupation government and, with Governor Forbes's help, sold large tracts of Filipino land to US companies, such as a fifty-eight-thousand-acre purchase by the American Sugar Refining Company. When it came to tariff policy, the same sweetheart deals applied. The occupation generally favored the interests of American companies exporting to the Philippines. These companies wanted their products to enter the country duty free. They claimed that the Philippines was no longer a sovereign nation; it was run by the United States and therefore should not be subject to duties and tariffs. The US Supreme Court weighed in on the matter and conducted the mental gymnastics necessary to support their interests. The justices argued that while the Philippines was not a foreign country, it was also not incorporated into the United States. This, they concluded, meant that the US Congress could set whatever policy it wished with regard to this new experiment in colonialism. Congress, not surprisingly, sided with its powerful constituents and eliminated tariffs (or dramatically reduced them) on most of the goods flowing from America to the Philippines. Filipino goods were not so lucky. To protect American beet and sugar companies, US Congress hit the Filipinos with a tariff on their goods entering the United States.

The same pattern seen in land and tariff policy was repeated in the area of transportation. The occupation was under pressure from Secretary of War Elihu Root to release railroad franchises "at once" and to provide "access to large provinces rich in valuable materials." He called the idea of railroad building "a most attractive field for investment capital." The US Congress subsidized these deals by guaranteeing up to 5 percent profits on any American corporate investment in railroad construction in the Philippines. This nationalized corporate risk and secured private profit. Two American companies won bids for the railway construction, but, after securing their profits, they lost interest in the project and sold the railroads to the Philippines for prices they could not afford. The occupation government passed on the several hundred thousand dollar obligations to the Filipino people.[26]

Education in this context was destined to fail. The lopsided policy decisions in favor of capital and to the detriment of the Filipino people had obvious consequences. It meant that there would be no stable sources of revenue to support domestic concerns, such as education. The sale of Filipino land was conducted between two American parties without the interests of the people in mind. Tariff policies failed to raise revenue for the Filipino people and worked against them when attempting to sell to American markets. Railways that were dreamt up by foreigners, but hardly of interest to the average Filipino, ultimately became some of their largest financial liabilities. None of this was conducted within an environment conducive to the modeling of democratic principles. All of this worked against the financing and support of education for the majority of the nation's children.

Filipino leaders, like lawyer and Philippine Assembly member Manuel Quezon, knew this was happening and were constrained by the occupation in what they could do or say. They had good reason to view American commercial interests as forces of bald exploitation and had learned that US corporate profits in the Philippines were created at the expense of the Filipino people. "We are against the ownership of large tracts of land, either by corporations or by individuals," declared Quezon, "for it is incompatible with the real prosperity of the natives." He called the sale of these large tracts of land "contrary to the will, wishes and interests of the Filipino people... The Philippines cannot endure competition from the corporations."[27]

At bottom was the Filipino struggle for the establishment of an educational system and a democratic form of government that was free from the clutches of American commercial interests. According to Quezon,

> Free trade between the United States and the Philippines would attract powerful American companies to the Philippines and would make American capital the absolute owner of our market... Large American companies would bring as a result the monopoly of the wealth of the country by them is a fact that is beyond all doubt; they would first take possession of our market, through lack of competition, and then our agriculture.[28]

For Quezon, there existed a tension between capital and a free democracy. Without the ability to develop independently, there would always be strong US capital forces that would interfere with the internal development of markets, whether in agriculture, industry, or education. Most American officials were blind to this. Taft, when he first arrived in 1900, said that "nothing will civilize them so much as the introduction of American enterprise and capital here." What Filipinos like Quezon could not help seeing, at least in these cases, was the savagery of capital and the denial of an educational system that would support the formation of a truly democratic society.[29]

* * *

McKinley's decision to war with the Philippines began with a strong, commercial rationale that permeated the work of the Philippine Commission. It influenced the thinking of Taft and Forbes, Atkinson and White, and subverted the efforts of Barrows and others. The efficiency progressives eclipsed in number and power the humanitarian progressives. In the end, it was White's legacy, not the one briefly attempted by Barrows, that won out. White succeeded in directing Filipino funds toward an expansive program of industrial education that lasted for decades. In 1910, primary school children who trained under an industrial curriculum numbered approximately 350,000. This increased to almost one million by 1924. Only in 1945, the year before Filipino independence from the United States, did all secondary high schools offer a general academic curriculum. In the four years after the United States fully withdrew its occupation government, secondary enrollments more than doubled.[30]

A hallmark feature of this and other US occupations was the recognizable gap that existed between the occupier and the occupied. This was true of Cuba, where the desire to be free from ongoing external influence ended in a radical revolution. It was true of the Philippines, where children witnessed radical shifts in the curriculum from the utilitarian to the democratic and back again. The people voted with their feet and their resources as soon as liberty was theirs. The same was true for another island, one in the Caribbean, that has neither received its independence from US occupation nor formed a completely autonomous government, an island that has hung in a state of perpetual political limbo.

CHAPTER THREE

CULTURE AND CITIZENSHIP

As assistant secretary of the US Navy, Theodore Roosevelt wanted Puerto Rico—badly. What's more, he had a way of getting what he wanted. When he decided the United States should have the Philippines, he set the nation on a warpath without approval from his superior, Navy secretary John D. Long, in February 1898. Roosevelt sent "peremptory orders" across the Pacific that had all but declared war against Manila; Long fumed and called him a "bull in a china shop" for doing so. This wasn't enough for Roosevelt, though, as he turned back to his map of the Caribbean. "Don't make peace," he cried out to Senator Henry Cabot Lodge, "until we get to Porto Rico." Roosevelt's land lust was great—as great as any that gripped American expansionists at the time—and he wanted to stall whatever peace process might have been in the offing with Spain. Don't worry, Lodge replied, "we mean to have it." He must have flashed his broad, toothy smile when he learned that it took a mere twenty-three days for US forces to control the island, long before any treaties were signed with the Spanish government.[1]

Roosevelt knew who to send to Puerto Rico: General Nelson A. Miles, a tough bastard who didn't get along with the "Rough Rider." They loathed each other, but he had just the reputation Roosevelt was looking for. Miles's long history with the US military began when he enlisted as a union soldier in the 1860s. He rose through the ranks and became an army commander leading campaigns against Native Americans in the 1880s. His most notorious work on the western frontier included the massacre of hundreds of native women and children as well as the slaying of tribal leader Sitting Bull. A few years before accepting his Puerto Rico assignment, he went to war with labor, dispatching troops against the Pullman strike riots of 1894 and gaining favorable attention from American industrialists. When he turned his guns toward Puerto Rico, Miles wasted no time. He finished the invasion and conflict in just over three weeks, established an occupation government in San Juan, and raised the American flag in the capital to make the transition of power perfectly clear. Miles then published two open but conflicting letters to the Puerto Rican people that sent wildly mixed messages about the intentions of the US military occupation. His first letter gave the impression that American officials would take a hands-off approach. "It is not our purpose," declared Miles, "to interfere with any existing law and customs." He might have assumed that the occupation wouldn't last very long; or he might have thought that the occupation would quickly incorporate local, civilian rule. Neither turned out to be the case. In his second one, Miles sharply announced that American officials had "absolute and supreme" control over the island and demanded that the Puerto Rican people "yield obedience to the authority of the United States." This was the Miles that Roosevelt knew.[2]

When he declared absolute and supreme control over the island, Miles meant it. This included virtually all political and economic functions of the state. It also meant that the occupation would take control of education and, with it, the lives of Puerto Rican children and the island's destiny.

At first, the people had mixed responses to Miles's letters. At a citizens' rally in the San Juan Theater weeks after the declaration of US rule, Puerto Ricans drafted and approved resolutions calling for the establishment of universal education based on "the best models of the United States." These citizens argued that an American-style public school system would be an improvement over the Spanish system. Under Spanish rule, the first compulsory program of elementary education had been introduced in 1865 by military strongman Governor Gelix de Messina, but it wasn't evenly enforced and not applicable to the secondary (or "superior") level. Although Spanish officials founded hundreds of schools in the decades leading up to the US intervention, Spain clamped down on education as its power began to wane. For Puerto Rico, this meant political repression, censorship of textbooks, and cutbacks to school funding that marked the decline of the public school system. Local support kept the system alive, with help coming from local school boards and the founding of two normal schools (one for men, the other for women) on the island. Even so, the Spanish government openly used schools as tools of imperialism and political dogmatism. The purpose of education, they declared, was "to teach them to love the fatherland so that they may grow to be loyal subjects of Spain." Puerto Ricans understood this well and, with the establishment of a US military occupation, they had high hopes that all of this would change.[3]

Although drawn to the idea of bringing America's "best models" of education to Puerto Rico, these protesters wanted nothing to do with Miles's occupation. They called for an "immediate termination of military and inauguration of civil government." That was in October of 1898. The first Puerto Rican governor was elected in 1949. Few, if any, of these protesters could have predicted what the next fifty years would entail for Puerto Rican self-governance. During the interim, the United States secured control over the island through the Foraker Act (1900) that allowed a US-appointed governor to oversee the activities of a limited, elected House of Representatives and the Jones Act (1917) that gave the island a Senate and imposed US citizenship on all Puerto Ricans. Along the way, a steady stream of US-appointed governors and education officials flowed in and out of the island. Each made their mark on the lives of students, teachers, and school communities. The first two decades of the American occupation were instrumental in establishing the foundation for what became the Puerto Rican public school system and the island's political economy that supported it.[4]

* * *

The first push for educational reform came from General Henry V. Guy. He started out as a provincial commander under Governor Miles during the initial invasion and occupation. When he replaced Miles as governor in December 1898, Guy made clear that he wanted English instead of Spanish as the official language in the school system. He started out slowly by opening a small school staffed by American educators during his first year as governor. The school, with its few hundred students, became a practice run for a larger project that involved sixteen American supervisors he appointed to oversee educational policy and practice throughout the island's sixteen districts. Through these supervisors, Guy declared English instruction one of the highest priorities of his administration and redistributed Puerto Rican tax dollars to prove his point. He established a two-tier pay scale that paid American teachers 25 percent more than native ones. Sooner or later, Guy stated in a circular in January 1899, all teachers "shall be expected to learn English." A few months later, Puerto Rico had a new "Code of School Laws" that dramatically changed education as they knew it. The new code authorized coeducation, abolished school fees, codified an age-graded school system, mandated caps on teacher-pupil ratios, provided free textbooks, centralized the system under an education bureau, and regulated teacher qualifications and their salaries. Of all these reform efforts, Guy believed the most important was changing the language of the nation through education.[5]

It surprised no one when Governor Guy put like-minded officials in charge of the newly established Bureau of Education. Victor Selden Clark, an economist from Columbia University, was one such official who continued Guy's advocacy of English instruction and even took matters a step further by suggesting that all students, from kindergarten to the university, were to immediately begin instruction in the foreign language. "The great mass of Puerto Ricans," he quipped, "are as yet passive and plastic… Their ideals are in our hands to create and mold." Students were to read from English-language textbooks and, ideally, to be taught by American teachers. The Americanization of the island began in earnest under Guy and Clark, not only with language instruction, but also through the mandated celebrations of American holidays, such as Washington's birthday, the Fourth of July, and Thanksgiving. They coupled these celebrations with the diffusion of symbols of American culture throughout the Puerto Rican school system, including US flags, portraits of American heroes, and sketches of battle scenes from American history. Clark helped Guy put English instruction and American culture wherever possible in the island's schools.[6]

What did surprise most Puerto Rican teachers was the way Clark moderated his views during his tenure as director of the Education Bureau. By the time he wrote the official "Teacher's Manual" for the school system, a few months into his term, he argued for bilingual education and no longer advocated an "English-only" approach. His previous position most likely became untenable, impractical, and unenforceable, given the scarcity of English-speaking teachers on the island. Whatever the reasons, it must have taken many by surprise and indicated that the English-only approach was, at least initially, a failed policy. The occupation didn't moderate much else, though. American education officials still discriminated against native teachers, mandating higher salaries to the seventy American teachers they had imported. These officials argued that American teachers should receive higher compensation because of the travel expenses they had incurred. Since the occupation controlled the state's revenues, it could redistribute wealth in this way. The message received by tax-paying Puerto Ricans was that islanders would have to subsidize their own Americanization.[7]

Clark knew that the moderated views on language instruction would most likely not save the occupation from backlash produced by the discriminatory pay policy, but he chalked it up to empire building. He was well aware of mistakes made by the Spanish in Puerto Rico when selecting their own officials for higher pay and how this had become a drain on the island's tax revenues. Teachers, he noted, "felt and resented keenly, as did all Puerto Rican officials, the appropriation of the best positions in the island by the Spaniards. They do not want to see this repeated in the case of America, and they see in the incoming of American teachers simply an invasion for spoils." These concerns, however, changed nothing in terms of occupation policy. Governor Guy and the rest of the occupation government supported Clark's view that the great masses of the island were for US officials to "create and mold." If it meant some "disfavor" from local boards of education for handing higher-paying teaching jobs to Americans, so be it.[8]

As Clark's efforts began to pick up steam, politicians in Washington took an interest in what was happening on the island. They set up two commissions—the "Porto Rico Commission" and the Carroll Commission—to investigate political, economic, and educational developments under the American occupation. President McKinley put two lawyers and a businessman in charge of the first one. Much of what the Porto Rico Commission had to say about education centered on faulting Spain for the poor quality of the island's school system prior to the US invasion. They charged the Spanish government with intent to keep the Puerto Rican population uneducated because "ignorance was supposed to render [islanders] more readily subject to obedience and control." What's more, the report blamed the overly pleasant tropical weather for inhibiting the development of the island's work ethic. Tropical heat, they suggested, stifled intellectual growth and even played a role in the 90-percent illiteracy rate. Environmental factors outweighed hereditary factors in the potential "natives" had for improvement. The islanders were capable of "quickly becom[ing] as intelligent as any others given the same opportunities." Because of this potential, the commission argued, the United States had an obligation to intervene and occupy. In fact, they pushed for something even more permanent in their report. "Porto Rico," they stated, "is now and is henceforth to be part of the American possessions and its people are to be American." Their educational policy recommendations followed from this annexationist logic. What the island needed was an influx of American teachers who would help with the task of "Americanizing" the island. The report was well received by military officials who gained two valuable points of justification for the US occupation of Puerto Rico: it highlighted the sky-high illiteracy rates, casting Puerto Rico as being in no position for self-rule; and it also supported the efforts of these officials in pushing English language in the schools. If Puerto Ricans didn't already know how to read Spanish, the argument went, what harm could there be in teaching them a new language?[9]

The Carroll Commission followed in the footsteps of the first investigation. Headed by US Treasury Department official Henry Carroll, these commissioners also blamed the tropical climate for what they described as "lack of will force." Carroll was more cautious, however, with the idea of Americanizing the island and defended bilingual education. He and his commission feared that pushing and forcing American values on to Puerto Ricans could result in a backlash and instability for occupation forces.[10]

Both reports recognized the difficulties faced by the military occupation. On the one hand, they celebrated the control the United States now had over the island. On the other hand, they understood the necessity of developing some semblance of self-rule. The Porto Rico Commission alluded to this by recalling the failed, heavy-handed approach of the Spanish colonial enterprise in the country. Carroll's report mentioned it directly, acknowledging that "an end of military rule is desired by the people" and recommending "local government after the pattern of our territories" because by doing so "she will gain by her blunders, just as the cities and States in our own glorious republic are constantly learning." Both reports called attention to the absence of self-governance and warned the occupation about the potential problems a military government would create over time.[11]

The occupation cherry-picked what it wanted from the reports. American officials appreciated the emphasis on illiteracy and the implied justifications for US rule over the island. They also moderated their views, in the case of Guy and Clark, on English-only instruction and began leaning toward bilingual education. But the occupation pressed forward undeterred with the Americanization project. They continued to infuse the Puerto Rican schools with symbols and imagery of American culture. And they continued to privilege American teachers over their native counterparts. They did all of this unilaterally, through the US-run military government, and kept Puerto Ricans largely out of this process.

* * *

From 1900 to 1921, Puerto Ricans demanded a greater role in making decision about their children's education by working with and sometimes protesting against the six education directors of the Bureau of Education that came after Clark. All of these directors vacillated to varying degrees between keeping strict control over the system and allowing more authority to Puerto Ricans.

The first three directors—Martin Brumbaugh, Samuel McCune Lindsay, and Roland Falkner—all made their way to Puerto Rico from the University of Pennsylvania. Brumbaugh, an education professor there, was handpicked by President McKinley to lead the Education Bureau after Clark in 1900. In practice, he outdid Guy and Clark in viewing education as a tool for Americanization. His main objective was to create an education system that would instill patriotic sentiments and a "zeal" and "enthusiasm for the Republic." By the time Brumbaugh took office, regulations required that every city or town with a graded school employ at least one native-speaking English teacher. This he saw as a gift, rather than a burden. He went so far as to say that the fifty American teachers who had arrived during his first year "have come as a solemn and sacred sacrifice for the Americanizing of the people of Porto Rico. These are true patriots and are worthy of the highest commendation." Brumbaugh's zealous patriotism inspired him to prescribe celebrations of the US flag across the island. These celebrations came complete with salutes, the singing of the national hymn, and, on a specified date during the school year, all-day performances including patriotic readings, patriotic songs, and marching band exercises. "No school has done its duty," he believed, "unless it has impressed devout patriotism upon the hearts and minds of all children." He believed naming schools after celebrated US figures would help the Americanization process along and soon Puerto Rican students began attending institutions named after Washington, Jefferson, Adams, Lincoln, Grant, Longfellow, and Mann. McKinley approved of Brumbaugh's work and sent $200,000 to support the opening of additional schools along these lines.[12]

Brumbaugh was pleased to see Puerto Rican students performing mandated flag celebrations and attending institutions named after American politicians, but he grumbled about not having enough control over the system. He particularly disliked the school boards, calling them "fatal to the advancement of schools." Taking aim at these local decision-making bodies, Brumbaugh drafted and successfully lobbied the occupation to pass *An Act to Establish a System of Public Schools in Puerto Rico* in January 1901. This act granted him power to appoint supervisors, reform the curriculum, control examinations, and determine requirements for teacher licensing and certification. It also allowed him to make unilateral decisions about textbooks, school equipment, and the design of school buildings. But most importantly, he reserved for himself the right to "formulate such rules and regulations" as he may "from time to time find necessary for the effective administration" of the island's schools. With this act, Brumbaugh effectively dissolved the last vestiges of local control over schools and school policy.[13]

Brumbaugh's top-down rule over the school system created significant blowback, as the commissions had predicted. Local papers ran articles calling Brumbaugh's moves "despotic" and accusing him of being a "czar that had come here to run the schools." Puerto Ricans were incensed that his education act had been designed and implemented on their behalf, but without their input. He appointed himself "sole authority to erect schools, appoint teachers, and purchase supplies—and this Commissioner is not beholden to the people of Puerto Rico whose money he spends." Brumbaugh's response was to deny the accusations. They had misread his intentions, he said, and deliberately misrepresented his views on every topic and in every way. He even accused his critics of treasonous propaganda, for "no loyal citizen should talk or write" against the occupation as they had. Although he admitted that American teachers were paid more than their Puerto Rican counterparts, these people "needed us" and they "are reaping the benefits of the change." And all this change had a purpose. Brumbaugh's goal was to see the "speedy placing of a new star in the azure field of the glorious flag of freedom." What he wanted more than anything else for the island was complete annexation and incorporation into the United States. With 733 schools under his control with an average daily attendance above twenty-three thousand students—as well as a school budget that absorbed over one-fourth of the Puerto Rican national budget—he believed the occupation was well on its way toward Americanization for annexation.[14]

Brumbaugh's term came to an end with the appointment of Samuel McCune Lindsay in 1902. Lindsay was a sociology professor at the University of Pennsylvania and, when he arrived in Puerto Rico, he quickly undertook a study of the island's schools. He conducted a survey and found four basic kinds: graded, agricultural, industrial, and special schools. Graded schools offered an academic and, in some cases, college preparatory curriculum. Agricultural schools included a smattering of academic course work, but mostly provided a Hampton-Tuskegee model education. Industrial schools centered on the mechanic arts. And the special schools offered night classes, nursing programs, and arts education. After surveying the island's school system, Lindsay described his greatest challenge as one having to do with finding a sufficient number of qualified teachers to fill positions across the island. He viewed the normal school (later the University of Puerto Rico) as critical to this end and vital to "the engrafting of American institutions upon a Spanish American stock." The normal school was "the most important of all [legislation]" in getting teachers in the classroom and as a vehicle for Americanization.[15]

After conducting the school survey, and discovering the problem of teacher shortages, Lindsay decided to expand an occupation-run program of summer institutes. These institutes provided basic teacher training, especially English instruction, to Puerto Rican school teachers. He believed that the people of the island needed English because "commercial prosperity depends on their adoption of the English language." What distinguished Lindsay's approach to language policy, however, was his view that it should be optional, rather than mandated. He encouraged Puerto Ricans to learn English in these summer institutes, but didn't require it. He explained to teachers through publications that this was a "purely voluntary" part of the examination for licensure and that it had "nothing whatever to do with the teacher's certificate you hold or the renewal of the certificate." This was a significant departure from previous administrations. It's clear he wanted to change perceptions about this approach to Americanization during his tenure as Education Bureau director. But Lindsay didn't change everything. He kept the status quo by having Puerto Rican teachers recite the Pledge of Allegiance every morning among other patriotic exercises and expressions. Americanization for annexation was still very much part of the goal during Lindsay's tenure and nothing made this more obvious than the display he sent to the St. Louis Exposition of 1904. Lindsay's education representative at the show highlighted the efforts that had been made in the Americanization of Puerto Rican children. The display included descriptions and visual examples of children in the public schools who "learn loyalty to the American flag and are proud to consider their land a part of the great Republic." By the end of his time in office, Lindsay had successfully increased the number of students who were learning "loyalty" to forty thousand in over eleven hundred schools.[16]

Following Brumbaugh and Lindsay, Roland Falkner made the same journey from Philadelphia to San Juan in 1904. He had been a business professor at the University of Pennsylvania, and his areas of expertise were in accounting and statistics. Like Lindsay, he too conducted a survey of the school system as soon as he arrived, but Falkner's was about school completion (e.g., grade levels completed by Puerto Rican students) rather than types of schools. He found that students rarely continued past the fourth grade. Applying a factory model of organization to the school system, he interpreted the numbers to represent inefficiency and, as a result, he decided to slow down school construction across the island. "To borrow a simile from modern industrialism," he told his colleagues, "it may be said of the educational problem in Porto Rico, 'It is not so much to extend the plant as to increase the output.'" While putting the breaks on school construction, Falkner also began to examine the textbooks reaching Puerto Rican children. He found that these texts failed to take the environment and conditions of the island into consideration. "Not one of them," he noted, "has been prepared with a special view to our needs." Some of these textbooks, for instance, used "peaches" to illustrate math problems, even though most Puerto Rican children had never been exposed to the fruit.[17]

Falkner's sensitivity to the Puerto Rican context when it came to textbooks didn't transfer to language instruction. In a reversal of Lindsay's "voluntary" approach, he establishment what became known as the Falkner Policy. The new policy made English the primary mode of instruction in Puerto Rico. This was no longer a course requirement for students; it was now the dominant method of communication in all subjects. To support this plan, he continued to pay teachers with English skills more than other teachers and developed a program of English classes that ran all year long. He believed the year-long program would be more effective than the summer institutes. Falkner also mandated a "two strikes" rule that gave teachers only two attempts at passing the English examination. If a teacher failed a first time, he or she could take it a second time after a three-month period. If failed a second time, "the Department of Education may suspend them from duty." Falkner issued an addendum to the rule, stating that teachers who had not passed the exam after two years faced the cancellation of their teachers' licenses or diplomas. The crackdown on English-language requirements, he argued, would lead to speedy changes. In one sense, he was proven right; it hiked up the rate of organizing among and protesting by Puerto Rican teachers. Contributors to Puerto Rico's leading teacher periodical, *La Educacion Moderna*, called the Falkner Policy a disaster. They noted that it put Puerto Rican children, many of whom spoke Spanish only, with an American teacher who was required to teach strictly in English. Critics dubbed the new rules as "inhumane, erroneous, and disturbing." Falkner finished his term in the middle of this storm of criticism. Puerto Ricans were not only agitated by his language policies, but also disappointed in the anemic school expansion with only a few dozen schools constructed and approximately sixty-five thousand students enrolled.[18]

The Falkner Policy became the standard by which the last three directors of the Education Bureau—Edwin Dexter, Edward Bainter, and Paul Miller—were measured. Dexter had been a professor of education and dean at the University of Illinois before arriving in San Juan in 1907. He continued the Falkner Policy, and in some instances made them more severe. Dexter reorganized the number of school districts, increasing them from 19 to 66 and requiring a significant increase in the number of American supervisors for each district. Through these supervisors, he demanded that "failure on the part of such teachers to pass the coming [English] examination may result in suspension from duty." This move was part of Dexter's policy of mandating English instruction beginning in the first grade. English-only instruction shot up from 67 percent to 90 percent in the graded school system as a result, making the transition from Spanish to English almost complete during his time in office. Several other dramatic increases occurred during his term including enrollments that rose from 71,000 to 160,000 and average daily attendance from 44,000 to 114,000. He also increased the number of students receiving manual instruction from 0 to 6,329 and agricultural instruction from 0 to 8,723. The feather in his cap, as far as annexationists were concerned, was the meteoric rise in schools with English-only instruction that shot up from 202 to 947. He too was an annexationist and saw the increase in English-only instruction as a prelude to granting US citizenship to Puerto Ricans. Dexter wanted "ultimate statehood for the island" and celebrated the Fourth of July in 1908 with 1,000 schoolchildren dressed in red, white, and blue as they sang songs (*Star Spangled Banner, America*) and paraded through the streets.[19]

Edward Bainter, like the directors who came before him, also pushed for Puerto Ricans to receive US citizenship as soon as he took up his duties at the Education Bureau in 1912. His approach to English-language instruction was twofold. If they passed the English exam, they would no longer have to attend mandatory English classes. At the same time, he continued to enforce the two-strikes rule that came with the Falkner Policy. Teachers could only take the English exam twice. But Bainter could hardly have predicted that his policies would be challenged by the increasingly powerful Puerto Rican House of Delegates. The political sands had shifted underneath Bainter. In a victory for English-only critics, the House of Delegates passed a law abolishing annual classes in English and the yearly English exam. This inspired the Puerto Rican Teacher's Association to hold assemblies and demand that the Education Bureau "establish Spanish from now on as the medium of instruction in all public schools." Bainter, caught in the rise of a Puerto Rican pride movement, complicated matters for himself by supporting the expulsion of a San Juan Central High School student for collecting signatures among fellow students in support of a bill that required Spanish to be used in all public schools. When newspapers learned of Bainter's position, the Unionist paper *La Democracia* saw this student, among others, as "unjustly persecuted by the Department of Education." In the end, Bainter tried to defend his position by describing the student as a notorious troublemaker, but critics simply replied that "it is not a matter of a pupil being disrespectful of a teacher, but of a Mr. Bainter who has been disrespectful to the country." The flare-up, in part, set him sailing home before the end of his term. Bainter fulfilled three of his four-year term, leaving abruptly and resigning without advance notice.[20]

Puerto Ricans expected more "use of the rod, instead of moral suasion" in the Americanization of the island after Bainter's departure. When they learned that Paul Miller would be his replacement, the mood quickly changed.[21]

President Woodrow Wilson handpicked Miller for the job of Education Bureau director in 1915. He had already served as the principal of the normal school at Rio Piedras, and was therefore already familiar to Puerto Rican teachers. Miller had a sterling reputation as principal, with reports stating he had "many friends" among the island's teachers and that he was "generally liked," had their "respect," and was held in "high esteem." It probably helped that he spoke Spanish fluently, having previously been a foreign-language professor at the University of Wisconsin. Miller had every reason to believe he'd succeed where others had failed. Given his background in foreign languages, teachers likely hoped he'd relax the English-language requirements and waited to learn what kind of policy he would propose. Miller replied to all this enthusiasm about his selection by stating that "I desire to work with you rather than over you." He was a known quantity and, given the initial enthusiasm, they looked forward to working with him too.[22]

Miller began cautiously. He continued to offer summer institutes for the diffusion of English because he wanted them to have "a good knowledge" of the language. At the same time, he relaxed some of the requirements on the books that mandated English-only in primary schools. Miller removed English instruction for arithmetic from first through fourth grades. Teachers of first and second grades were now permitted to use the Spanish American Primer. This slowed down the transition from language to language, with English-only classes beginning in the fifth grade. "The elimination of English reading from the first and second grades," he warned, "is in no way to be construed as a change in attitude by the Department as to the advisability of teaching English." They would still have to know the language by fifth grade and supervisors in the third grade would be responsible for making that transition as smooth as possible.[23]

The honeymoon didn't last. Miller and the island's teachers clashed over the handling of two developments: demands coming from the Puerto Rican Teacher's Association for Spanish-only instruction in all grades and the onset of World War I. The Teacher's Association demanded that Miller end the English-only language policy; they no longer wanted a bilingual program and believed that Miller might be open to this change. Their hopes were dashed when he flatly rejected the request. While he may have understood their concerns as well as he understood their language, Miller was swept up in war mobilization. "There never was a better time...for teaching fundamental morality and lofty patriotism," he said, and referred to teachers as "efficient propagandists, ready and able to take part in the molding of public opinion along patriotic lines." School communities began to strike as a result of his position on the language policy and in opposition to the occupation government. These strikes set off a chain of events that resulted in Miller ordering the suspension of all students involved "indefinitely." But it wasn't just students who were targeted. Teachers who assisted student strikers were also "liable to suspension." University students erupted in protest and in solidarity with the school communities, launching what's now referred to as the "Young Turks" protests. These Young Turks demanded that Puerto Rican political leaders in the House of Delegates call for an "open declaration of independence for Puerto Rico." Students across the country followed this lead and formed literary societies to organize further protests. Occupation officials viewed one of them—the Jose De Diego Society—as particularly threatening and forced schools to dissolve the organization. Miller's most inflammatory decision during this period, however, had to do with a graduating senior at Central High School who brought the Puerto Rican flag to graduation exercises. Miller demanded that police "remove the enemy flag from the place." Students left the assembly in droves with the flag held high. Newspapers ran stories on the "abusive power" by the occupation government and called for Miller's removal.[24]

Although Miller began his work as Education Bureau director with widespread teacher support, his term ended with demonstrations and efforts to see him removed from office. Critics viewed him as "*persona non grata* to the Puerto Rico society." Political events during his tenure and beyond the bureau's control created a fluid environment in which rapid changes occurred. Washington passed the Jones Act, giving Puerto Ricans the "rights and privileges accorded our own citizens in our own territories." The declaration of these "rights and privileges" came without any political input from Puerto Ricans themselves. Some native politicians claimed that the Jones Act denied "the capacity of the people of Puerto Rico to direct their own destinies" by drawing the nation further into the sphere of American influence and territorial control. More importantly for teachers and schoolchildren, the Jones Act dramatically empowered the already powerful Bureau of Education in Puerto Rico. Occupation officials applauded this increase in authority over education that would save education from "the somewhat unskilled handful of well-meaning Puerto Ricans" The Jones Act, according to the governor at the time, offered the occupation "a firmer grip upon the educational system of the island." With all of this control in hand, the occupation government made a surprising appointment following Miller's removal. The next director was a native-born Puerto Rican lawyer and former teacher, Juan B. Huyke. This appointment marked the beginning of the complex American governance over Puerto Rican education. The American occupation continued to wield and exercise authority over educational policy, but it did so through native-born representatives. Huyke's term marked the beginning of the use of client-state officials to accomplish the tasks desired by the occupation government.[25]

* * *

During these first decades, from Governor Guy's educational reforms to the appointment of Huyke as Education Bureau director, the school system suffered from the economic policies created by the occupation government. The revenue sources upon which these schools relied were anything but stable, creating sometimes extreme differences in pay between native and American teachers or extreme variation in school construction from director to director.[26]

At bottom, external economic interests interfered with the revenue sources Puerto Rican schools relied on most. US Treasury official Henry Carroll, who led one of the initial Puerto Rican commissions, recognized the significant draw that the island would have for American corporate, industrial, and agricultural interest during the US occupation. For him, Puerto Rico represented a perfect release valve for the pressure created by the overaccumulation of capital in the United States. It would give great opportunities for American investors and would "furnish a field for American capital and American enterprise, if not for the overflow of population." With the closing of the American frontier, the limitless expanse that once was the United States no longer seemed so limitless. Carroll understood this to mean that America needed an empire—new terrain for exploitation—for its capital and for its people.

The greater the influence of external economic interests, however, the less schools received for significant improvements in literacy, grade completion, teacher compensation, and school expansion. In each of these areas, with the exception of school construction (and average daily attendance), the occupation made few substantive academic gains.[27]

US political and corporate interests, meanwhile, made tremendous gains that overwhelmed Puerto Rico's political economy during the first decades of the US occupation. The Foraker Act—as much as an economic instrument as a political one—denied the island the ability to negotiate treaties with other countries, gave the United States control over the island's tariff rates, and required partial distribution of tariff revenues to the United States. Meanwhile, the occupation government selectively enforced those Foraker provisions that proved pesky to American corporations, such as restrictions on the sale of land to foreign companies to five hundred acres. By 1930, less than 1 percent of the corporate-owned farms violated this rule, but they controlled over one-third of all Puerto Rican land. Absentee ownership and manager-operated farms skyrocketed during the early occupation and led to almost half of all farm lands being rented or managed by foreign interests. This pattern forced small farmers out of business, impoverishing the locals, while providing a land bonanza to well-connected US corporate sugar interests, such as the four corporations—Central Aguirre, South Porto Rico, Fajardo, and United Porto Rico/Eastern Sugar—that controlled approximately a quarter of all cane fields and half of all corporate-managed lands on the island. Seventy-five percent of their profits—the wealth produced by Puerto Rican labor on their native soil—flowed out of Puerto Rico and, for the most part, into the bank accounts of American shareholders.[28]

Tobacco went the way of sugar. Favorable tariff policies for the commodity gave it a leg up and attracted the interest of US producers and processors. Not long after 1898, the United States dominated the Puerto Rican tobacco market with over 80 percent of the production and processing controlled by two US corporations—The Porto Rican-American Tobacco Company of New Jersey and the New York Tampa Cigar Company. Porto Rican-American, by 1930, was purchasing 50 percent of the island's crop, making it the single most powerful manufacturer in Puerto Rico.[29]

US bankers, as a result, benefited disproportionately from the American occupation. After two decades, over one-fourth of the island's wealth was foreign owned with the vast majority of this in US hands. After three decades, four North American banks—American Colonial Bank, National City Bank of New York, Bank of Nova Scotia, and Royal Bank of Canada—controlled 50 percent of Puerto Rican assets and much more in terms of farm, land, and industry debt. This tremendous redistribution of wealth northward occurred swiftly, with the first US bank—American Colonial—entering the Puerto Rican market two years after the start of the US occupation and, by 1910, becoming the single largest bank on the island.[30]

* * *

The wealth extraction from Puerto Rico removed a vital revenue source for internal developments, particularly those having to do with the Puerto Rican educational system. This wealth extraction was not a result of an invisible hand, with market forces dictating the terms of such things as teacher salaries, but in fact was the result of the very visible hand of US occupation policies that favored US corporate and banking interests through tariff controls, selective law enforcement, and denying the island the opportunity to freely negotiate with other countries. These policies ultimately proved detrimental to vast swaths of Puerto Ricans who were left impoverished and with an educational system that received a mere pittance when compared to the favors and attention given to US economic interests.

But at least racial antipathies didn't complicate matters in the occupation of Puerto Rico to any significant degree. The "tropical race theory" occasionally cited by US officials largely pointed to climate, weather, and an abundance of natural resources as the cause of perceived underperformance on the island. It wasn't so much a matter of Spanish or native blood, as sunshine, surf, and lush, fertile soil. This wasn't the case in another US occupation that began a few years before Puerto Rico elected its first native secretary of education, a short distance away in the Caribbean. Race colored just about everything, right from the outset, when the United States invaded and occupied the second oldest nation in the Americas, second only to the United States.

CHAPTER FOUR
HAMPTON CREOLE

"Dear me, think of it," said William Jennings Bryan in 1912, "Niggers speaking French!" At the time, Bryan was Woodrow Wilson's secretary of state, learning about Haiti, and in charge of US foreign policy toward the country and region.[1]

His lessons about Haiti came from the American manager of the country's most important financial institution, Banque Nationale. It's ironic that he turned to bankers for advice. Bryan loathed them, especially those known for loan-sharking and exploitation in Latin America. But he felt he had little choice. The very real possibility of an American invasion of the country increased during the first years of Wilson's term. The banker to whom Bryan turned and who helped him most was Roger L. Farnham.[2]

Farnham knew quite a bit about Haiti, but he was hardly a disinterested player in the events that were to unfold. As vice president of the National City Bank of New York *and* of Banque Nationale in Haiti, as well as president of the National Railway of Haiti, the stakes for Farnham were quite high. An American invasion and occupation of the country would be a significant boon for him and his circle of Wall Street speculators. Putting American combat boots in Port-au-Prince had the potential of turning their risky investments into stable, secure ones almost overnight. This was hardly the kind of justification that Bryan would appreciate, since it would require asking the American taxpayer to subsidize investment risks for the purpose of private profit. But he warmed to these New York financiers who wanted exclusive control of Haiti's debt and, to secure their investment in the country, Haiti's customs house as well. They convinced Secretary Bryan to send marines into Haiti the year before the 1915 invasion. In that mission, troops removed $500,000 worth of Haitian government gold from the Banque Nationale, shipped the funds to New York, and deposited them at National City Bank—all without a single shot fired. The idea was to force Haiti's European creditors, who'd made multimillion-dollar loans, to negotiate with the United States rather than Haiti. At the same time, American military officials began preparations for a full-scale invasion and occupation in case "local authorities admit their inability to protect foreign interests." Within the year, the opportunity to use the plans appeared when an angry Haitian mob turned against Haitian president Vilbrun Guillame Sam, whose term was marked by suppression of political dissent. President Sam's overthrow and assassination set the stage for the US invasion.[3]

While Farnham continued to tutor Bryan on American economic interests in Haiti, Wilson's team quickly began assessing the humanitarian crisis enveloping the country. The State Department spoke firmly of the "humane duty" the United States had in addressing the political disorder and potential famine. Stability, freedom, and democracy became the administration's refrain. These ideals, however, only reveal part of the picture; they hardly provided the sole or even primary impulses for invading and occupying a sovereign country. On twenty previous occasions since 1857, the United States had dispatched warships to visit Haiti's ports to protect American lives and property. What made Bryan's situation different in 1915 was the level of American investment in Haiti, increasing competition from European investors, a perceived threat from German military interests in the Caribbean, and Haiti's political and economic instability. At bottom, US economic and military interests commanded great influence over the decision to intervene and the decision to occupy.[4]

To Farnham's circle, the occupation meant greater financial control over Haiti. They assumed managing roles in the country's finances and wielded influence over how Haitian taxes would be spent under US governance. They also received a much sought-after prize for foreign corporate interests when the occupation rewrote the Haitian constitution. The constitution prior to the invasion explicitly made foreign landownership illegal. Haitians held sacred the idea that Haitian land was to be owned by Haitians. But this was an offensive legal obstacle to large-scale American agricultural, timber, and mining interests. In a conspicuous nod to these interests, the occupation government removed the obstacle. Franklin Delano Roosevelt, who was then assistant secretary of the navy, later admitted to personally having rewritten

Haiti's constitution, thereby opening the door to US corporate control over Haitian soil.[5]

Presidential candidate Warren Harding expressed disgust at corporate and military meddling in the affairs of other countries during the campaign trail in 1920. He told the American public that the United States shouldn't be in the business of writing a constitution for a sovereign nation, much less trying to "jam it down their throats at the points of bayonets." After campaigning against this "rape of Haiti," little changed once Harding won the election and moved into the White House.[6]

The occupation, beginning with Wilson's invasion in 1915, continued largely unchanged over the course of five US administrations because each delegated much authority to American military commanders. And these commanders held a tight grip over the country. By controlling the government revenues and customs houses—in addition to Haiti's land policy and constitution—American officials had veto power over the provisional, parallel Haitian government. The occupation had the power to withhold the salaries of Haitian politicians and to revoke funds for unauthorized projects. Haitian leaders quickly learned it was futile to resist US decision making when the power of the purse was not theirs. The one area of Haitian life the American military government in Haiti didn't have explicit control over was education. Absent from any of the original postinvasion agreements signed between the US and Haitian governments was mention of schools, colleges, or universities. The agreements, intended to legitimize the authority of the occupation, allowed for an almost complete transfer of control over Haiti, except for education. That oversight left an opening. It gave Haitians a sense of control over the future of their country not found elsewhere.[7]

* * *

When it came to education, occupation officials shared much in common with what Farnham envisioned for Haiti. What the country needed, he believed, was a "good deal of development" through foreign capital and "some time to educate the Haitian to become a good laborer." As he understood it, with the aid of the right institutions, Haitians could be trained to provide the labor force needed to support American banking and commercial interests.[8]

If there was one person who could make Farnham's vision a reality, it was General John H. Russell. He was the most powerful man in Haiti and led the occupation for over a decade. As head of American forces in the country, he had authority over the government's revenue and almost complete influence over the Haitian government. The US government created the special position of "High Commissioner" of Haiti in recognition of his achievements. With all of this influence came the responsibility of charting a course for developing the nation's institutions and infrastructure. Russell embraced the Farnham view of things when he said that "education and civilization march hand in hand. The introduction of railways and good roads and the opening of certain agricultural sections by foreign capital will, in time, have a civilizing effect on the natives." Russell wanted American capital to pour into Haiti; he wanted businesses, industries, and large-scale agricultural interests to serve as Haiti's most powerful educator. His faith in American capital was highly colored by his lack of faith in Haitian potential. "The peasants," he said, "who form the mass (85%) of the population and who have so long been held by their literate brothers in a backward state, have the mentality of a child of not more than seven years of age reared under advantageous conditions." According to the general, American investment was the solution to the country's problems.[9]

Russell's views on capital and the Haitian "mentality" had immediate consequences for Haitian education. His policies hardly budged the 95 percent illiteracy rate the occupation had inherited. School enrollments increased from 3 percent to 25 percent, but this was underwhelming considering the goal of Haitian self-rule and the stagnant literacy rates. Despite unflattering statistics, Russell decreased the total education budget by 20 percent when comparing funding for 1914 ($423,000), the year before the US invasion of Haiti, with that of 1920 ($340,000), the second year under his command.[10]

Russell had little interest in promoting literacy or traditional schooling, but instead favored programs that would benefit the work of foreign capital such as industrial and agricultural education. As head of the American occupation, he speculated about the nature of the mind to support his preference. Mass literacy education, he asserted, "does not teach them to think. When reading the mind is passive. It requires argument to be active; and reading a party paper presenting only one side of the case, they think only one line." He suggested that literacy had little to do with democracy and struck reading instruction from his list of priorities. Far more valuable, Russell claimed, was teaching "each individual a trade, to make each citizen an asset." According to him, only two kinds of schools had any place in Haiti: "The industrial school is necessary for the proper education of the entire mass of the children of the cities of Haiti. In the same manner, the agricultural school is necessary to the entire mass of children in the rural districts." While this hardly tells the whole story of Russell's thinking in terms of American capital, education, and democracy, it clearly offers insight into his policies. It's as close as he ever came to explaining why he made the most significant education-related decision of his career.[11]

In 1922, Russell began one of the largest educational reform efforts in Haitian history. After failing to convince the Haitian government of the need to create a national network of industrial and agricultural schools, Russell decided to take matters into his own hands. He radically increased funding for the Department of Agriculture with the intent of starting an entirely new system of education, one that would compete with the traditional, classical schooling offered by the National Schools under Haiti's Ministry of Education. With these new funds, he established the "Bureau of Technical Service of Agriculture and Vocational Education" as a division within the Agriculture Department. The division was to supervise the development of new institutions for technical education. His goal was for the program to rival and eventually overtake the entire educational infrastructure under the Ministry of Education.[12]

This ambitious reform required someone to head up the necessary tasks and manage the day-to-day bureau affairs. Russell personally selected George F. Freeman for the job. He found Freeman through an advertisement that began with three qualification requirements that captured an unintended irony: "White, no racial prejudice, agricultural expert."[13]

Freeman had a solid background in science, became the darling of foreign capital interests in Haiti, and established a poor track record in terms of race relations. He had a doctorate in science from Harvard University, where he developed an interest in large-scale agricultural production. Before arriving in Haiti, he had been chief of the Division of Cotton Breeding at the Texas Agricultural Experiment Station. Almost as soon as he became Haiti's director of the Technical Bureau in 1923, Freeman began using funds at his disposal to support the interests of American investors through the establishment of experiment stations. Research, instruction, and support offered by these stations came from an American staff selected by Freeman who were known for speaking only English. By default this arrangement favored large-scale foreign interests while marginalizing French-speaking natives and their small farms. The significance of Freeman's operation increased as American sugar and coffee companies consolidated and expanded their landholdings in Haiti. Over 170,000 acres of prime farmlands were acquired by these investors under the US occupation. The power, resources, and tactics of these large-scale operations had the predictable consequence of wiping out small-scale Haitian farmers. Many who once owned their land soon found themselves working as laborers for foreign companies. Freeman's prejudices shaped his understanding of the situation. These black natives were not suited for self-rule, he believed, and if Haitians were to advance they would need to view themselves first as "human instruments" of commercial interests. Only then might "true leaders and teachers" follow to govern and educate the masses. He practiced what he preached and turned the experiment stations into tools for industry, but the stations were just the beginning.[14]

Russell had Freeman use the Technical Bureau to carry out a total reform of Haitian education. To do this, Freeman received what amounted to a blank check. He also received important words of support from Russell, who stated that if reforms were to succeed then traditional "primary and secondary instruction must necessarily await [funding]" because "the energies of the Haitian Government at present should be directed along lines of agricultural development and training and vocational instruction." Over the objections of the Haitian government, Freeman began by establishing the École Centrale d'Agriculture in 1924. Its purpose was to train agricultural technicians and to serve as a centerpiece for the proposed network of agricultural and technical institutions. Following the École Centrale, the bureau invested heavily in the construction of farm schools and industrial schools that began appearing across the country. They would be, Freeman argued, better than the old, classical schools that draw "a child's mind to fanciful dreams of better things far away." The new schools taught about the here and now—farming, shoemaking, iron works, masonry, and bricklaying—with a curriculum divided in two parts. Approximately half of the instructional time centered on manual labor and the other half on basic reading, writing, morality, catechism, civics, and hygiene. To pay for ongoing school construction and fund their operations, the budget for Freeman's division had to increase significantly. Russell happily complied. By 1929, Freeman was receiving 4.5 million gourdes for a total of 69 agricultural and vocational institutions. This was more than two

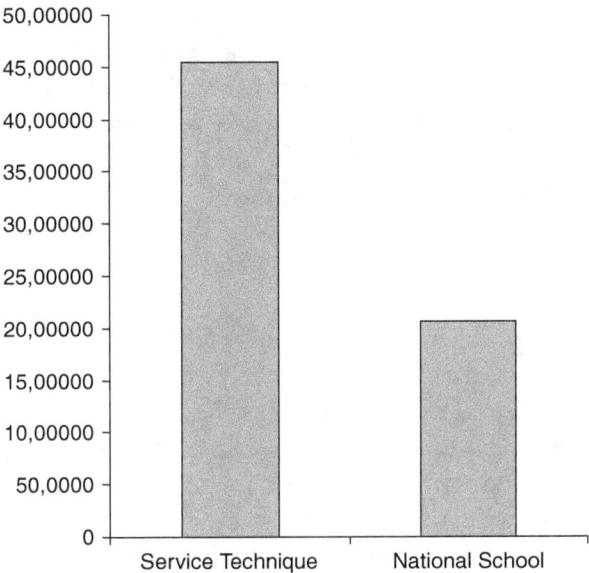

Figure 4.1 US military occupation government budget allocations (in Gourdes), 1928–1929.[16]

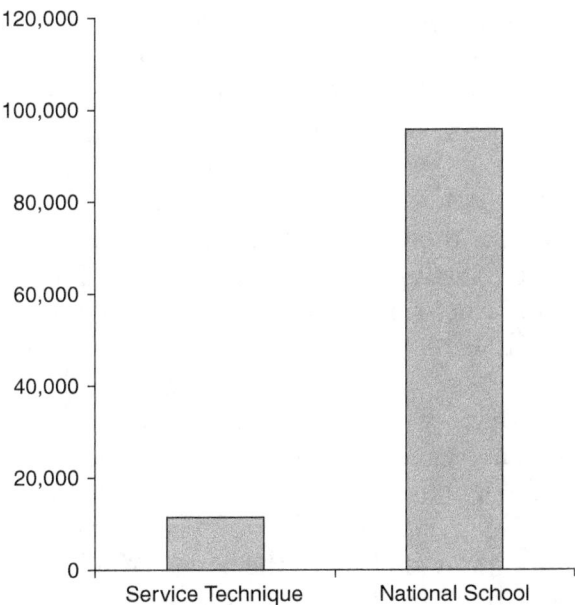

Figure 4.2 Haitian student population distribution, 1928–1929.[17]

times Russell's allocation to all other public schools combined, including 608 public elementary, secondary, and postsecondary schools.[15]

With this redistribution of Haitian funds, Russell had circumvented the democratic process that would have required working with the Haitian government on educational policy. He succeeded in building the schools he thought Haiti needed most.[18]

* * *

But there was a problem. Haitians, by and large, rejected Farnham's vision of the country's future, Russell's educational policies, and Freeman's agricultural and vocational schools. No matter how many schools the Technical Bureau opened, they still needed students to fill the classrooms. And while denied the formal democratic process, students could vote with their feet. Very few (10 percent of the Haitian student population) ever enrolled in the Bureau's new programs. The National School System, on the other hand, with 90 percent of the nation's students, had to make do with a budget considerably less (approximately 60 percent less) than that of the bureau.[19]

What Russell had dismissed too quickly was Haiti's well-established system of classical or traditional education that was a central part of Haitian culture; this tradition wasn't likely to change in a year or two or even in a decade. The country's classical education had formed roots under the shade of French colonialism and had become part of the Haitian social order. Haiti established a national Ministry of Education in the 1840s, around the time Horace Mann was proposing public education for the state of Massachusetts. Before the American occupation, Haiti had also created the office of the École Communales that provided for a network of rural and urban schools and, eventually, the National School System. The most prized form of education was the classical, Latin-Grammar schooling offered at the lyceums. Haitians viewed them as pathways to higher learning and social mobility. The few lyceums that existed offered a strictly academic curriculum with moral and religious instruction, language and literature studies (French, Latin, Greek, Spanish), history, geography, philosophy, law, political economy, and applied mathematics. While a small percentage of the population ever received this kind of education, it held an important place in the Haitian conception of education, democracy, and social progress.[20]

This historical and cultural reality was Russell's greatest blind spot, even though he had been warned. Haiti's president Louis Borno understood what the people wanted and told Russell that the educational reforms were likely to fail. Borno pleaded with him to reconsider the disproportionate emphasis on technical education; he wanted Haitians to have greater access to classical education through the National School System. Russell ignored Borno's concerns and suggestions. "Any change in the American policy at this time," he told Borno, "would be a tremendous blow."[21]

As funds continued to pour into the Technical Bureau, large budgetary discrepancies came into plain view. Salary differences between National School System teachers and those in the Service Technique caused an uproar. Teachers in the National Schools were native Haitians and received approximately $4–6 dollars a month. The vast majority of Service Technique teachers were white American educators and received ten times the salary with ranges between $40–90 dollars a month; some received wildly disproportionate salaries of $4000–5000 per year. The Haitian press, such as the *Nouvelliste*, was outraged and described the Service Technique as a symptom of the occupation's general disregard for the people: "There exist great fiascos which cost the Haitian people large sums of money...As for The Service Technique de l'Agriculture, they kept spending money, and spent it badly." The British minister to Haiti also couldn't help noticing that Freeman's instructors were "made up to a great extent of men and women who neither speak a word of French nor have any special qualifications as 'experts,' but who have been dumped on the unfortunate Haitian budget at unnecessarily high rates."[22]

Outcries over discrimination in teacher pay contributed to a groundswell of dissatisfaction over the American occupation and Haiti's loss of autonomy. The occupation's management of Haiti's internal revenue fell under increasing scrutiny. It placed Russell and other occupation leaders under pressure to explain their actions. As Haitians saw it, the disproportionate funding of the Technical Bureau came at the expense of the National Schools that still operated out of rented buildings, had poor-quality teaching materials, and offered teachers rock-bottom salaries at about 15 cents per day. Worse still, Haitians made the inflammatory discovery that Russell had used "surplus" funds in the nation's budget to make advanced principal repayment to a $40-million New York–backed loan. This move gave the impression that extra loan payments to Wall Street mattered more than repairing the crumbling National School System. Tensions skyrocketed.²³

* * *

Widespread Haitian frustration ultimately exploded over what started out as a small student protest in October 1929. The protest spread across the country and caught the occupation by surprise. It ignited the same fuel of repressed political dissent that led to the mobbing of President Sam. This time Freeman, Russell, and Borno were the targets.

The crisis began at Freeman's flagship École Central de l'Agriculture. Poor enrollments there proved to be an embarrassment to the entire technical education plan. To increase enrollments, Freeman received funds for a scholarship pool. The idea was to attract students by giving them a generous financial aid package that would enable them to attend. Midway through the fall semester of 1929, Freeman decided to make an across-the-board cut of 20 percent to the scholarships students were receiving. He moved the "savings" to an experiment station and demonstration farm in the city of Damien. Students were expected to absorb the difference. When they learned of this decision, students formed a committee and met with Freeman in October 1929. It didn't go well. Freeman remained unmoved by their concerns and told them that if they were unhappy, they could simply leave the school. They immediately responded by striking. Classrooms emptied and students marched approximately five miles to Port-au-Prince. Their objective was to appeal to the Haitian minister of public instruction, Charles Bouchereau, who they hoped might be able to represent their concerns to the American occupation. To their dismay, Bouchereau came across as siding with Freeman, telling them that they had to return to classes the next day. If they failed to do so, they would be automatically withdrawn from school. He threatened them with a loss of their seats and aid at the institution. But this move only aggravated the situation. Students became more resolved to fight Freeman and what he represented—American control of Haiti. They declared their intention to continue the strike.²⁴

Word spread quickly across the country that students had taken a stand against the occupation. During the month of November, Haitians from virtually all walks of life began to show their support and take a stand themselves. The Haitian League of the Rights of Man demanded an investigation into the Freeman controversy. Newspapers talked of his "drastic action against young men and girls." Students attending Haiti's professional schools of law, medicine, applied sciences, and teacher education signed formal declarations of support for the École Centrale rebellion. Students at a reform school joined the uprising with a hunger strike. Some Haitians took to the streets and even stoned Freeman's home. Others, including students and staff at the École Centrale and at the Service Technique school in Damien, began to demand Freeman's resignation. Toward the end of November, coordinated demonstrations were organized in Jacmel, Cap-Hatien, and St. Marc. Students in those towns left classes and poured into the streets to protest against the occupation. The strike turned into a movement that reached the very heart of the occupation. Haitian employees in the customs houses, banks, and commerce divisions under occupation control left their desks and protested against the military government's treatment of Haitian students.[25]

Russell, Freeman, and Borno attempted to deal with the crisis by increasing student financial aid in December 1929, but it was too late. Russell began blaming the strike for what appeared to be the beginning of the end of the occupation. He feared that protests were "rapidly spreading throughout Haiti" and wanted to suspend freedom of the press because "invitations to disorder were daily printed." Meanwhile, student and parent groups asked to meet with Freeman. The director refused their request, creating an uprising among faculty and staff at the École Centrale. They threatened to resign if Freeman continued to rebuff requests for a meeting. When he finally agreed to one, observers described it as "apparently acute." Nothing came of it, prompting Borno to step in and replace Minister of Public Instruction Bouchereau with Hannibal Price. He hoped a change of guard might appease critics. Price immediately tried to stem the crisis by guaranteeing École Centrale students jobs upon graduation, returning scholarships to their original amount, and working the press to promote the latest round of concessions.[26]

None of these moves slowed the Haitian protest movement. It had taken on a life of its own and transformed into demands for the end of the American occupation. Russell panicked. He ordered marines in Haiti back to their barracks, requested more troops through contacts at the State Department, and prepared for battle. In a show of force, he ordered select military units to parade their equipment and machine guns across the country. He hoped the population would back down. They didn't. About one thousand Haitians charged a group of marines stationed on the outskirts of Cayes, resulting in the death of five Haitians and the wounding of twenty others.[27]

* * *

The occupation's collapse appeared imminent. Borno, aware that his own presidency depended on the occupation, tried to arrest twenty political opposition leaders, but Russell refused the order. News of the crisis reached Washington and President Hoover responded by requesting a special Commission to investigate the situation. He got two of them: the Forbes Commission and the Moton Commission. The first was made of an all-white group and the other, with the exception of one member, was all-black.[28]

W. Cameron Forbes led the first commission. He was the same Forbes who'd previously served as governor of the Philippines during the early stages of that occupation. He was the same Forbes who came from a prominent business family that had amassed fortunes in the railroad industry and the Bell Telephone Company and believed that believed that attracting American investment to the Philippines was more important than building up schools. It was a belief much like the ones held by Farnham, Russell, and many others of their generation. As for schools that best suited the Filipino, Forbes claimed that "we want men taught to work with their hands...we want to see agricultural schools and arts and trades schools in greater abundance." These were the experiences and propensities Forbes brought with him to the Hoover Commission. His charge was to examine the general social, political, religious, and economic conditions of occupied Haiti. His team was to provide an honest assessment of the conditions on the ground and whether it was time for the US military to pull out.[29]

The Forbes Commission traveled on the Navy's USS *Rochester* and spent ten days in Haiti to gather information for their report. Forbes placed some of the blame squarely on

> the failure of the Occupation to understand the social problems of Haiti, its brusque attempt to plant democracy there by drill and harrow, its determination to set up a middle class—however wise and necessary it may seem to Americans, all these explain why, in part, the high hopes of our good works in this land have not been realized.

Forbes also commented on the "racial antipathies" of the occupation that "lie behind many of the difficulties." American military forces understandably, implied Forbes, didn't know how to respond to "a highly cultured, highly sophisticated" society made of the "Negro race" that had enjoyed freedom and developed "race-conscious leadership." The report recommended that Borno should step down and be replaced with an interim president until a general election could be held. It favored a gradual military withdrawal and selective replacement of US occupation officials with others more sympathetic to the Haitian people. At the same time, the Forbes Commission defended the rights of foreign landowners, such as US corporations, who had acquired large tracts of land under the occupation. The commission believed that these acquisitions should remain legal and intact, although they supported the desire on Haiti's part to rewrite the constitution or reform land policy for all future land acquisitions.[30]

The Moton Commission was led by Robert Moton, president of the Tuskegee Institute. A graduate and later "commandant" of the Hampton Institute (1891–1915), Moton worked at the Tuskegee Institute as Booker T. Washington's successor. He was well-known for having turned Tuskegee into a college-level institution. Moton had spent a lifetime in technical and industrial education for the African American community.[31]

The selection of a black committee under Moton raised eyebrows among the African American press. Some considered it a "Jim Crow" move that segregated the white, politically oriented Forbes Commission from the black, technical education-oriented Moton Commission. Others questioned whether Moton was in a position to do much good in assessing the true educational needs of Haiti. Still others saw this as a transparent attempt by Hoover to win black votes. Whatever the case, many viewed the Hoover administration as "anti-Negro to the bone" for separating the two commissions.[32]

When called to serve on Hoover's Commission on Education, Moton wanted to silence critics by demonstrating that both commissions were of separate but equal importance. So he made a simple request. He asked for the two committees to travel together. Acting secretary of state Joseph Cotton worried about "the embarrassment and complications which would ensue if we ask the Navy to provide accommodations for Dr. Moton on the *Rochester*." The State Department, however, gave the excuse that the Moton Commission should wait to go to Haiti after political tensions had subsided. Since tensions were in large part over educational policy, Moton agreed to wait. Once Moton's group was given approval to go, he made another simple request. He asked for the same mode of transportation given to the Forbes Commission. Moton wanted the *Rochester*. He claimed that the America black press would dub the Hoover administration as racist if denied the request. This fell on deaf ears. The State Department replied that the navy might have a minesweeper that could be made available to them. Feeling "Jim-Crowed," as one member put it, they decided to travel by commercial steamer. Their visit to Haiti lasted twenty-four days.[33]

Moton's Commission had a narrow charge—to study the state of Haitian education and offer recommendations. Freeman was still director of the Technical Bureau at the time. When he discovered that a black commission would review educational policies in Haiti, he immediately submitted his resignation. He told Russell he was "very anxious to leave at once." The timing and urgency of his hasty departure raised suspicions among the Moton Commission, especially after they discovered that after fifteen years under US occupation only about 25 percent of Haiti's school-aged children were attending school. They blamed the poor enrollment figures on the lack of school facilities. The entire country had approximately eleven hundred schools that served one-fourth of an estimated four hundred thousand school-aged children. Student-teacher ratios were 70:1 at the elementary level. The commission identified low teacher salaries, lack of equipment, and inadequate teacher training as important factors contributing to the dismal state of Haitian education. But the primary reason for these "shortcomings" was the costly and misguided creation of a "distinct and separate system of schools" run by the Agriculture Department. Moton's team recommended the creation of a unified system under the direction of Public Instruction, increases in teacher salaries based on preparation, Haitian-based teacher training, school-building programs, and a freeze on the expansion of Service Technique schools.[34]

While calling attention to the Service Technique, dubbing it a wasteful educational reform effort, Moton believed that problems ran deeper in occupied Haiti. It wasn't just an issue of mismanagement and ill-conceived educational policy. His real concern was in the occupation's general approach to Haiti, influenced as it was by

American business interests. "Had there been less of a disposition," he argued,

> to deal with the island as a conquered territory and more to help a sister state in distress, less of a desire to demonstrate efficiency and more to help others to the efficient direction of their own affairs, less of enforced control and more of helpful cooperation, the United States might today have greater reason to be proud of her intervention in the affairs of a struggling neighbor.[35]

Moton's concerns displayed a sensitivity to the gap between rhetoric and reality. He understood that the US intervention began with a hopeful, humanitarian spirit, but was soon overtaken by the spirit of enterprise and efficiency. Here Moton suggested that capital eclipsed compassion.

Unlike the Forbes report, which was met with a positive reception, the Moton report never had a chance. It was shunned by W. W. Cumberland, a former financial advisor to Haiti, as "maliciously erroneous." A former Service Technique official said the report sounded like "Nigger to Nigger" to him. The State Department demanded revisions to Moton's final document. When Moton refused the order, state issued a public, preemptive warning about the commission. They described Moton's assessment as riddled with "misconceptions" and "incorrect information." What's more, there was a virtual blackout of Moton's report. It wasn't announced to the public when it was released.[36]

Many in Congress followed the commissions carefully, weighing the benefits and drawbacks of leaving a military government in place in Haiti, but others, like George Huddleston from Alabama, believed all this business about commissions and reports was a waste of time. Huddleston didn't think a collection of "high hats and long-tailed coats" poking around the countryside would reveal anything new. To his mind, the truth of the matter was that the United States invaded and occupied not for uplift or "political tutelage" but because of greed from the American business community. Why else, he wondered, do Americans control the "only really valuable harbor in Haiti," the most fertile lands in the country, the market on some of the "cheapest labor in the world" at 20 cents per day, and the nation's debts and bonds purchased at "great discounts." The intervention began by executive order and should end by the same means, he argued. Commissions would just delay the process of ending the intervention in Haiti.[37]

Huddleston had a clear understanding of the economic influences that intersected with the US occupation, but he spoke too soon when it came to his assessment of the value of commissions. Whatever their reception, the commissions had the net effect of rapidly accelerating the transfer of power to Haitians and the complete withdrawal of American troops in 1934. The original treaty allowed for the occupation to last until 1936. The commissions helped trim that by two years. Until the riots and protests, there was no indication that the United States was preparing for withdrawal. The commissions exposed what many in Congress had originally feared. Some had become resigned to the fact that Borno was merely "a puppet" of the occupation. Others viewed the occupation as little more than an "attempt to justify the imposition of our will and authority upon another people." President Hoover and Congressional leaders were indicating that they'd had enough, and the commissions gave them cover for their positions. Russell attempted to defend the occupation from criticism. After fifteen years under US rule, Haiti's infrastructure improvements included 153 rural clinics, 11 modern hospitals, the registration of 2,800 automobiles, a tripling of the nation's bridges, and 800 new miles of road. Russell had also built up the Haitian Gendarmerie, the country's military police, to just under 3,000 strong. The country, he thought, was unmistakably better off.[38]

* * *

But of all the criticism that came from Capitol Hill, there was one critical point Russell had failed to address. It had to do with the problem of education and democracy. Hamilton Fish III, Representative from New York, stated frankly that "we have not lived up to our agreement to try to educate the Haitian people to some form of self-government." The legacy of efficiency over humanitarianism continued for decades, as the United States supported oppressive dictators friendly to foreign corporations, like Papa Doc Duvalier, and quickly removed humanists, like Bertrand Aristide, who ran a popular social justice opposition movement unfriendly to the business community.[39]

The US occupation in this sense never left. But while it was there, during the first year of the Haiti intervention, officials began to talk about another occupation opportunity across the border on the other half of "Hispaniola."

Chapter Five
By Executive Order

Unlike Haiti, there were no bloody riots or political assassinations offering a prelude to US military action in the Dominican Republic in 1916. Unlike Haiti, Wilson had far less claim to a "humane duty" to intervene next door.[1]

At stake, however, was Wall Street's transparent, yet tenuous, economic penetration of the Dominican Republic that had a long and storied history. It began when late nineteenth-century American speculators took over approximately $4 million of the nation's debt through a company they had formed for the purpose: The San Domingo Improvement Company. By the opening of the twentieth century, the company pushed for US intervention, primarily through the State Department, whenever these speculators did not receive expected repayments. In 1903, state obliged them by agreeing to serve as broker for what they claimed were $4.5 million in outstanding loans. A few years later, state's involvement became official with the Dominican Treaty of 1907, a treaty that required turning over control of the nation's customs houses to American banking and government officials. Under the treaty, approximately half of the annual customs receipts would be handed over to US officials serving on behalf of financial titans—such as National City Bank of New York (now Citi) and Kuhn, Loeb, and Company—that had replaced the San Domingo Improvement Company. It also required that any new foreign loans sought by the Dominican government be approved by New York bankers by way of the US government. The deal transformed the Dominican Republic into a "financial protectorate" and placed the country in a $40 million debt peonage. Discovery of accounting fraud, unclaimed interest, and other recalculations eventually brought the total down to $20 million owed to American creditors.[2]

The entanglement among financial speculators, the State Department, and the Dominican Republic through the Treaty of 1907 became a critical factor in the events leading up to the invasion and occupation. When the country's internal politics struck an overly nationalistic, anti-American tone, bankers called on the US minister to the Dominican government to issue demands. In November 1914, when demands were not met, threats soon followed.[3]

Dominican election results in 1914 revealed a mood unsettling to Wall Street speculators. The results signaled a desire to move toward economic independence from the United States. William Russell, American minister to the country, issued a set of demands that few viable, sovereign governments could reasonably accept. He demanded that the Dominican Republic turn over all economic policy to an American advisor and allow the United States to take control of the country's military forces. This was rejected across a bitterly divided Dominican political system. In 1916, strongman General Desiderio Arias took control of the capital and toppled the US-supported administration of Isidro Jimenez. According to the US government, this offered sufficient pretext for military action. American warships circled the island and threatened Arias with an ultimatum—leave the capital or risk war with the United States. Arias's late night departure was immediately followed by a takeover of the nation's capital by officer William Caperton and six hundred marines. By capturing and controlling all national revenue sources, including all customs and national tax receipts, military officials hoped to control a client government that would serve American economic and military interests. Military commanders used the power of the purse to issue demands about what kind of president should replace Jimenez and Arias and warned against the selection of an oppositional administration. Ignoring US demands and following their constitution, the Dominican Congress selected Dr. Francisco Henriquez y Varabajal for president. Dissatisfied with the choice, US officials responded by cutting off all funds to the Dominican government. The State Department refused to recognize the selection and approved the dissolution of Dominican democracy to be replaced with an American military government.[4]

The economic entanglements and the pattern by which American officials skirted democratic processes continued throughout the US occupation. The first governor, Captain Harry Knapp, took charge of the new military government in November 1916. He removed native Dominicans from top-level and executive cabinet posts and replaced them with American military officers. Knapp "suspended" the Dominican Congress and set a precedent by issuing "executive orders" that functioned like decrees. Many had to do with the regular functioning of the government. Others had to do with civil liberties, such as Knapp's censorship of the press and suspension of weapons permits. His replacement in 1918, General B. H. Fuller, perceived almost no limits to his authority. Fuller attempted to stamp out the national pastime of cockfighting and also tried to rename the country—all by way of decree. He didn't last long and was followed by Rear Admiral Thomas Snowden, who clamped down further on the press and expanded trials by military court. The last two governors, Rear Admiral Samuel Robison and Brigadier General Harry Lee, presided over the end of the occupation and the transfer of power back to the Dominicans. Over the course of the eight-year military occupation, 821 executive orders went into effect at the direction of the US military. Together, their work left a legacy that influenced the nation's political and economic destiny across the twentieth century.[5]

* * *

When it came to education, the same forces affecting other aspects of Dominican life influenced such matters as school reform and higher education policy. The occupation's rule by decree and the nation's long-standing economic entanglements shaped the course of Dominican educational history under US rule.

During the first year of military occupation, Harry Knapp's administration turned to the issue of education after consolidating control in the country. He described the status of Dominican education as "deplorable" and soon began to issue incontrovertible executive orders to reform the nation's school system. Knapp had his eye on four basic problems: illiteracy, enrollments, attendance, and rural education. Illiteracy was a fairly easy target. The country suffered from a 90-percent illiteracy rate when the occupation began. If handled properly, the rate would decline rapidly. Success in this area had the potential of giving the occupation credibility—or, as some scholars have argued, assisting the occupation's drive for legitimacy—among Dominicans as something other than an economically motivated colonial enterprise. To remedy the literacy problem, Knapp would have to address the dismal school enrollment figures. Less than 10 percent of school-aged children signed up at the beginning of the academic year at the outset of the occupation. What's more, of those enrolled, a mere 40 percent actually attended. And of those attending, the vast majority lived in two major cities—Santiago and Santo Domingo. The widely dispersed populations in the rural districts saw little in the way of formal schooling or training.[6]

To address these problems, Knapp issued his first education order at the very beginning of 1917. The order assembled a special Commission on Education to investigate the status of the country's schools and to offer recommendations for the establishment of a national system. By doing so, the military government struck a collaborative tone since the commission was composed entirely of Dominicans—six "distinguished" Dominicans—selected by Knapp and his circle. Their charge was to submit a report to the occupation that would form the basis of a new national system of education. In practice, however, Knapp considered this committee more of a public relations move than anything else. His concern had to do with how Dominicans would perceive the relationship between the occupation and educational reform. "I thought it was wise," he stated, "to have their own views uncolored by any appearance of pressure from outside." Appearance of independence struck Knapp as more important than actual independence. To the commission, he assigned "one of the firmest friends of the United States in the country," Alfredo A. Nouel Bobadilla, archbishop of Santo Domingo. Knapp put Monsignor Nouel, as he was best-known to the public, in charge of the education commission.[7]

Although stacked with "friends" of the occupation, Knapp viewed the commission's work and their final report as nonbinding. The military government retained decision-making authority as to what kind of education Dominicans would receive. Long before receiving a final report, Knapp enacted plans that expanded elementary education but slashed secondary schools. When it came to higher education, he showed special contempt for the country's "two so-called universities, neither of high rank." The University of Santo Domingo, derived from one of the oldest universities in the Americas, and the University of Santiago, opened in 1915, offered the only postsecondary instruction in the country. Santo Domingo had a professional focus while Santiago had both professional and liberal arts programs. Neither institution escaped Knapp's plans for restructuring and redistribution of Dominican taxes.[8]

Before the commission had completed its investigation, Knapp had already begun implementing wholesale changes to the system. He had shut down the University of Santiago and suspended any nonprofessional programs at the University of Santo Domingo. This was in concert with his vision that "less attention will be paid to higher education" and that the "efforts will be bent toward reducing illiteracy rather than to providing for the needs of a limited class of students in professional and literary subjects." He had already fired the superintendent of education for lacking "proper balance" and being "full of theoretical ideas" and "whose conversation is grandiloquent," replacing him with a much younger substitute—Julio Ortega Frier. Knapp considered the younger, twenty-nine-year-old teacher to be more agreeable and compliant. He liked that Frier had been "educated in the United States" and that he was "a man young enough to be ambitious to make a reputation." A recent graduate from the Ohio State University, Frier served not only the military occupation in several offices but also the military dictatorship of Raphael Trujillo after the United States left the country.[9]

Ahead of the commission's report, Knapp had also selected the Dominican Republic's chief education official. He appointed marine officer Rufus Lane as secretary of justice and public education. Lane had no previous experience with administration or governance of public education, but he did have a law degree, which likely served him well in his role as justice secretary. His own educational background included attending the US Naval Academy and graduating from Columbian Law School (now George Washington University) with a bachelor of laws degree. According to one observer, Lane "broke no academic records" at the Naval Academy, graduating nineteenth in his class, and was considered one of "three bottom men" of his cohort. His views on education, however, aligned closely with Knapp's. He showed little interest in public secondary education or the normal schools that provided for teacher training. Lane scaled both areas back significantly across twelve provinces, calling them a "drain on the public treasury." By executive order, without a vote or democratic process, the US military government "suppressed" the operation of normal schools and closed all but two of the secondary schools—one in Santo Domingo and another in Santiago. Lane also introduced new high-school graduation policies.

Students were now required to demonstrate "excellence" in academic performance in basic as well as advanced courses.[10]

By the time the Commission on Education submitted their report in December 1917, the military government had already established the main features of a new national system of education. It was now centrally-controlled, streamlined to focus attention on elementary education, and largely in the hands of Secretary Lane. Knapp thanked the committee for their "painstaking" and "thorough" work and told them that he would draw "essentially" from their plan to build on his own.[11]

* * *

Knapp's most-anticipated school reform laws had to do with compulsory education and the creation of a new code of education. These laws directly impacted the lives of students, teachers, and families and defined the nature and character of the Dominican educational system.

Knapp decided a full year after the initial invasion that Dominicans should have a strongly enforced compulsory education law. Although Dominicans already had compulsory education laws on the books, the low enrollment numbers and scant attendance suggested that there was little, if any, enforcement. Knapp signaled that the military government would not tolerate noncompliance. He established mandatory education for those between the ages of seven and thirteen in his "Ley de Instruccion Obligatoria." This law outlined the penalties and fines for parents, guardians, school inspectors, and school administrators found guilty of ignoring the issue of truancy. Parents who failed to register their children within one month of the start of classes now received a fine of five pesos or, if unable to pay, five days in jail. The fines doubled if parents failed to comply within ten days of the first penalty. Ten pesos, at the time, was equivalent to two months of a teacher's annual salary. The law granted a few exceptions, such as illness or death of a family member and, on rare occasions, work. Child labor, if absolutely necessary for families in extreme poverty, rose to the level of exception. Knapp called this kind of extreme situation "la necesidada imperiosa." The imperative necessity would have to be shown and proven. Otherwise, the "Ley de Instruccion Obligatoria" required children not only to attend school but also restricted them from employment through child labor protections. These restrictions, added to the compulsory education law, prevented businesses from hiring school-aged children. Businesses that violated the new policy would be subject to fines of up to one hundred pesos.[12]

The compulsory education law created a predictable dilemma that the occupation struggled with and never adequately addressed. An increasing number of students in the classroom required a corresponding increase in facilities constructed and teachers hired. When Knapp claimed that the educational situation he inherited was "deplorable," he spoke from the belief that the occupation could correct the situation—that it was their burden (or in the words Rudyard Kipling, the "White Man's Burden") to fix the problems of the native population. Yet the compulsory education laws, that on paper suggested progress, ran straight into some hard statistical realities. There were roughly seven hundred and fifty thousand Dominican citizens at the time of the occupation. Of this population, two hundred thousand were school-aged children with between fourteen thousand and eighteen thousand enrolled and attending. During the first year of the compulsory education law, Knapp promised the Dominican people that funds would be made available to construct new schoolhouses and end the policy of using rented facilities. But the occupation struggled to find the resources to accommodate even forty-five thousand students. The law also created an environment in which enforcement of fines, jail time, and other punitive measures could be used with malicious intent against the parents of the over one hundred and fifty thousand children left without a schooling infrastructure. It empowered school officials, inspectors, and other agents of the state within a social order known for its "caudillo," or family-based, politics. Dominicans responded to this law in creative ways by taking matters into their own hands through a grassroots movement, but the fruits of their labors didn't begin to appear until Rear Admiral Snowden took over the military government.[13]

In the meantime, Knapp attempted to handle the sharp increase in the demand for teachers caused by his compulsory education laws by mandating education for teachers as well. Since the closing of most secondary schools and training programs, the occupation failed to anticipate the sharp drop in the number of qualified educators to take up available positions. Knapp decided that a summer school program for them would fill the void, but this did not go over well. As summer 1918 approached, he ordered compulsory training sessions for all new as well as existing teachers. The goal was to prepare for the coming academic year. Ultimately the idea and implementation of these sessions "caused some dissatisfaction," Knapp confessed. The training program aimed to assist teachers with the modernization and standardization of the curriculum, textbooks, school governance, and classroom instruction. Teachers received a crash course in the revised program of study that was then in the process of being implemented. The new curriculum affected all levels of education and changed completion and graduation requirements. Pedagogical methods were emphasized with an eye toward bringing school teachers up-to-date with contemporary practices. Julio Ortega Frier took the lead in promoting what he viewed as the latest in classroom methods, drawing from his studies at Ohio State. Missing from the program, however, was teacher input. The "dissatisfaction" with the mandatory classes had to do with the top-down, occupation-driven demands placed on Dominican educators by a foreign power. After Knapp's administration and the end of the occupation, educators pushed for greater autonomy suggestive of their resistance to education by decree.[14]

Despite the desperate need for teachers, Knapp resisted following a tradition established in other US occupations—the tradition of importing American teachers. In every previous military occupation, including Cuba, Puerto Rico, the Philippines, and Haiti, American officials recruited US teachers to help establish new systems of education. The largest, oft-cited project of this kind occurred in the Philippines. In this case, hundreds of teachers, known as the Thomasites, boarded the USS *Thomas* with the goal of Americanizing the occupied Pacific islands. Knapp decided against doing the same in the Dominican Republic and stood firmly against pressure to declare English as the language of instruction. "Some question has been raised as to the method which I adopted,"[15] he stated, but

> I have been strongly of the opinion that the education of the Dominican people was a matter to be undertaken in their own language (Spanish); and that any attempt to force upon them either the English language or such methods as were, with great propriety, undertaken in the Philippines and Porto Rico, would not bear the good results that were

to be hoped for from a system devised by Dominicans of high attainments for their own countrymen. I have not, therefore, looked with sympathy upon the idea of importing a large number of American school teachers unfamiliar with the Spanish language, valuable as their services would have been.[16]

In short, he preferred "leaving public instruction in the hands of Dominicans themselves."[17]

This sentiment, however, didn't prevent Knapp from Americanizing the system through his Code of Education. As Knapp grappled with the problems created by the compulsory education law, he dramatically changed what happened inside the classroom through the code's four-part legal framework: (1) *Ley Organica de Ensenanza Publica* (Law of Public Education); (2) *Ley General de Estudios* (General Law of Studies); (3) *Ley Para la Ensenanza Universitaria* (Law for University Studies); and (4) *Ley Para la Direccion de la Ensenaza Publica* (Law of Educational Governance).[18]

The first three laws decreed an American-style system of education that made public-private, church-state distinctions. They defined the differences between public (*oficial*), private (*particular*), and hybrid (*semi-oficial*) schools across the education spectrum, including primary, secondary, normal, vocational, special, and university levels. Private schools were largely free from state control, with the exception of elementary programs and the prohibition against cruel and degrading punishments for students of any level. Public schools were to be tuition free, without fees of any kind, and open to all students. The law declared that those attending public schools would be free of religious instruction. "No student at a public school," wrote Knapp, "can be forced or obligated against the will of the parents, tutor, or guardian, or against the student's will, to receive religious teachings or subjected to religious practices." Public schools were also prohibited from engaging in "political propaganda" or requiring students to engage in what the military government called "politica militante." This stipulation would have served Knapp and other occupation officials well, since it gave them permission to close a school that engaged in militant political acts contrary to the wishes of the military government.[19]

Knapp's first three laws also prescribed a detailed curriculum to be followed from primary to graduate education. The primary and secondary curricula were overwhelmingly academic, rather than vocational.

This was a significant departure from the pattern established in the occupations of Haiti and elsewhere that emphasized manual, industrial, and agricultural studies. Primary classes included writing instruction, Spanish grammar, weights and measures, Dominican geography and history, world geography, ethics, mathematics, civics, physical and natural sciences, hygiene, anatomy, physiology, manual labor, drawing, and music. All high-school students took a common core of languages, mathematics, science, history, and geography. After completing the core, students would select concentrations or majors in one of three fields: *Filosopfia y Letras* (Humanities), *Ciencias Fisicas y Naturales* (Physical and Biological Sciences), or *Ciencas Fisicas y Matematicas* (Physical and Mathematical Sciences). Normal school programs consisted of pedagogical methods, history of education, school, law, and organization and governance. Those wanting to teach elementary education had to be at least sixteen years of age and a graduate of upper elementary school. Those wanting to teach high school had to be at least twenty years of age and a graduate of high school in one of three areas of specialty. Most of the vocational programs under the general law had more to do with university studies than school curricula. Vocational programs, as the occupation defined them, were the professional schools of medicine, law, and engineering. The final area covered by these laws—university education—focused exclusively on the University of Santo Domingo, prescribing a full catalog description of the rules and regulations applicable to the institution. It defined the courses of study, the responsibilities and authority of the rector and deans, the procedures of faculty governance, as well as the admissions, examination, and graduation requirements of students. Knapp's Code of Education, in short, handed teachers, professors, or administrators a complete, readymade system. He left very little "in the hands of Dominicans themselves."[20]

The fourth law—the Law of Educational Governance—revealed more about Knapp and the military occupation than all the others. It showed, unequivocally, that Knapp wanted to retain final authority over the entire system, creating a highly centralized bureaucracy in the process. The law referred to Knapp as "el Poder Ejecutivo," or the executive power. Through the occupation's power to issue executive orders, this law established what was called the Consejo Nacional de Educacion, or National Education Council. Their charge was to oversee the establishment, organization, and maintenance of Dominican education. The first sign that Knapp wanted to keep firm control over the system was in the formation of this body. "The first members of the Council," he wrote, "will be named directly by the Executive Power." He planned to stack the governing body with friends of the occupation. But even so, he made it clear that these members were to stay on a tight leash. If at any point the decisions made by the council conflicted with the interests of the military government, the actions of the council would automatically be considered "null and void in all of its effects" and "nullification will be declared by way of Decree." Through the council, Knapp controlled all levels of education—primary, secondary, special, normal, vocational, and higher education—including the exams given, programs offered, formulation and modification of curriculum, and any other governing function related to personnel decisions and staffing. The council would have the power to select, for example, the rector of the University of Santo Domingo and dismiss the same if viewed as oppositional to the occupation government. Through this body, Knapp also controlled the superintendent of education, who at the time was the handpicked Julio Ortega Frier. The superintendent's office was charged with implementing the plans of the council, inspecting the nation's schools, making and maintaining budgets and contracts, and preparing regular reports to the council. Continuing the precedent established by Knapp, the law stipulated that the selection of the superintendent would be made directly by the executive power, thus bypassing the council.[21]

To safeguard against any missed opportunities for keeping the council in his sphere of influence, the law reminded all education officials that the occupation government held the power of the purse and that Education Secretary Rufus Lane would oversee all their actions. The salaries of the members on the council, the superintendent, and any ranking school official would be determined by the "Presupuesto Nacional," or national budget, that was created at the sole discretion of the military government. At any time the military government could use this power to maintain strict conformity to the interests of the occupation. Moreover, Knapp declared that the National Education Council served at the pleasure of Secretary Lane. Lane received ex-officio status on the governing body and oversaw the drafting of their bylaws. The final product and any future modifications were to be submitted for approval to the executive power.[22]

* * *

Knapp completed his educational reforms just as his stay as governor was coming to an end in mid-1918. He transferred power to an interim military governor until Rear Admiral Thomas Snowden took command of the Dominican Republic in February 1919. When Snowden assumed control of the country, he inherited Knapp's centrally controlled system of education, compulsory education law that had turned into an unfunded mandate, promises of school construction and teacher shortages, and a fully prescribed curriculum from elementary to graduate school.

What Governor Snowden also inherited were economic entanglements that complicated the story of Dominican education under US rule. Knapp had years before briefly alluded to these entanglements in his first official communications with the State Department at the start of the military intervention. He suggested that Wall Street's influence was pernicious and would thwart the efforts he was undertaking to stabilize the political and economic conditions of the country. "In connection with the $20,000,000 bond issue," he said referring to New York bank loans that bought out all foreign creditors, "I invite attention to a feature of the agreement with the bankers that appears to me to be vicious." Knapp explained that it privileged bankers before all else, requiring any surplus funds to be used to pay down the debt. What's more, he noted, "the monthly charge upon the Dominican Government, instead of gradually decreasing by the absolute retirement of funds, goes on at a uniform rate of $100,000 per month, five percent interest and one percent amortization on the $20,000,000 loan." The financial sleight of hand was called a "sinking fund" that appeared to allow the retirement of the $20-million debt all at once, but that, in practice, continued to generate interest for speculators and rising debt levels for the Dominican government. According to Knapp, "the arrangement is an admirable one for the bankers but a very bad one for the good of Santo Domingo... For the government of a country like Santo Domingo, it is hard to conceive of anything worse."[23]

Knapp's concerns were ignored and passed on to Snowden's administration, establishing a precedent of rubber-stamping agreements that benefited American economic interests at the expense of the Dominican people. Unlike Knapp, however, Snowden faced increasing pressure due to a global economic downturn in the price of the country's single most important commodity: sugar. The economic downturn gave way to a massive uptick in lobbying by American financiers and sugar interests that called on Snowden to create favorable trade policies for them.[24]

The most important economic policy decisions of Snowden's tenure—the ones that most deeply affected Dominican education—had to do with tariff and taxation policy. According to a study conducted during Knapp's administration by Yale professor Fred R. Fairchild, 90 percent of the state's revenue came from customs receipts. Fairchild recommended direct taxation of the people of the Dominican Republic. He concluded that any system that relied almost exclusively on indirect taxation placed an unjust burden on the poor, for it increased the price of basic, imported goods needed by the poor and left the wealthy untouched. With this situation in mind, Snowden began preparations for a complete overhaul of the country's tariff and taxation policy and thereby reformed how schools and institutions of higher education were funded. His goal was to rework the pattern by which imported goods were taxed and to construct one of the first systems of direct taxation in the Dominican Republic's history: the property tax. The aim was to offset the reduction in revenue from lowered tariffs with the increase in revenue from property taxes.[25]

To handle the question of imported goods, Snowden assembled the Dominican Tariff Commission of 1919. Their stated charge was to "recommend an appreciable reduction in the rates of duty on imported articles which are not produced in quantity in this country and which are ordinarily classed as necessities in contrast to articles of luxury." The commission, however, was dominated by North American and Puerto Rican representatives and the tariff policy they came up with, and that Snowden put into effect, mirrored the interests these members represented. The most conspicuous beneficiaries of this reform were sugar estates, such as the Barahona Company. Barahona, a New York–based corporation organized in the year of the US invasion, acquired nearly fifty thousand acres during the occupation, making it the second largest sugar estate in the country. They had a strong interest in the results of the new tariff policy. Items that received free entry status included agricultural machinery, industrial machinery, vehicles, tools, and building materials. Approximately 250 other items made it on the free list and the rest were reduced by an average of 38 percent. This created a very favorable trading situation for American sugar interests within the country and US exporters who controlled the largest share of Dominican trade. For Dominicans, however, the new policy cut in half the country's greatest source of revenue. Washington hinted at the possibility of offering a reciprocal trade agreement, meaning a tariff reduction for Dominican goods in the United States, to help smooth out opposition. But in the end, the State Department reneged on this once the occupation government had decreed the reforms recommended by the commission. What Dominicans did receive was a letter from state that "noted with satisfaction" the passage of the new Dominican tariff law, but "sincerely regretted" being unable to respond in kind.[26]

This asymmetrical relationship hurt Dominicans worse still after the failure of the Property Tax of 1919. Taxation of property was considered "a most radical measure" according to US minister William Russell, "and no former Dominican party in control would have dared to undertake it." The military government began to study the issue through its reform of land policy. Snowden assembled a commission to make recommendations on how to assess titles and tax properties. US citizens comprised the entire six-member board, all of whom were appointed by Snowden, including Secretary Rufus Lane. At the head of the committee stood J. H. Edwards, a receivership official who was well-connected with the sugar industry. His land title policy that favored the agricultural companies over Dominican peasants in the rural districts became law. After winning virtually unanimous support for his proposal among the commission, he resigned to become president of a corporation that owned five hundred thousand acres of land across the Dominican Republic. Lane stood as the lone voice of opposition and resigned in protest over the Edwards proposal, but nothing came of his protest. With land title policy settled, including the establishment of Dominican "land court" dominated by US judges, Snowden moved on to the issue of taxation. After a year of preparations, he unveiled the *Ley de Impuesto sobe la Propiedad* (Property Tax Law) in 1919. He wanted to place "the burden of taxes upon those best able to bear them," but soon found that those best able to bear them also stood in the best position to resist taxes. Large sugar estates were the first to oppose the new measure. They banded together to form the Sugar Association of Santo Domingo, led and dominated by North American owned companies. They petitioned the military government, the US Navy, and the State Department. Snowden ultimately capitulated and gave the sugar barons Executive Order No. 545. This order reduced the tax and eliminated a graduated rate based on size of estate. The largest sugar companies saw their tax rate reduced from 2 percent to 0.5 percent. This was accompanied by an increased tax on "improvements" to the land, but none of these taxes led to any significant source of state revenue. On the contrary, the sugar corporations led a popular, "nationalist" boycott of all property taxes. Enforcement of the law faded and the property tax disappeared altogether a few years after the end of the occupation.[27]

The combined forces of falling sugar prices, slashed tariff receipts, and a failed property tax created a perfect storm that left the national school system in tatters. Snowden had hoped that the property tax would provide an American-style local funding stream for Dominican education. Nothing of the sort happened. The economic reforms of 1919, including the elimination of a business tax called the *Ley de Patentes*, led to a slowdown in school construction in 1920 and a complete shutdown of the system in 1921. At first Snowden expressed optimism that "it is expected that for the future all municipalities will be able to take care of themselves, they having been empowered to collect a land tax which will suffice for their needs." Projecting a successful land tax, he reworked the national budget accordingly. At the same time, he reported that "only a shortage of funds prevents the erection... of schools for secondary education."[28] Just before the collapse in funding, Snowden proudly remarked that almost one hundred thousand children were attending primary school. After dissolving the funding infrastructure, he discovered that his policy had a hand in creating a half-million dollar shortfall in education.

Once the tariff and tax policies went into full effect, Snowden saw the amount of funding for education drop from $70,000 to $20,000 per month. "As a consequence of these reductions," he reported, "the schools are loosing about 30,000 children." Cutbacks led to the closing of the "Musical Lyceum, the Academy of Drawing, Painting, and Sculpture of Santo Domingo, the professional schools for girls of La Vega, San Francisco de Macoris, Moca, Monte Cristy, Puerto Plata, all night schools for illiterate persons, all preparation schools for teachers, and two hundred and thirty-six rudimentary primary schools." Universities also felt the budget cuts resulting from the economic environment. The university suspended "practical lessons in the laboratories." Normal schools in Santo Domingo and Santiago had to "close the final classes and to reduce the number of subjects offered to pupils." What's more the "schools offices have suppressed many employees and the personnel of the primary graduate schools has been reduced to one-half."[29]

* * *

Education funding reached a crisis point in 1921 when the entire national school system was shut down completely for one month. Snowden "intended to close the schools for some time and to maintain the school offices" but ultimately issued orders to "completely close down the schools service. Lessons were suspended on May 20, 1921." The same occurred in the first quarter of 1923, when schools were "closed for some time…due to lack of funds for maintenance." As such, between the start of Snowden's tariff and tax reforms and the end of the occupation in 1924, schools operated intermittently and without any stable sources of funding.[30]

During the occupation's final three administrations of Snowden, Robison, and Lee, virtually all public works projects, such as school construction, road building, and other public improvements, were called off. They operated in the red and appealed to Wall Street for loans to finance basic governmental operations. They cut 90 percent of the teams of engineers and laborers, to the tune of some five thousand men, who had been contracted to rebuild the nation. As schools were shutting down, the military governments decided to sink deeper into debt rather than return to the previous tariff system. Snowden borrowed $1.2 million just to keep his administration afloat in early 1921. Later in the same year, the military government demanded more and received another emergency infusion of $2.5 million. Even so, by December 1921, the military government had only enough to cover 50 percent of their budget. In March 1922, they received another $10 million loan used partly to retire debts incurred in the previous year and partly to bailout tobacco companies, finance the completion of one highway, and to build up the Guardia Nacional that served as a national police force. Each of these loans carried unusually high banker fees, such as an initial 10 percent cut of the 1922 loan. As the United States began to hand over the country to a provisional Dominican government, the nation barely limped along. In the final year under US rule, the government operated at a loss. To avoid embarrassment and the appearance of mismanagement, Washington approved a final loan of $2.5 million. Each of these loans were made by the US military government and passed on to the Dominican people who would be held responsible for paying back these debts for decades.[31]

While the occupation shut down public works projects and loaded the government with debt burdens, Dominicans took it upon themselves to construct schools they wanted rather than wait for the occupation to do it for them. They weathered the maelstrom created by education decrees and economic reforms through the creation of "Sociedad Populares de Educacion," or Popular Societies. This was a grassroots movement by Dominicans concerned about the state of their children's education. Amid budgetary crises and unfulfilled promises of school construction, Dominicans turned to each other through this movement to support the construction, furnishing, and maintenance of school facilities. Hundreds of these societies emerged throughout the country and were responsible for the construction of over three hundred schoolhouses. They became more than a place for children; they also served as centers of community organizing and enrichment. Members met in these schoolhouses for "reading, lectures, and other social and cultural work" and these meetings became an "immense success." While officials in the military government were pleased because the Popular Societies would "contribute to the task of pacifying those towns," Dominicans likely saw the movement as an empowering, democratizing effort that addressed community needs and that stood beyond the reach of US economic control.[32]

The Popular Societies often stepped in when the military occupation left a void. This is particularly telling in the various, often conflicting, accounts provided by the military government relative to how many schools were in operation under US rule. During his tenure Snowden claimed to have in operation 783 rural schools, 131 primary schools, 6 secondary schools, 11 professional schools, 54 night schools, 2 correctional schools, and 1 university. This left an ambiguity in his reports about how many were simply rented facilities, how many were the work of the Popular Societies, and how many were built by the military government. In 1921, for instance, the military government celebrated the opening of 15 schools. During the same year, Popular Societies had built 60 schools within a three-month period. When a storm hit the island and leveled 3 school buildings in Seybo and 3 in Samana, it was the "Popular Societies of Education [that] have in some places undertaken the reconstruction of the buildings destroyed." This was at a time when the military government's reductions meant "the slowing down if not the complete cessation of some of the work already begun which would have contributed to development and public welfare."[33]

Just as Popular Societies were expanding and becoming "very active in purchasing and constructing school buildings," the military government took an opposite turn. It "abolished numerous [education] offices of the service" to save tens of thousands of dollars in Dominican tax revenues controlled by the US occupation. As a result, "it became necessary to decide on the closing of various schools and the suppression of some teachers of graduate schools and messengers in school offices."[34] The military government, in effect, began to rely on the work of the Popular Societies and spoke in glowing terms about their accomplishments. The State Department learned that

> the reductions in the school service have shown once more the enthusiasm of many guardians for Public Education. Some rudimentary schools, which were to be closed owing to the savings made in the National Budget, will most probably continue to function through the offer made by some guardians to take care of the expense entailed by the maintenance of those schools. Private persons and teachers have likewise offered their services to gratuitously serve the grades that were being suppressed for economical reasons. This attitude of teachers and private persons will permit the retention in the official schools a large number of children who were running the risk of being deprived of their education.[35]

The Popular Societies relieved the military government from some of their education-related responsibilities, but, in the end, they couldn't free the occupation from the kind of education legacy American officials ultimately left behind.

* * *

The US occupation of the Dominican Republic was presented to the America public as a humanitarian mission, but from the start the United States had great difficulty explaining the humanitarian nature of this mission. Military governors and State Department officials spoke in general terms about the mismanagement of the nation's finances and democratic institutions and how such circumstances were the root of the country's purported problems. They began with confidence that they could fix such things as the "deplorable" state of Dominican education. But governmental mismanagement lacked salience when it came to explaining why the United States invaded and occupied a sovereign nation. The murky rationale offered in the US Occupation Proclamation of 1916 had mostly to do with economic issues, such as debt repayment, rather than military or humanitarian concerns.[36]

In the end, education by decree failed to teach much about democracy; and the tariff and tax reforms that benefited US interests and the wealthiest in Dominican society did little to encourage elites to take a share of responsibility for the general welfare. According to one observer, the kind of laws promoted by the occupation gave "people with money an advantage over those who had little or none." In terms of Dominican economic policy under US control, American banking, industrial, and agricultural interests had the upper hand. The commissions established by the military occupation succeeded in satisfying American economic interests, but had failed to promote democracy through education.[37]

One of the most revealing discussions of the actual purposes of the occupation appeared in Thomas Snowden's *Santo Domingo: Its Past and Its Present Condition*. He published the work to clarify why the United States was in the country in the first place and what priorities the occupation had established. He conceded that his objective was "to comply with a desire on the part of certain bankers and businessmen." At the top of his list of priorities were ones that satisfied the needs of American speculators: "to free the country from debt [and] to establish the finances upon a sound and enduring basis." Only after mentioning these priorities was the need for education recognized. And even then, he stated that the kind of training the next generation of Dominicans needed was "in American ideals and standards of personal honor and morals" so as to "succeed in steering the ship of state without further wreck." Ironically, Snowden's evidence of mismanagement by the Dominican government that became the pretext for the US takeover was his assessment that the nation had been "overdrawn by the sum of $14,234.63." This, of course, paled in comparison to the occupation's own mismanagement that left the country in a multimillion dollar debt peonage to American bankers.[38]

What's remarkable about the story of Dominican education in light of such a military occupation was the determined self-agency displayed by the Popular Societies movement. It resembles a similar form of self-agency that African Americans promoted in what has been described as a system of double taxation. African Americans in the US south during the progressive era faced two kinds of education taxes: one to fund public schools that they could not attend due to segregation and another imposed on themselves for the construction and maintenance of schools that they created in their own communities. Dominicans similarly faced what could be described as a form of *triple* taxation. They were taxed by the military government for education established by decree, taxed again through the subsidization of tariff policies favorable to US corporate interests, and taxed a third time through the Popular Societies that drew on the local energy, efforts, and resources of Dominican citizens.[39]

Despite the intentions of the Popular Societies, the legacy left by the US occupation was entirely unsustainable. The military government quickly found itself in its own budgetary crises and mismanagement as a result of unintended as well as intended educational and economic reforms. In the end, US rule failed to produce a lasting school system, a secure funding source for that pillar of democratic society, a substantive infrastructure, and a change in the minds of elites about their share of responsibility in the educational welfare of the masses. Once US forces left, Dominicans immediately returned to their previous tariffs and ignored "agreements" with the United States that prevented a return to such tariffs. By 1930, the school system had stabilized through a combination of national, provincial, and local sources of support and served approximately fifty thousand children.[40]

After withdrawal from the Dominican Republic, and later Haiti, the United States began to cool its empire-building engine that had been turned on with the War of 1898. During the economic doldrums of the 1930s, that came with sky-high unemployment at home and little appetite for further adventurism abroad, the United States got out of the military occupation business outside of the Philippines and Puerto Rico. Not until World War II did the United States reopen this business for a new Asian and European clientele.

Chapter Six
Greatest Generation

Harry Truman gave Douglas MacArthur explicit instructions when it came to the US occupation of Japan. He wanted the general to assume the role of Supreme Commander for the Allied Powers and, in this role, he wanted MacArthur to take complete control of the country. "The authority of the Emperor and the Japanese Government," Truman stated flatly, "is subordinate to you as Supreme Commander...Since your authority is supreme, you will not entertain any question on the part of the Japanese as to its scope." So began the occupation that lasted from 1945 to 1952.[1]

This was hardly the first time that Japan had experienced an imbalance of power with the West. Since the mid-nineteenth century, the United States had used its seafaring forces to extract treaties from Japanese officials that favored American military and commercial interests. US president Millard Fillmore made the first moves along these lines by sending a special squadron—the famed Black Ships under Matthew Perry's command—for the sole purpose of opening Japanese markets and ports. The highly imbalanced arrangements that resulted, such as the Treaty of Kanagawa and the Treaty of Amity and Commerce, undermined Japanese sovereignty, causing domestic turmoil. Signed under threat of attack, the agreements required the opening of ports to American ships and missionaries, mandated assistance to any shipwrecked US vessels, fixed low tariffs favorable to US commercial interests, and determined future Japanese foreign policy by automatically ascribing to the United States any diplomatic agreements Japan settled with any other foreign power. These treaties ignited a political powder keg that gave rise to the Meiji Era centered on the creation of a strong, centralized, modern, and militarily powerful Japan. The Japanese desire to develop a fleet capable of dealing with Western powers accelerated with the US occupation of the Philippines after the War of 1898. Through this modernization process, Japan retained its monarchical system based on *Sonno-Joi*—a widespread ideology highlighted by a desire "to expel barbarians and revere the *Tenno* (Emperor)." The country sought to increase its technological capacities, expand its educational opportunities, and build on a highly meritocratic system, while also retaining the mysticism of the Tenno's divine right to lead the country. This was the Japanese reaction to American presence in the region. It was also the dominant force that shaped the Japanese state MacArthur took over at the end of World War II.[2]

MacArthur was to mid-twentieth-century Japanese education what Perry was to mid-nineteenth-century Japanese foreign policy—with one crucial exception. Educational reform during the US occupation of Japan incited only minor dissent. For the most part, the transformation of Japanese schools, colleges, and universities into American-style institutions failed to provoke sustained domestic turmoil and, at times, it received a positive reception. In the preface to a sweeping educational reform proposal by the US occupation, Japanese translators called it "one of the most distinguished pieces of educational literature in the world."[3]

Part of the reason for this smooth reception was the way MacArthur used established institutions, such as the Tenno system, to further US interests. This decision had few supporters at home. By the end of World War II, the majority of Americans believed Hirohito, Japanese emperor and head of the Tenno system, should be executed for war crimes. MacArthur thought otherwise. He saw a well-maintained system of power and influence under Hirohito that could provide a vital tool with which to reform Japanese society. While exempt from charges of war crimes, the US occupation forced Hirohito to take a more ceremonial role as the country's monarch. The Japanese constitution, which once read that "[t]he Empire of Japan shall be reigned over and governed by a line of Emperors unbroken for ages eternal," now read, under the US occupation, "The Emperor shall be the symbol of the State and of unity of the people, deriving his position from the will of the people with whom resides sovereign power." As a figurehead, American forces found useful the authority he had over the Japanese people who strongly valued obedience to authority. Another reason for the lack of dissent had to do with Japanese beliefs about merit and hard work. Existing meritocratic values fit well with US-imposed democratization of educational institutions. Pressure to respond to Western powers before World War II had launched a dramatic push for the cultivation of native talent in industry, technology, and the military. The sense of urgency fueling the need for progress and power also enhanced Japanese desire for access to education. By the 1920s, the country had already flirted with the idea of free, universal, and high-quality secondary schooling for all citizens. The US occupation's proposal for democratizing the school system resembled to a large extent the kind of proposals the Japanese people had seriously considered and debated long before the start of the US occupation.[4]

* * *

MacArthur wasted little time in using Japanese values and traditions to advance the US occupation's educational reform efforts. Viewing his charge as having to "rebuild a nation" and the Japanese nation as "the world's great laboratory for an experiment," the three most dramatic education-related changes he enacted had to do with religion, the structure of the school system, and the democratization of higher education. All along the way, he used Hirohito and the Tenno system and the specially created Civil Information and Education (CIE) Division to create alliances with the Japanese Educational Reform Committee (JERC) and the Japanese Ministry of Education (JME), although at times critics from both JERC and JME helped to derail key educational reforms.[5]

Early in the occupation, MacArthur succeeded in taking the unusual step of blurring distinctions between church and state, creating clear and provocative entanglements between the two. He made the decision to not only encourage the creation and spread of Christian churches, but also to financially support their interests. He used US and Japanese funds for the promotion and distribution of Bibles to "every hamlet in the country" and favored Christian missionaries by granting them visas well in advance of all other civilian visas issued by the US occupation.[6]

While using his US-appointed position as supreme commander to promote the interests of Christianity, he used the same to squeeze Japanese religion out of the school system. The occupation banned two central belief systems from educational institutions as well as Japanese public life: Shintoism and Shushin ethics. Shintoism, an indigenous, polytheistic religion, had been around long before the Meiji Era, but was in part used by the Meiji to promote nationalist sentiment and a positive view of the emperor. By World War II, Shintoism represented a combination of polytheism and Confucian ethical codes of honesty and responsibility. It had become a common feature of school life. After the war, US occupation forces removed Shintoism from the schools and prohibited school-sponsored field excursions to Shinto shrines. Shushin ethics, meanwhile, was one of the most important subjects taught in Japanese elementary schools. It provided a form of moral education that drew from Confucianism and general ethical principles. It emphasized such moral virtues as loyalty, piety, health, civic-mindedness, and family honor. The occupation removed the subject and rituals from the curriculum, textbooks, and school activities for fear it might be used by the state for political purposes.[7]

Both actions—the active support for one religion and the active suppression of another through the military occupation government—caught the attention of observers, particularly those monitoring American-style constitutional reforms enacted by MacArthur. "The concern of the American military with Japanese religions," noted William Woodard, an official with the CIE, "was definitely out of the ordinary. Respect for local customs, including religion, as a basic principle of military government and involvement, not to say interference, in the religious affairs of an occupied country is clearly ruled out by army regulations." Particularly troubling to Woodard and others was the inherent hypocrisy of the occupation's actions. While the supreme commander issued directives to "separate religion from the State, to prevent misuse of religion for political ends, and to put all religions, faiths, and creeds upon exactly the same legal basis," MacArthur nevertheless showed a willingness to play favorites when he supported the Christianization of the Japanese people.[8]

While the occupation removed native traditions from the school system, it also made sweeping moves to restructure Japanese education. To that end, the occupation began with the establishment of the CIE division that started with nineteen members and increased to approximately 140. Robust support for the division signaled that MacArthur had a significant interest in reshaping the Japanese educational system. CIE officials, once settled, directed their attention to the issue of teaching personnel. They developed a twenty-three-question survey to vet all school staff. This vetting process led to a flood of resignations before the survey reached even 5 percent of school teachers and administrators, with over one hundred thousand school officials taking themselves out of the system to prevent the shame of receiving a dismissal notice. While vetting and restaffing schools, CIE officials received two US educational "missions" to Japan, the first in 1946 and the other in 1950. The first mission included twenty-seven American scholars who drafted a report that included four major recommendations for the occupation: reeducate the people; reorganize the multitrack system in order to increase access to higher education; democratize Japanese school governance; and democratize and rebuild Japanese higher education. The second mission returned to the country to evaluate the progress made on these fronts.[9]

The occupation handled the issue of reeducation by targeting what officials believed to be the greatest difference between the US and Japanese people, a difference over the primacy of the individual. CIE officials believed Japanese culture subordinated the individual to the state. Some officials reported that the system they sought to change "supports an authoritarian social and political regime" and has the effect of producing "obedient members of the state." Ironically, the CIE decided to make explicit use of the Japanese "habit of obedience to authority" and "uncritical acceptance of the teachings of their leaders" to promote a US form of Japanese individualism. They took advantage of the self-initiated purgings that were based on subordination of self for the interest of the state. They removed Japanese religious teaching and practices and, for a time, Japanese history, geography, and martial arts. And they used their authority to replace these courses and activities with a social studies program that included politics, ethics, and civics as well as a brief experiment with *romaji*—an unpopular version of Japanese introduced in the schools that used the English alphabet. The CIE handled the *Kyoiku Chokugo* in a similar manner, a school ritual that involved recitation of a script pledging allegiance to the Japanese Empire and the hanging of Tenno's portrait. Occupation officials, rather than forbidding this long-standing practice, leaned on the Tenno to "produce a new rescript" and, with the new, symbolic ritual in hand, made it optional rather than mandatory throughout the Japanese educational system.[10]

When it came to reorganizing and democratizing the schools themselves, CIE members took on the multitrack system and its administration. Rather than have specialized and segregated schools reflecting different classes in Japanese society, the occupation sought to create comprehensive, coeducational schools in which all segments of society learned together. This they hoped would lead to the cultivation of democratic values and ideals. The successful reform of schools along these lines was in part due to positive responses coming from the Japanese people themselves who sent petitions in support of the idea. It resembled a "secondary school for all" movement that had been promoted in Japan during the 1920s. This movement sought to democratize access to higher education. The US Educational Mission to Japan expressed a similar sentiment by stating that "recognition of the right of access to higher learning must be made clearer to the people and to the administrative powers controlling higher education, as the prerogative and special advantages of the few are relaxed and redefined for the many." For this reason, the US occupation eliminated the *Koto Gakko*, or network of elite secondary feeder schools for the prestigious Imperial University. The old network created an impression that access to prestigious universities required attendance to one of these feeder schools. The occupation wanted to break up this monopoly and, through a new system of high schools, democratize channels of access to the old university system.

To support this goal, the occupation assisted Japanese officials in establishing a new administrative structure through the School Board Act of 1948. The idea was to create a "lay educational agency" that functioned much like school boards functioned in the United States. One leading CIE official, Joseph Trainor, believed that "a major requirement for its reform and reorganization" would be to decentralize power over the schools, then held by the Ministry of Education, through "some agency or agencies closer to the people themselves." Not everyone in CIE agreed with him. Some expressed a "distrust in the ability of the Japanese people" for this kind of democratic self-governance.

In the end, the Act succeeded in promoting the democratization of school governance, but not in the way the occupation had anticipated. Those most affected by school-board decision making came forward to participate in these newly formed opportunities for participatory democracy, such as teachers unions that overwhelmingly supported the establishment of school boards. The act provided teachers and administrators with greater control over the selection of teaching materials and practices. This put them in the vanguard of Japanese democracy, as they made extensive use of this outlet for self-governance.[11]

For a time, the occupation sought to build on the school reform momentum with the lower schools to enact changes at the higher education level. Before the occupation, Japan had over four hundred postsecondary institutions that included colleges, universities, and normal schools for teacher preparation. The variety of institutions served separate segments of society, much like the class division that appeared in the school system. The universities ranged from prestigious, centrally run institutions to single-faculty universities, to private, city, and prefectural colleges. With an eye toward democratizing access to the best institutions, the occupation looked for ways to dissolve the sharp distinctions that existed within this system. They created multifaculty universities, folded normal schools into university-level programs of study, and brought the total number of higher education institutions to just over two hundred. This meant that approximately 50 percent of institutions in existence had been either absorbed by other institutions or shut down. What's more, the occupation made all higher education institutions—with the exception of women's colleges—coeducational. The occupation succeeded in making these changes and hoped that by doing so they would weaken the hold that the Imperial University had on Japanese imagination and political life.[12]

* * *

Despite their many successes, the US occupation did face stirring opposition in one important area of educational reform: how Japanese university systems would be run. The CIE office saw the first hints of resistance when their attention turned to the restructuring of colleges and universities, a kind of resistance they hadn't seen at the lower levels. The proposals for greater access to the university system and raising the status of select programs, such as teacher education, gave rise to an opposition movement. Those who opposed the reforms worried that university studies would be negatively affected in terms of quality and rigor. Faced with an occupation force that sought to expand, democratize, and open the doors to the country's most revered universities, the first to come forward with their objections were the elite institutions. As quickly as the CIE higher education reforms were implemented, the Imperial University responded by adding graduate-level studies in an effort to distinguish itself from the newly created institutions. The Imperial University was the only institution in the country at the time capable of offering graduate course work.[13]

But it was in the attempt to reform control over Japanese higher education that ripples of opposition turned into waves of protest. The occupation wanted for colleges and universities the same kind of democratic form of governance it had created at the lower levels through the School Board Act. At the forefront of these efforts was Walter C. Eells, a Stanford PhD known for his expertise on junior college education. At sixty-one years of age, he accepted the assignment to serve as CIE's chief of higher education policy. His unpopular decisions and handling of higher education, dubbed by Japanese observers as the "Eells Typhoon," generated great controversy, particularly over two matters: his "Outline of Proposed Law Governing Universities" and what came to be known as the "Red Purge."[14]

Eells's "Outline" came out the same year as the School Board Act. It proposed an American-style system whereby power over universities—previously held in large measure by the Japanese Ministry of Education and university faculty—would reside with governing boards established at each university. These boards, comprising members appointed by government officials, alumni associations, and the board itself, would alone have the power to appoint and dismiss presidents, deans, and faculty, determine enrollments, and set budgets.[15]

Several Japanese university leaders weren't pleased with this outline at all. Seven of them from the prestigious Imperial universities heard about the ideas in the planning stage, before it was published, and sent a petition to the CIE. They cited the board model of governance as an "extremely grave problem" that they feared entrusted those potentially without academic experience or training with the "heart of university research and teaching." They demanded "careful consideration" of this matter because the application of this American-style system "ignores the tradition and the advantages of university autonomy in our country." They noted the need to preserve faculty rights, for instance, in selecting the teaching staff of the university and decried the placement of such powers in the hands of a board that could politicize university appointments and destroy the very core of Japanese higher education. Around the same time as the petition, Nanbara Shigeru, president of the Faculty Senate at Tokyo University, paid a special visit to the CIE higher education office. Nanbara's opinion had special significance. He served not only on the faculty of Tokyo University and as faculty senate president, but also as chairman of the JERC, a special committee of Japanese scholars who served as consultants to the educational reform efforts coming from the occupation. The CIE had a favorable view of JERC for its assistance in helping to implement significant changes to the primary and secondary system. When Nanbara walked into the CIE office to express his opposition to the idea of university governing boards in the clearest possible terms, they had reason to listen. One CIE official present in the meeting with Nanbara described the chairman as stating "unequivocally" that the issue of board control was "the most momentous ever to face the Japanese universities and the one most fraught with danger."[16]

Tensions came to a head after the Ministry of Education published a Japanese translation of Eells's "Outline" in 1948. Faculty at one university immediately responded by passing a "correction" to Eells's work. JERC followed this correction with a counterproposal of their own. Other organizations and institutions, such as Tokyo Technical University, the Japanese University Accreditation Association, and the Association of Technical Colleges, supported these alternative plans and rejected the idea of boards filled with "industrialists, businessmen and city men." They wanted nothing to do with governing boards "occupied by such people" and forcefully noted the corrosive effect that "local bosses" would have on institutions of higher education.[17]

Eells and his cohort brushed off these initial protests. He described the many objections he'd received as "not necessarily valid." His views on the matter had everything to do with his understanding of the American system and his belief that "universities belong to the people and should be responsive to them." Despite the objections he received from the Japanese academic community, he moved forward with plans for transforming Japanese higher education governance into a version of the US model. His colleague, Arthur Loomis, claimed that Eells's "Outline" was "in excellent shape." He pushed to have the outline turned into law as soon as January 1949. A few month past this target date, the outline was on its deathbed and fell into obscurity. And years later, the CIE chief at the time recalled about Eells's proposal that "perhaps it wasn't as appropriate for Japan as we thought."[18]

The demise of the outline coincided with the rise of student protests. At Tokyo University, students published a pamphlet criticizing the "colonistic restructuring" Eells had proposed. They objected to the idea of having "local political bosses and local business capital" handling the affairs of university life. National student organizations produced pamphlets and drafted proposals of their own. They pushed for returning all of the major university decision-making authority to established faculty governance bodies, including those previously held by the Ministry of Education, and added to this the stipulation that faculty governance bodies should include some student participation, membership, or representation. When students saw that their proposals didn't have much effect on the CIE's course of action and decision to move forward with the outline, they began to strike. Joining them in spring 1949 were supporters from an "Umbrella Association for Countering the University Law," a Tokyo-based group that represented politicians, scientists, women's groups, and unions for teachers and railway workers, among others, and that coordinated strikes and protests throughout the country. Reports indicated that seventy-five thousand students from 105 schools had participated in these strikes.[19]

The combination of university, student, and union protests torpedoed Eells's "Outline." "Strong opposition undoubtedly prevails," commented one higher education consultant with the CIE who recommended against introducing the new governance structure for fear it would "endanger the whole university situation." Eells ultimately agreed with this and, by 1950, stated that "the decentralization and democratization of public higher education is not being planned at present." As he watched the slow-motion sinking of his proposal, Eells turned his attention to what he believed facilitated the kind of protests and union organizing that thwarted his plans for higher education. He blamed the rise of communism in Japanese education.[20]

Before university leaders, students, and unions exercised their power against his "Outline," Eells showed little concern for communist ideas or faculty in educational institutions. He placed his full support behind the US occupation's Civil Liberties Directive (1945) that granted the Japanese people "freedom of thought, of religion, of assembly and of speech," which to his mind included all political ideologies, doctrines, and parties. He backed the release of thousands of wartime prisoners who had been members of the Japanese Communist Party (JCP) and who had actively protested against going to war, advocated peace, opposed Japanese militarism, and fought for universal suffrage rights. He believed, in fact, that the JCP's platform of establishing "a people's democracy" accorded well with the US occupation's efforts to democratize and decentralize Japanese education. To suppress their views because they are communist would be "little different from the hated wartime 'thought control'" experienced by Japanese academics and activists during the lead up to World War II. "As long as freedom of opinion is provided for in the Constitution," noted Eells, "it is quite inconsistent to deny similar freedom of belief and freedom of expression to mature, thinking students and professors at the university level." He described "interest in communism" as a "normal and healthy attitude in a university community searching for truth."[21]

Everything changed for Eells after tens of thousands of university students took to the streets against his "Outline." This was hardly the only factor. World events, including the spread of communism in China and Korea as well as the rise of the Soviet nuclear program, certainly contributed to his changed views. But the widespread campaign against his reform efforts began to take on new meaning for Eells. They looked more to him like manipulation by communist leaders rather than expressions of democracy and freedom of assembly. These student groups, he claimed, were "not interested in the development of democracy in Japan." When he learned that JCP members had attended a national university student conference, he concluded that these students were taking orders from the JCP. When he also learned that JCP membership nationwide had exploded from around one thousand to over one hundred thousand members during his tenure with the CIE, he began to panic.[22]

The CIE responded to escalating concerns over the rise of communism in Japanese higher education by sending Eells on a whirlwind, typhoon-like tour across 138 of the country's universities in 1949 and 1950. He kicked off the tour with a controversial address at Niigata University's July commencement in which he called communism a "dangerous and destructive doctrine since it advocates the overthrow of established democratic governments by force." Communist teachers and professors, he urged, should be dismissed from Japanese schools and universities. His speech caused a stir among academic circles, mostly because it resembled the kind of witch hunt and purging that the Japanese had suffered before the occupation. "We have a bitter experience of 'thought control' during the war" suggested one university president, and, as far as universities were concerned, "we do not want to repeat the same mistake." Eells stuck to his remarks. University leaders sought clarification about whether this constituted an order and if the CIE officially supported the remarks. Both Eells and the CIE left sufficient ambiguity about occupation policy to cause great concern among school and university leaders. Two months after the speech, over five hundred school teachers affiliated with the JCP were fired. Presidents from almost seventy leading universities gathered to coordinate a response to the speech, but concluded only that a speech did not in itself establish formal occupation policy. The president of Tokyo University called for academic freedom to prevail and argued in defense of university autonomy. Short of faculty openly promoting communist beliefs, the Japanese academic community had little appetite for controlling the political beliefs of its members, at least at the higher education level. Of the almost two hundred documented communist or communist sympathizing professors, an estimated forty professors were actually dismissed.[23]

* * *

Within days of Eells's controversial Niigata speech, MacArthur announced that the occupation would wind down its operations. This signaled the beginning of Japanese independence and marked the imminent end of the occupation. MacArthur wanted to begin relaxing the control the United States had over "almost every phase of Japanese life." Educational policy would increasingly be handed over to the Japanese and it would no longer be used to influence the economic ideas of its teachers and professors in favor of future trade and market relations with the United States. The occupation had by this time succeeded in securing these economic interests—the maintenance of a "free-market" trading partner or, as some later called it, "Japan, Inc."—through industrial concentration, a defense treaty, and the continued presence of US military bases in Japan. Although the Japanese followed a form of state-guided capitalism following the end of the occupation, they were squarely within the US economic and political sphere of influence.[24]

That Eells and the CIE failed in their attempts to revise the governance of Japanese higher education or to purge all communists from its faculty is not surprising given the transition then occurring. The occupation's CIE office, nevertheless, could boast to the second Educational Mission to Japan that they had responded to many of the charges given to them by the first mission, including the reeducation of the Japanese people, the reorganization of schools, and the democratization of school governance. What Japanese officials, teachers, professors, and occupation critics knew barely, if at all, was that halfway around the world in another postwar occupation, overwhelming resistance to US educational reform efforts were being successfully organized with a German accent.

Chapter Seven
Zero Hour

Even as allied forces began taking control of the first German town of Aachen, Franklin Delano Roosevelt showed little interest in postwar planning meetings in the fall of 1944. With the war still on, his attention was elsewhere. Officials from state, treasury, and the US military kept raising the issue with the president during the early stages of American control over Germany in World War II. They wanted him to review their ideas about the kind of US occupation government they envisioned for the country. He offered them a curt reply: "Speed on these matters is not essential at the present moment... I dislike making detailed plans for a country which we do not yet occupy." They disagreed. Without an occupation plan, many wondered, how would the United States govern Germany's core political, economic, and educational institutions when the time came?[1]

The problem with FDR's absence in postwar planning was that each agency went its own way and, as a result, some fundamentally different ideas about what the occupation would look like began to take shape. State and treasury, for instance, were deeply at odds. State officials had in mind a quick and efficient reconstruction of Germany. They wanted to create an environment that would lead to a speedy recovery of Germany's infrastructure, health, welfare, education, and sanitation. The German state, they believed, would have great difficulty coming out of the rubble left after the war without such an environment. In part, their intentions had to do with the welfare of the German people. But their other concern had to do with the USSR. State officials wanted Germany strong enough to create a buffer between western Europe and the emerging Soviet state. They had serious concerns about the postwar expansion of communism, and Germany, as they saw it, would be key in limiting that expansion. Treasury, meanwhile, took a different position. Secretary of Treasury Henry Morgenthau called for a "harsh peace" to teach Germany a lesson after having started two world wars, caused a holocaust, and dreamt up an Aryan belief system centered on world dominance. Morgenthau wanted to punish Germans by allowing them to suffer for a time the consequences of the war they had started. The Morgenthau Plan, as it became known, envisioned giving the US occupation license to allow Germans to experience disarray in public works, sanitation, and public health. As such, state and treasury couldn't both have their way and FDR missed early signs of the impending clash.[2]

State also had disagreements with the War Department, but these had more to do with timing than with fundamental differences. War officials viewed state as the agency best equipped to handle the long-term affairs of a US occupation government, at least in the case of Germany. But they didn't want state meddling in their operations in the short term. The differences between state and war became a matter of sorting out what constituted short-term versus long-term planning.[3]

Most of these conflicting views coming from the Departments of State, Treasury, and War were left unresolved as FDR became consumed with the war itself and with his own flagging health. Germany's future had to wait.

By the time the war ended, FDR was gone, Harry Truman was in the White House, and the allied forces carved up Germany into four sections. The British and the Soviets split the northern half of the country, with the British in the northwest and the Soviets in the northeast. The French and US occupations divided the southern half, with the French in the southwest and the United States in the southeast. All four allied forces took a share of Berlin then located in the Soviet zone. This partitioning of the German state presented a novel problem for the United States. In no previous military occupation had the United States shared control over a people or nation. These conditions forced the United States to take into account the kind of planning activities undertaken in other zones. It also prompted German citizens to question discrepancies that would inevitably emerge between allied governments. Most notably, the British ceded control to German officials early on in the occupation, particularly over matters like educational policy. The United States, meanwhile, had grand plans for educational reform, denazification, and reeducation. For the first time, a US occupation government faced pressure not only from the citizens of an occupied land, but also from other occupation governments. American plans for German education were caught between these twin pressures.⁴

* * *

The War Department took the lead in handling all education-related matters in the American zone. They created a low-level office of Education and Religious Affairs (ERA) under the Public Health and Welfare Division. ERA was initially deemed a section (1945), then a branch (1946), and finally a division in its own right (1948). Since the US military occupation assigned generals to the high-status divisions, low-level offices like ERA had civilian heads and a high degree of autonomy from military influence. ERA had both these qualities, an initial staff of ten, and the power to impact the educational lives of approximately twenty million Germans in Bavaria, Greater Hesse, and the northern areas of Baden-Württemberg.⁵

German citizens in the American zone and elsewhere throughout the country held deeply rooted educational values that stretched back to the Weimar Republic. Under the pre-Nazi system, long-standing class divisions that existed in the broader society also existed in the schools. German schools typically didn't follow these class divisions for the first four years—from ages six to ten—of a child's education; all children attended the *Volksschule*. But once they completed this basic mass-education program, students faced a two-track system—one for vocational education and another for college preparatory studies. Even among the elite, in the preparatory track there existed an 80-percent attrition rate, especially at the most distinguished *Gymnasium* schools that focused on the classics—Greek and Latin—as well as humanistic, cultural, artistic, historical, and scientific studies. The ones who completed the secondary program received the distinction of *Abitur*. When the Nazi regime came to power, this two-track system continued. Mass primary schooling, class stratification at the secondary level, and the continuance of the *Gymnasium* remained largely the same. The crucial difference was that the new regime turned secondary schools into centers of nationalistic and fascist sentiment. These schools began supplying the managers and officials of the new Nazi state.⁶

The tiny ERA office, under the command of the War Department, had to decide what to do with the educational system the Nazi regime left behind. While state, treasury, and war all pulled in different directions over this and many other questions, ERA chief John Taylor quietly took the lead, piloting the low-flying office undetected while others fought larger battles over the character of the occupation as a whole. While each region within the American zone operated with increasing autonomy, with their *Land* directors (or regional governors) and local ERA branches, Taylor initiated the first occupation-wide educational reform. That's what the military government had selected him to do as ERA head from 1944 to 1947.[7]

Taylor had the ideal resume for the job. This former educational administrator had completed a PhD at Columbia University with dissertation research on Weimar youth groups. What's more, he'd taught in Berlin before the war and had practical experience on the ground with German students, educators, and administrators. All of this meant that Taylor had important scholarly credentials, leadership experience, vital language skills, and credibility among both the German people and US occupation officials. But Taylor was not the occupation's first pick. He was little known and had none of the star power some officials wanted for the ERA. His lack of recognition limited the influence he had, especially in meetings with his superiors. Throughout his term, they continued to search for candidates with higher profiles. State Department officials further complicated his charge with the creation of a special group called the General Advisory Committee (GAC). This group consisted of education professors, experts on German history and culture, as well as German refugees who gathered to offer recommendations and suggestions on the direction education should take in occupied Germany. Their reports created an uneasy, and largely unwelcome, relationship with ERA.[8]

Taylor faced three immediate challenges he believed his supervisors and GAC had dismissed or misunderstood: staffing, denazification, and resistance. These problems made his job among the most difficult and unenviable of the entire division. They were also problems that he continued to face long after June 1945 when the first handful of schools reopened in the American zone.

* * *

His staffing difficulties stemmed from the reality that 80 percent of all male teachers in many communities had reported for active military duty under the Nazi government. By some occupation standards, simply having this military background immediately disqualified these teachers. Disqualification, in some cases, meant that they would never return to the classroom again. Those who supported this policy warned against having former Nazi soldiers in the school system. They feared that these former soldiers would inevitably expose German children to Nazi propaganda. By other occupation standards, reporting for military duty alone wasn't a sufficient reason for disqualification for a teaching position. A final decision would depend on peer-references, acts committed while on military duty, and the degree to which these former Nazi soldiers subscribed to the ideals of the Nazi party. Taylor had to navigate through changing, often conflicting standards and policies while also having to staff schools as soon as possible.[9]

The War Department, at first, established a black-grey-white staffing policy that Taylor attempted to follow, even though inconsistencies in its application appeared across the American zone. The black-grey-white policy stipulated clear distinctions between Germans on a continuum from former Nazis to anti-Nazis. Blacklisted Germans were typically those who had held a high rank within the Nazi party or who were guilty of war crimes. Lower-level civil servants in the party would undergo further vetting, but could potentially receive a "grey" listing. Germans who had no affiliation with the Nazis or who had actively worked against the regime were placed on the "white" list and could immediately assume duties in the US occupation government as civil administrators.

In the end, this policy impacted the ERA more than any other office, branch, or division. Schools needed German teachers, while other sectors of the occupation could make do with American or European officials. Taylor worked with the policy for a time, but realized that few qualified teachers would be available to staff the schools if it were implemented according to the strictest interpretation of the black-grey-white code. Over 90 percent of educators had joined the Nazi association for teachers, not all of whom did so voluntarily. He turned to housewives as the logical alternative to disqualified male teachers. Yet German housewives with the proper training proved to be too scarce for reopening all schools across Bavaria, Hesse, and the rest of the American zone. He then challenged the strictest interpretations of the policy. To his mind, permanently categorizing Germans in this way denied them the possibility of change through reeducation. He not only believed they could change, but also planned and depended on it. When most elementary schools opened in October 1945, with

80 percent of eligible children enrolled, he faced a dire staffing crisis. Student-teacher ratios hovered between 80:1 and 120:1. What's more, the American zone had seven universities and an assortment of specialized technical and professional programs, most of which had not yet reopened. These institutions were also at a standstill, in part because of the vetting process for readmitting faculty.[10]

For a time, a more lenient staffing policy replaced the stringent one during the first year of the American occupation, but it backfired once media outlets reported on various former Nazis who had slipped through the cracks and made their way back to school or university positions. The War Department responded to such reports by conducting crackdowns and purging faculty, at times eliminating 60 percent or more of an institution's teaching staff. These crackdowns crippled important areas of study in medical and scientific programs. Once the media fervor died down, these vastly understaffed areas left Taylor and the ERA demanding once again a more lenient process of vetting candidates for teaching and research positions. As occupation officials let up on the process, after recognizing grave shortages, the cycle of lenience, scandal, and purge would repeat.[11]

* * *

While ERA attempted to navigate around the shoals of staffing policy, the State Department's GAC kicked off the second major challenge facing Taylor and his cohort: denazification. GAC had come to specific conclusions about what kind of denazification efforts the occupation should implement. The harshest statements by far came from German refugees in the group. They had the most pessimistic view of the potential for reeducation. Paul Tillich—theologian, philosopher, and refugee—called for a blanket dismissal of all German teachers. He recommended starting with a complete purge, while holding out the possibility that some teachers might be reinstated at a later time. His views on universities were equally severe, believing that the entire system should be shut down until a proper faculty could be recruited. By proper, Tillich meant a faculty receptive to the kind of democratic principles the United States was attempting to export to occupied Germany. Alfred Doblin, also a German refugee consulting with GAC, agreed with Tillich. "Educating Germans is almost hopeless," he argued, "because the majority of the professional classes are Nazis."

Others on the committee were a bit more hopeful. Smith College professor Walter Kotschnig suggested that the solution to reeducating German teachers was to send them to teacher-training programs in the United States. This would help reorient and internationalize their perspectives on education, schooling, and society. For Taylor, these ideas and recommendations left unresolved the immediate problem of filling the overwhelming vacancies he was charged with filling. He believed he had little time to respond to this challenge, to wait for the system to survive a complete purge, or to hold out for German educators to study abroad. Taylor sank into the realities on the ground and operated with the belief that reeducation and redemption would happen under the occupation government's guidance.[12]

Taylor's larger denazification concern extended beyond teachers and their training and had more to do with the kind of materials children received in school. It didn't take long for ERA staff members to recognize that many German texts from the Nazi era posed serious problems for education under US occupation.

These texts were shot through with language aimed at stirring nationalist sentiment and promoting the interest of a fascist state. Such language inevitably conflicted with the goal of denazification and, no matter how desperately the schools needed texts, Taylor couldn't use them. But he surprised his staff with a solution. As a graduate student at Columbia University, he had conducted research on the Weimar Republic while working with a professor on a project that involved collecting pre-Nazi era textbooks for Columbia's International Institute. He thought that if he could get his hands on some of these texts, they just might make suitable replacements. Taylor contacted the International Institute with an urgent plea to have approximately 250 Weimar period textbooks microfilmed and shipped to him as soon as possible. They prepared and sent the collections as fast as they could. Once he received them, Taylor raced to a local newspaper plant to print 40,000 textbooks. Without these texts, as he well knew, German classrooms would remain in limbo and perhaps become breeding grounds of anti-American sentiment. GAC experts from Stanford and Columbia ultimately weighed in on the issue of denazification of school materials. They took the view that entirely new textbooks were needed and that they would be willing to write them. That was the only way to be sure to eliminate blatant propaganda and nationalism from these materials that appeared even in the Weimar texts. As GAC debated these goals, Taylor turned to the almost two million Germans students waiting for action. The 40,000 textbooks he had printed offered a stop-gap solution until more acceptable texts could be produced.[13]

At the very moment Taylor faced critical staffing shortages and the dilemma of denazification, the GAC officials assembled a special "mission" for the purpose of conducting a systematic study of German educational problems and solutions. Taylor and the ERA staff wanted little to do with this mission. Taylor believed it was too early to evaluate what they'd done and it was too soon to change what they'd started. Under pressure from his superiors—such as occupation governor general Lucius Clay, who had praised the idea of a mission ever since he received a copy of a report by a similar study conducted in Japan—Taylor finally relented and agreed to help mission members with their study in summer 1946.[14]

Among members of the special commission were educational experts, representatives from unions, and religious leaders—all headed by their chair, George Zook, a former commissioner of education under FDR. The report they produced came to be known as the Zook Report. The authors argued that the German school system was structurally incompatible with a democratic society. First on their list of reform priorities was the two-track system that perpetuated inequalities. "This system cultivates attitudes of superiority in one small group," they argued, "and inferiority in the majority of the members of German society, making possible the submission and lack of self-determination upon which authoritarian leadership has thrived." Requiring children and their families to make lifelong career choices at the age of ten worked against what the Zook Report described as a common culture necessary for a democratic society. They called for a unified system of education that combined all elementary, secondary, and vocational programs. It was to be available to all students and offer academic opportunities for any interested in preparing for higher education. These reforms, as they saw it, would break down class distinctions and create common experiences and coursework that would erode the notion that there were higher and lower social and political stations in German life. Higher education under this plan would serve more than elites.[15]

The Zook Report challenged long-standing social, political, and educational values and attracted a great deal of attention when it appeared in October 1946. Some of the most incisive critics were officials within the State Department. "I do not believe that democratic practice," argued one official, "requires the integration of vocational education with general secondary education under the same roof as the mission recommends." Another suggested that the report was too eager "to fasten on the German educational system all the details of the American system."[16]

* * *

The problems raised by the Zook Report critics were not lost on the German people and touched off the third major problem of Taylor's tenure at the ERA: resistance. The most powerful German opponent to US-backed educational reform was Alois Hundhammer.[17]

As minister of culture and education for Bavaria, Hundhammer rose quickly through the ranks of civil administration under the US occupation and gained a powerful position within months of the establishment of the American zone. He'd risen to power just as the US received the results of the Zook Report listing the objectives for a wholesale educational change to German schools, colleges, and universities. His rise also occurred as the British had begun to cede power over to the Germans at a much faster rate than the Americans.[18]

Hundhammer's dealings with the ERA were highly influenced by the internal, mixed reception of the GAC study and developments in the British zone. He began by flatly ignoring the Zook Report's demands for educational reform. In his first official statement on the matter to the American occupation, he failed to acknowledge US demands for reform and left the preoccupation system intact. His second statement did the same, even though occupation officials had given him direct instructions to incorporate such changes as the implementation of tuition-free secondary school, modification to the two-track system, democratization of higher learning, and the elevation of teacher preparation to university status. When pressed about the lack of attention to these changes, he conceded and promised a course of action that never saw the light of day. He kept the two-track system as it was and even mandated a profession of Christian or Catholic faith from all teachers, thereby excluding Jews, agnostics, and any other person of faith or nonfaith. Although Hundhammer claimed to have developed a tuition-free secondary program, parents complained that they were pressured to make "donations."[19]

Hundhammer's strategy of resisting the ERA and other elements of the US occupation proved highly effective. His delay tactics bought him time to win public support. Bavarians began to understand the lack of consensus within the occupation government about educational reform—the kind and the extent. This left a leadership vacuum that Hundhammer filled as quickly as it presented itself. As his popularity as minister of culture and education increased, the occupation's authority began to wane. Occupation officials attempted to regain control by calling Hundhammer to account for the lack of progress. By then, he had gained enough credibility in the eyes of both Bavarians and the US occupation to make it difficult to imagine proceeding without him. Nevertheless, they pressed him hard and threatened his career in the process. "I am a soldier," came his reply, "I know how to take orders."[20]

What the United States soon discovered was that he was also a clever administrator with an eye for seeing opportunities even in the face of adversity. His next move crystallized his power and left the occupation with few options. Hundhammer put together a plan that was sure to satisfy US demands for educational reform, but that was also sure to cause an uproar among Bavarians. He got on Bavarian radio and announced what the US occupation wanted, but, more importantly, described in painful detail how much the reorganization of programs would cost the German people. Given the dire hardships Bavarians faced at the time, including starvation, homelessness, and illness, the costly educational reform effort made the US occupation appear frivolous and out of touch. Bavarians came out in protest against the occupation and Hundhammer became the linchpin between these citizens and US officials. It left American administrators with two options: dismiss Hundhammer and face even greater public resistance or soften their stance and work with the popular, if cunning, minister. They chose to work with Hundhammer and the result was another round of delay tactics and manipulation of public opinion that achieved exactly the results he wanted. The one point of concession gained by occupation officials, at least as far as they could see, was in the promotion of free textbooks and tuition-free secondary education. On these, Hundhammer relented. But he counted on using social and cultural pressure to force some students out of academic secondary programs so as to preserve these primarily for elites.[21]

Despite all the efforts of the occupation, the realities of teacher shortages, lack of materials, and resistance from German leaders like Hundhammer made substantive reform an unlikely possibility. Taylor and the ERA staff had to contend with immediate realities that left them scrambling to work with an ever-changing policy for recruiting teachers, professors, and civil administrators. After a year of work in Bavaria, the occupation decided to see how far along education had served the purpose of denazification and reeducation. They sent out a questionnaire to be completed by grade-school children. The survey discovered that Nazi beliefs had far more staying power than they had expected. When asked whether national socialism was a bad idea or a good idea executed badly, over half of schoolchildren believed it was a good idea executed badly. A mere 3.5 percent believed it was a bad idea; the rest were undecided. Even though the US occupation focused on denazification, the restructuring of the educational system, improving teacher training, promoting university reform, and building networks for cultural exchange, Germans found ways to preserve long-held systems and traditions.[22]

* * *

As Taylor's term at ERA came to a close, the occupation named his replacement, Richard Thomas Alexander. The change of guard in 1947 came with great promise. Alexander had the kind of international recognition they had wanted for the position. A professor and dean at Columbia University, he was widely considered to be the leading expert on German education in America. He had studied the country's educational institutions, policies, and practices for decades and had even mentored John Taylor through his doctoral studies. Alexander knew that the German system stood "in sharp contrast to the practice in America," particularly in the way German elites claimed for themselves "the privilege of excluding others from its ranks." He applauded the American enthusiasm for promoting democracy in Germany and the efforts the United States had made in opening the door to German self-governance in each of the regions under US control.[23]

By the time Alexander arrived, however, Hundhammer's impact could be felt across the rest of the American zone. The minister and his fellow German representatives, including the various ministers of education in each province (or *Lander*), secured enough power to block reform and to make substantive changes to schools, colleges, and universities virtually impossible. The US occupation soon realized that while they raced to give Germans an opportunity to exercise democratic self-governance, Germans used that power to thwart the United States' larger aims of reeducating the German people.[24]

In Greater Hesse, the occupation worked with Minister of Education Franz Schramm. He'd signaled to American officials his willingness to work with them by instituting summer workshops for teacher preparation, banning corporal punishment from the schools, and submitting early (by comparison) a school reform plan in 1946. Schramm wanted to keep the two-track system, but suggested that a "German Unified School" plan would address the United States' interest in democratizing the schools. Under Schramm's unified schools, large schools would house all levels, tracks, and student backgrounds. The idea was to put all groups under a single roof while maintaining the stratification within the school through differentiated programs. For a time, the comprehensive school idea appeared to hold great promise. Given the kind of resistance faced in Bavaria, this proposal had the potential of turning the tide against resisters and moving the United States closer to its broader goals of facilitating the transition from fascism to democracy. Unfortunately for the United States, the plan began to fall apart as officials in the Ministry of Education changed and as parents began to protest reforms that they interpreted as lowering educational standards. New German leaders called for greater differentiation at younger ages, in direct opposition to what US officials had advocated. As a result, and as late as 1949, no real progress had been made in educational reform, leaving one frustrated US official to declare to Erwin Stein, then German minister of education, that "your German school system is just as dangerous as those war-materials factories." By then US influence on educational matters had seriously eroded and enforcement of educational change seemed counterproductive to the maintenance of postwar German democracy.[25]

In Bremen and Baden-Wurttemberg, the ministers of education were inspired by the resistance seen in Bavaria. They followed the same aim by way of a different course of action. Christian Paulman, minister of education in Bremen, pushed for the kind of changes the United States wanted and submitted a plan that would extend universal elementary education from four to six years—although the United States demanded nine—and also included other democratizing features to be implemented in the Bremen region. The way Paulman managed to get these controversial reforms passed in 1949 was by failing to include an implementation schedule. Without an implementation schedule, the reforms became suggestions rather than initiatives to be enacted. Theodor Bauerle, minister of education in the Baden-Wurttemberg region, faced a 65 percent dismissal rate among his teachers as a result of denazification, leading to student-teacher ratios of 150:1. Bauerle kept the two-track system and early differentiation among students, but he too borrowed a page from Hundhammer in using delay tactics to avoid implementation or even serious consideration of school reform. When pressed by US officials for reform plans, he loaded education bills with the most expensive features, assuring that they'd receive scorn from the public and be defeated by German representatives. What's more, the region was slated to be unified with the French zone that had largely ceded control over educational matters to the Germans. With the coming unification, Bauerle and other German officials successfully delayed educational reforms until the end of military occupation.[26]

* * *

Berlin was altogether a different story. Soviets had entered and occupied the capital seven weeks before the rest of the allied forces had arrived.

They had already created a school system before the first Berlin meeting of all allied forces called the Kommandatura in August 1945. The Soviets had an educational law that shared much in common with US goals—an eight-year mass education program with differentiation occurring after that. Other distinctive features included early foreign language requirements for all students and a history curriculum that, while Marxist, as one American official noted, was "technically suited to the democratization of education." The United States and the Soviets worked out agreements on, made revisions to, and ultimately settled on a final approval of the Berlin reform, while the French and British protested the lack of German input on the matter. These were not easy negotiations. Soviet representatives wanted to infuse in the history curriculum economic interpretations that linked capitalism, imperialism, and warfare in lessons geared toward the denazification of Berlin youth. The United States argued for a broader course to replace the traditional history curriculum, a course that would include the social studies subjects of psychology, sociology, economics, geography, civics, and world history. That they made compromises acceptable to both parties, especially as tensions between allied powers increased, showed that there was a common desire to use education for the transformation of German society. The key remaining educational disagreement between the Soviets and the rest of the allied forces had to do with private schools. The United States and the British refused to concede on the Soviet idea of shutting down private schools in Berlin. With there being very few private schools, the Soviets made concessions and the Berlin School Law went into effect in June 1948.[27]

In a sense, US officials envied the accomplishments of the USSR in Berlin, given the difficulties faced in the American zone. The Soviets had followed a "plan" similar to that "in the States," as one US representative in Berlin noted, but that it was "very quick and drastic." They had accomplished virtually all the major reforms the United States had wanted in the American zone and more, such as providing for compulsory education up to the age of eighteen, free books, free tuition, coeducation, and relatively late differentiation. The Soviets had succeeded where the United States had not and most of those changes came as a result of the highly militarized nature of the occupation of Berlin.[28]

After World War II, the Cold War put the two superpowers—the United States and the USSR—at the center of a global standoff that created hot wars through proxy governments and rebel fighters on almost every continent. The contrast between the Soviet and American zones during the occupation of Germany began to appear around the world with the Soviets continuing to rely not only on their military strength and the enforcement of direct change to those satellite countries within its orbit, but also on the establishment of strong, comprehensive, universally accessible systems of education. The United States, meanwhile, would turn to indirect, covert approaches to influencing decision making in foreign governments and the public opinion of their people. The single best example of the differences between US and Soviet approaches to empire and education played out in the hills of Afghanistan.[29]

CHAPTER EIGHT

IN PERPETUITY

As airline jets penetrated the World Trade Center's twin towers and media pundits began describing the smoldering buildings as lit cigarettes on September 11, 2001, President George W. Bush sat reading *The Pet Goat* in front an elementary class in Florida. An advisor whispered in his ear that the United States was under attack, informing him of events as they unfolded, but Bush continued to stay with the children another seven minutes. He appeared unsure of what to do next. The towers eventually collapsed and the public was soon informed that this had been a terrorist attack that had cost the lives of approximately three thousand individuals. By the time he reached the rubble at ground zero, Bush knew exactly what to do. He climbed on a pile of rocks, draped an arm around a fireman, and spoke to a crowd of disaster relief workers, telling them that "I hear you. The rest of the world hears you. And the people who knocked these building down will hear all of us soon!" At no other time in his presidency did he have as much domestic and international support. This became his moment, a moment he used to direct the full force of the US military against Afghanistan and the Taliban regime.[1]

US intelligence agencies blamed the attack on Osama bin Laden, then in Afghanistan, although this figurehead of the Al-Qaeda network denied having anything to do with the attacks. Negotiations between Taliban leaders and the United States broke down, leading to a military build-up around Afghanistan that took a matter of weeks to assemble. Instead of sending ground troops and incurring large numbers of American casualties, Bush and his circle of advisors decided to use a collection of warlords and their foot soldiers called the Northern Alliance for the major ground offensive. Many of these warlords had notoriously criminal reputations, but political and pragmatic interests trumped other concerns. "The Northern Alliance, whose members are little better than the Taliban," stated a women's group in Afghanistan in a direct appeal to Bush, "will again attempt to gain power in a new Afghan government. Although they have helped the United States in the ground war, that must not be allowed." Their protests were muffled by Afghan gunfire and tens of thousands of US missiles and bombs. In the end, Northern Alliance members with "real criminal and inhuman nature" received assurances from the United States that they would be part of the new Afghan government. Their representation in the *loya jirga*, the Afghan assembly formed in June 2002 to select leadership for an interim government, indicated that any restrictions on war criminal participation would be overlooked. Women's groups, such as the Revolutionary Association of the Women of Afghanistan (RAWA), warned that this would be one of the greatest mistakes for the future of Afghan women, education, and civil society. They, and many others who fought for broad representation in the *loya jirga*, spoke from a long, multigenerational history of experience with regime change.[2]

* * *

Women and school communities in Afghanistan experienced dramatic changes throughout the second half of the twentieth century. During the 1950s, Afghan government officials in the Ministry of Education began an effort to modernize and reform the nation's educational system. They contracted Teachers College, Columbia University (TCCU) to develop teacher training and curriculum reform that at first served only male students and teachers but, over a twenty-five year period, eventually liberalized education in the country. Under Afghan king Mohammed Zahir Shah, the ministry launched a series of progressive initiatives through his Constitution of 1964. While failing to receive much attention in the United States or elsewhere around the world, the constitution fundamentally changed the lives of average Afghans. The new law of the land granted women full equality "without any discrimination or preference...before the law." It also established education as "the right of every Afghan and shall be provided free of charge by the State and citizens of Afghanistan." Zahir's government created partnerships with the University of Wyoming and the University of Nebraska at Omaha, in addition to TCCU, leading to new programs in teacher training, curriculum design, school construction as well as the creation of a new campus for Kabul University. Throughout the 1960s and 1970s, women's literacy increased as did the number of women's groups—such as the Democratic Organization of Afghan Women—that lobbied to end forced marriages and other patriarchal laws and customs. Primary education became compulsory where facilities were available and coeducation was common at least in Kabul.[3]

The decade-long Soviet occupation beginning in 1979 built on these initiatives through the Afghan Socialist Constitution. Under provisions made through the socialist constitution, 15 percent of government posts went to women. Women also accounted for half of the twenty-five thousand university student population (up from a total of ten thousand before the Soviet invasion), approximately three-fourths of the teaching staff across the country, and almost half of all physicians. Overall literacy rates increased from 10 percent at the beginning of the occupation to 45 percent male literacy and 14 percent female literacy by the time the Soviets left the country. Even Afghan critics of the Soviet occupation applauded the advances for "the public Afghan woman" as "schools were expanded throughout the country, and women went to them with great success."[4]

But a covert war launched by the United States against the Soviet occupation brought to power an extremist wing of Islamic militants called the mujahedeen that crippled these progressive developments. "It may take a century," noted one female physician about the war's toll on women and education, "for us to reach back to the level when I was a student in medical school" under Soviet control. This multibillion dollar war, the most expensive of its kind in modern history, funded not only armaments and weapons training that contributed to the destruction of 80 percent of the seven thousand schools in Afghanistan, but also educational programs intended to militarize the young. Textbooks created by the University of Nebraska at Omaha and backed by a $50 million US Agency for International Development (USAID) grant were worded to create soldiers rather than citizens. As a result, Afghan children read math problems framed in terms of targets, distances, and numbers of casualties. Some questions attempted to teach the mathematics of velocity while normalizing gruesome violence: "The speed of a Kalashnikov bullet is 800 meters per second. If a Russian is at a distance of 3,200 meters from a mujahid, and that mujahid aims at the Russian's head, calculate how many seconds it will take for the bullet to strike the Russian in the forehead." Others taught simple arithmetic in a similar way: "One group of mujahidin attack 50 Russian soldiers. In that attack 20 Russians were killed. How many Russians fled?"[5]

To some US officials at the time, this militarization and indoctrination of young Afghans through an extremist form of religious fundamentalism was a small price to pay. "What was more important in the view of world history?," asked National Security Advisor Zbignew Brzezinski about this violence-infused training and education. "The possible creation of an armed, radical Islamic movement, or the fall of the Soviet empire? A few stirred-up Muslims or the liberation of Central Europe and the end of the Cold War?"[6]

Long after the Soviets left, the mujahedeen continued to publish these textbooks under the Taliban regime that lasted until the US invasion in 2001. The leadership of the Taliban came largely from US and Saudi financed madrassas during the covert war with the Soviets. These madrassas were run by mullahs steeped in a Saudi Wahhabism that made women subservient to the will of men and followed a Badi system centered on honor, revenge, and hospitality. In its system of "justice," women were punished for not wearing burqas, and women, including little girls, were the satisfactory compensation for crimes between men. The US State Department, when responding to these injustices, followed the lead set by American energy and finance corporations who wanted to negotiate with the Taliban to develop natural gas interests in the region. When the Taliban rolled into Kabul, the State Department's deputy spokesperson and assistant secretary of public affairs, Glyn Davies, saw "nothing objectionable" with the power grab. After a year of their rule, another state official saw a bright future for US investors with the rise of an Afghan dictatorship that would "probably develop like the Saudis" with "pipelines, an emir, no parliament and lots of Sharia law. We can live with that." Executives from US gas giant Unocal helped shape this view. They argued that the rise of the Taliban was a "very positive" development and that the United States should recognize the new regime promptly so as to "lead the way" for "international lending agencies" to finance the extraction of "tremendous uncapped hydrocarbon reserves." All the while, literacy overall declined under the Taliban; women's literacy descended to the new low of 4 percent. What's more, the regime shut down the university in Kabul in the mid-1990s. Along with it, they decided to close all girls schools in the country. Until the US invasion, women's education went underground and was kept alive in home-based programs. Some members of the ruling Taliban were discovered to have provided such home-based programs for their own daughters, while denying it to the rest of Afghan society.[7]

* * *

The bombs, missiles, and other instruments of war the United States brought to Afghanistan in 2001 came with a wave of hope and optimism in the United States. It was to be the start of a new Afghan social order. Speaking to Virginia Military Institute cadets, Bush said that "Americans always see a greater hope and a better day, and America sees a just and hopeful world beyond the war on terror." Justice and hopefulness, to his mind, would depend on Afghanistan developing a stable government, the degree to which that government could train and develop a national army, and the establishment of a system of universal education "for boys and girls which works."[8]

Not long after this speech, Bush turned his attention elsewhere in the Middle East and made his wife, Laura, his representative to humanitarian efforts in Afghanistan. She had previously taught second grade for three years and served as a librarian for another three and she drew on these experiences during her time as first lady. To kick off her new responsibilities in Afghanistan, Mrs. Bush gave a speech in 2001 at the United Nations about the need to establish human rights in the country. "A major focus is on education," she stated. "Prosperity cannot follow peace without educated women and children. The United States is committed to helping the Afghan people redevelop their education system." She celebrated an initial $50 million US development fund earmarked for Afghan health, education, water, and sanitation programs and held up a backpack decorated in the imagery of the American flag as an example of the humanitarian efforts under way. Forty thousand of these backpacks, she proudly announced, would be distributed to Afghan children through the new fund. Over the course of the Bush presidency, Mrs. Bush made three visits to Afghanistan, the first of which came before her husband made his first trip to the country. Her visits were intended to represent the United States' commitment to human rights in the country and to US-backed Afghan president Hamid Karzai at crucial times when his legitimacy had come under fire. The first lady received praise from Karzai for her support and for having "personally attended all international conferences on

Afghanistan." She also came to see the progress that'd been made with billions of dollars in USAID grants, one of the main sources of US funding for Afghan reconstruction.[9]

By the time the *loya jirga* met and inaugurated the new government of Afghanistan, USAID had already begun contracting with the Louis Berger Group for reconstruction in the country. The New Jersey–based firm had a long history with government projects, beginning in the 1950s with domestic and foreign road-building and construction contracts. As an engineering consulting firm, they built roads across the United States, Burma, Nigeria, and elsewhere, wharfs for Norway, subways for Sweden, a pipeline for Kazakhstan, economic programs for Iran, Cambodia, Liberia, and Nicaragua, as well as agricultural training for the Philippines. In the decade leading up to the invasion of Afghanistan, Louis Berger had almost $150 million worth of development projects around the world through US government grants. The first contract they received from USAID for postwar Afghanistan was an "Infrastructure Assessment" followed by a "Vulnerability Assessment Map" project. These projects came to less than $6 million, but paved the way for Louis Berger to receive a much larger project.[10]

The single largest USAID contract for Afghan reconstruction, with a budget of $300 million, ultimately went to Louis Berger. Their charge was to "oversee" such projects as road building, well-water drilling, and school construction. They also had the responsibility of destroying the country's old currency as the Afghan government created and began circulating a new one.[11]

It wasn't long before controversy began to surround the Louis Berger contracts, especially ones having to do with school construction. The contract stipulated that the firm would construct 135 buildings. Along the way USAID "removed all but 105 buildings from LBGI's contract because it was not satisfied with the contract's progress on the school and health clinic buildings that it had begun to reconstruct in 2003." The number fell two more times from ninety-three to ninety. Of these, twenty-three schools had an average cost-per-classroom of over $20,000. According to the Afghan Ministry of Education, this was an astronomical figure that came as a result of fraud rather than the use of high-quality materials. Some of the "model" schools cost nearly $600,000 to construct and raised questions about the misappropriations of funds, especially as some recently built Louis Berger schools began to fall apart. Two of these ultraexpensive schools experienced roof problems after the first winter. They weren't strong enough to handle the accumulation of snow. Berger blamed the local government for this, suggesting that the problem was not in their design but rather in lax snow removal. They charged millions of dollars to replace all the school roofs, but denied any wrongdoing, poor planning, or poor design. While Berger charged approximately $600,000 for their schools, Japanese contractors working on Afghan projects funded by the Japanese government had already built comparable schools for under $100,000, or one-sixth the cost of a Berger school.[12]

Berger's primary reconstruction contract lasted from 2002 to 2006 and by the end of this period an audit could only verify the completion of ninety buildings with others at "various stages" of development. Nonprofit agencies—such as the Cooperative Housing Foundation International, Switzerland's International Organization for Migration, and the United Nations Office for Project Services—completed 421 schools and clinics in the same amount of time. Claims of corruption and fraud against Louis Berger and other for-profit US contractors triggered the creation of a new system of oversight for reconstruction companies called the Synchronized Predeployment Operational Tracker (SPOT). The SPOT system required contractors to submit data to a centralized system for oversight and management. USAID and the State Department waived this requirement for all eight major US contractors in Afghanistan, opening the door to further charges of corruption and fraud.

In Berger's case, US investigators launched a three-year audit of Berger's budgeting and accounting practices. The investigation led to the arrest of Scott Anthony Walker, a Berger official responsible for coordinating a contract valued at over one billion dollars. The investigation also led to two guilty pleas from former high-level Berger associates, a $69 million settlement for overbilling, and the resignation of Derish M. Wolff, chairman of the firm's holding company. According to Paul J. Fishman, the lead US attorney for the prosecution, "this fraud is about more than playing with the numbers to rip off the government. Funds that could have raised hope from the rubble instead padded the bottom line. This criminal conduct sends the wrong message to the world about what we stand for as a nation." In the case of USAID, a US Senate investigation revealed that rampant fraud was facilitated by rampant lack of oversight. Contractors stated that USAID officials did not visit sites "outside the wire" or beyond safety zones. Without direct oversight, agency officials relied on contractor reports and word of mouth information for their own assessments.[13]

Despite widespread fraud, the Afghan education system received much-needed attention and support from 2002 onward from the global community. Funding increased exponentially from the outset with a $4.5 billion reconstruction and aid package from donor nations that met at a conference in Tokyo in 2002. The Economic Cooperation Organization, including member nations Pakistan, Turkey, Iran, Azerbaijan, and the Central Asian Republics, created a reconstruction fund for the country. The Asian Development Bank came forward with a $500 million package for roads, agriculture, education, and energy. The neighboring government of Pakistan pledged $100 million independent of their work with other nations. The Swedish Committee for Afghanistan invested in schools, primary education, secondary education, and teacher training and ran schools in over twelve Afghan provinces serving one hundred and sixty-five thousand students. By 2010, China had donated approximate $200 million, including higher education scholarships, and Germany announced it had spent 1.6 billion euros in civilian reconstruction, about 10 percent of which went to culture and education. Of all the education projects most popular with donor nations, the category of vocational training came out on top.[14]

The influx of funding translated into an influx of contractors from around the world and the numbers tell a story of marked increases in just about every indicator. Education development in the country helped to build or reconstruct several hundred schools, train over fifteen thousand teachers, professors, trainers, and administrators, print almost 50 million textbooks in the native languages of Dari and Pashto, and fund the development of another 11 million curriculum textbooks. Between 2001 and 2010, school enrollments climbed from less than a million to an all-time high of 6.2 million. Females, effectively shut out of education under the Taliban, accounted for 35 percent, or 2.2 million, of the all-time high.[15]

While the absolute totals—in funding, school construction, curriculum development, teacher training, and school operations—appeared strong, Afghans themselves told a different story. Afghan Ministry of Education spokesperson Asef Nang stated that over six hundred schools remained closed in the country at the end of the decade, leaving almost three hundred thousand students without access to the education system. There were still thousands of schools destroyed during decades of war that still had not been rehabilitated. Moreover, some of the "schools" declared "constructed" appeared to be little more than makeshift facilities. Director of the Balkh Education Department of Northern Afghanistan, Mohammad Zaher Penhan, stated that approximately one hundred and sixty schools did not have classrooms and that students received instruction in tents. School statistics corroborated their story and suggested that many were still being left behind. By the end of the decade, according to UNICEF research, less than half of all school-aged Afghan girls enrolled (46 percent) and attended (40 percent) primary schools, while males enrolled (74 percent) and attended (66 percent) at a much higher rate. Even fewer Afghan girls enrolled (15 percent) and attended (6 percent) secondary school, while males continued to enroll (38 percent) and attend (18 percent) in greater numbers. Most surprisingly, the Afghan military had a 90-percent illiteracy rate after almost a decade of US occupation.[16]

War zone violence certainly contributed to the depressed numbers. By 2010, almost one thousand schools had been destroyed and hundreds of teachers and students killed as a result of insurgent retaliation against the US occupation. In one year alone, Afghans reported 670 attacks on schools, teachers, and students. This kept away many students who otherwise would have attended school. But other reasons had to do with misplaced funding. While Afghans received grants for US contractors to design and develop schools, such as a $3.5 million project to create the new English-language International School of Kabul, Afghan educators were denied salary increases. International donors rejected pay raises to teaching staff and the lack of incentives limited teacher recruitment efforts across Afghanistan.[17]

* * *

When US interests turned to university development, Afghans again questioned unilateral decisions made on their behalf. During a six-hour visit to Afghanistan, Mrs. Bush announced a $17.7 million grant to establish a new institution of higher education, the American University of Afghanistan. This institution, created with USAID government funds, launched the first private university in Afghanistan's history. By the end of the decade, the institution offered three undergraduate degrees—business, technology, and public administration—for students who could afford to pay nearly $6500 per year in fees, room, and board in a country where the average annual household income was approximately $300. Coincidentally, families involved in the poppy trade made approximately $6500 per year. Gulalai Bahrami, director of an elementary school in Kabul, bristled at such misallocation of funds. She noted that "even in Kabul there are schools where children attend classes in tents" and asked, "Do American children study in tents? And this is almost four years after the Taliban." Ashraf Ghani, a former finance minister for Afghanistan and president of Kabul University, also disagreed with the misallocation of funds and the privatization of higher education. "You cannot support private education," he argued, "and ignore public education." He viewed the new private institution as serving elite Afghans and absorbing funds at the expense of the public university already in existence.[18]

Far more expensive was the cost of the US-built National Military Academy of Afghanistan (NMAA), estimated at over $100 million. The vast campus stretched across five thousand acres in Kabul when designed and built. As the single most expensive educational institution in the country, it fulfilled Ghani's predictions. While Afghan faculty salaries stagnated at Kabul University, the United States promised almost endless support for a militarized form of postsecondary education with faculty from "all three [military] service academies" shipped periodically to the campus to provide support and training. Despite Mrs. Bush's attempts to focus on women's education, this disproportionately expensive institution discriminated against women. In 2010, one thousand cadets graduated from their training at the institution. None of the graduates were female. Five years after NMAA's founding, no female had studied in any of the five traditional undergraduate degree programs—English language, civil engineering, computer science, management, and law—the institution offered. That same year, US and Afghan official laid the cornerstone for a $200 million conglomeration of military academies called Afghanistan Defense University. "This university will teach student lessons on how to defend the country," said Afghan Minister Abdul Rahim Wardak, "and nothing else."[19]

* * *

The war against Afghanistan began in vengeance over the attacks of September 11, but was also presented to the American public as a humanitarian mission to liberate Afghan women from the tyranny of the Taliban. With the takeover of Kabul, US contractors poured into the country and racked up billions of dollars worth of fraud and corrupt dealing or, as the US Commission on Wartime Contracting dubbed it, "criminal behavior and blatant corruption." The country itself certainly held strategic interests in terms of its location in the region, especially in securing control over the proposed Trans-Afghanistan Pipeline that directs natural gas from the Caspian Sea to India. Senator Lindsay Graham claimed in 2011 that military bases would remain in Afghanistan "in perpetuity" to protect US interests. More immediately lucrative, however, were the reconstruction contracts themselves. The economics and politics of development contracts factored directly into the quality of schools, recruitment of teachers, and limited salaries that Afghan educators received. When asked about the misallocation of funds and the pervasive fraud in Afghanistan, Mrs. Bush and President Hamid Karzai dismissed the problem. "No, it was not something we were discussing today," came the reply. When asked if European donors would criticize the corruption, Bush and Karzai erupted into laughter when Bush replied, "Donors? You think European donors will be criticizing, or you think it will just be the journalists?"[20]

As such, US officials sidelined questions about fraud and pressed forward with plans to establish institutions and spend large sums without much oversight. They did this also without conferring in a democratic way with the Afghan people. As a result, many projects failed to win over their hearts and minds.[21] By and large, the reconstruction efforts that had the most potential for success came as a result of humanitarian progressives who worked on behalf of citizens, rather than contractors or promoters of privatization. Greg Mortenson, the once popular and later embattled author of the best-selling *Three Cups of Tea*, popularized a vision of successful school reform that depended on consulting with locals first and discovering what they wanted and needed most.

> Haji Ali spoke. "If you want to thrive in Baltistan, you must respect our ways. The first time you share tea with a Balti, you are a stranger. The second time you take tea, you are an honored guest. The third time you share a cup of tea, you become family, and for our family, we are prepared to do anything, even die. Doctor Greg, you must take time to share three cups of tea. We may be uneducated but we are not stupid. We have lived and survived here for a long time." That day, Haji Ali

taught me the most important lesson I've ever learned in my life. We Americans think you have to accomplish everything quickly... Haji Ali taught me to share three cups of tea, to slow down and make building relationships as important as building projects. He taught me that I had more to learn from the people I work with than I could ever hope to teach them.[22]

He wasn't alone. Mortenson's storytelling captured a reality—in humanitarian sentiment and effort—already present on the ground. Others like Professor Margaret Jo Shepherd of TCCU had long taken a similar approach when she led a textbook and curriculum initiative supported by the United Nations Children's Fund. "The aim of Teachers College," she explained, "is to help poor people and immigrants, and educating Afghans so they can make a difference." She and her team had completed eleven textbooks in four local languages ready for distribution in 2005. Most importantly, she noted, the spirit with which they created these texts mattered as much as getting them done at all. "We aren't trying to create a Western educational revolution here," she stated, "we want it in a way that helps the Afghans."[23]

Before any of these projects—whether successes or failures—got under way, American public concern over Afghanistan began to fade because attention had turned to another Middle Eastern country and to what became a $3 trillion elective war.[24]

CHAPTER NINE
PRIVATE MATTER

During World War II, the State, War, and Treasury Departments had years—approximately three years—to plan and prepare for the occupation of Germany and Japan. Despite the absence of presidential leadership or the changing of administrations, these departments knew what was coming. They knew they'd be called upon to develop a postconflict plan to help stabilize the social, political, and economic order in both countries when the time came. Such was not the case for Iraq during what the Bush administration dubbed the "war on terror." Serious disagreements arose between state's Colin Powell and the Defense Department's Donald Rumsfeld, but in the end no resignations came forward and the idea of invading and occupying Iraq with less than three months of planning prevailed. The administration alleged a connection between Iraq's Saddam Hussein and the Al-Qaeda network. It also alleged connections between Hussein and weapons grade nuclear material, or "yellow cake" uranium powder from Nigerian dealers. Although UN inspectors were on the ground, touring and scouring the country for evidence of weapons developments, the US government, media, and advisors to the president pressed forward. The link connecting the radical, Islamic fundamentalist group and the Arab state—that allegedly sought, if not already possessed, weapons of mass destruction—served as the primary pretext for the invasion and eventual occupation of Iraq.[1]

Bush created the Office of Reconstruction and Humanitarian Assistance in January 2003, and Rumsfeld gave retired general Jay Garner three months to lead the planning effort. "Ok, I'll do this for the next few months for you," came the reply, but "let me tell you something, Mr. Secretary. George Marshall started in 1942 working on a 1945 problem. You're starting in February working on what's probably a March or

April problem." The administration didn't wait as long as Garner had hoped. They began a "shock-and-awe" bombing campaign, invasion, and occupation in March that resulted in over a million Iraqi deaths and casualties as well as many times that number of displaced civilians.[2]

Garner's frustrations with the administration increased dramatically once US troops had secured Saddam Hussein's palaces and the Oil and Interior Ministries, but left much of the rest of the country in turmoil. Looting of hospitals, libraries, universities, social service centers, and the twenty-eight galleries of the National Museum went unchallenged. The concerns of Garner and others fell on deaf ears. The administration called complaints about the deterioration of conditions following the invasion as "henny penny" and "the sky is falling" rhetoric. Pushing Garner aside, state and defense decided to create a new organization "on the fly" called the Coalition Provisional Authority (CPA) that would take complete control of the country's social, political, economic, and educational institutions. It replaced ORHA and retained all decision-making authority between April 2003 and June 2004.[3]

West Virginia senator Robert Byrd stood out among congressional leaders who chastised the administration's handling of the entire affair. Incensed that "the President asked Congress for authority to launch an invasion against a sovereign nation that did not constitute a clear and imminent threat to the safety of the American people" and that Bush kept Congress in the dark about reconstruction planning after giving Garner "his walking papers," Byrd lambasted the president for turning once again to Congress for approval of $20 billion for the mysterious CPA. Led by L. Paul Bremer, a former ambassador to the Netherlands with almost no experience in the Middle East, the CPA's charge remained classified as a National Security Directive. By May, when Bremer issued the first regulation in Iraq, its role became much more clear: "The CPA is vested with all executive, legislative, and judicial authority... This authority shall be exercised by the CPA Administrator." During the CPA's fourteen month rule, this US administrator held the reigns of power in Iraq before turning the country over to a transitional government.[4]

* * *

Bremer, known as an active supporter of privatizing public sector responsibilities, applauded the outsourcing of education reconstruction in Iraq to a small, private company called Creative Associates

International (CAI) through the United States Agency for International Development (USAID). For a total of three years of work, CAI received $109-million worth of contracts through a no-bid process. The secretive dealing led Senator Joseph Lieberman to decry that there had been "no competitive bidding at all," exposing taxpayers to potentially excessive rates, fees, and charges. More controversy erupted when an Office of Inspector General audit report revealed that the CAI contract violated federal regulations. USAID had no documentation "to support the decision-making process" used to select CAI and had failed to follow basic procedures to avoid "conflicts of interest" when the agency "invited" only one contractor to bid on the contract. The report called this contract and ensuing violations a "significant event" that needed further investigation, particularly after interviews with contractors produced conflicting accounts. Representatives for the agency and CAI dismissed the controversial findings. They admitted not following "good business practice," but characterized the issue as a minor problem. "The only thing lacking," they argued, "was a written document explaining the thought process that went on." The reply to the audit failed to satisfy critics who described the dealing as a form of crony capitalism.[5]

CAI's background and connection to the Washington, DC business community likely had much to do with the favoritism it received. Four women founded the company in the 1970s after having run a day-care business together. During the 1980s, the company became a global, multimillion dollar operation with offices around the world. It had aligned itself with the policies of the Reagan administration and its efforts to thwart left-leaning, democratically elected governments in Latin America. The company developed programs for the Defense Department that helped US-backed Contra rebels to oust the Sandinista government. During the 1990s, CAI created "democracy promotion" programs in Haiti that, as one company representative described it, should aim for "democratship," or the establishment of some blend of dictatorship, democratic governance, and privatization in the beleaguered island nation. In other projects with two "well-known" oil companies, it has worked to "advance United States global interests." Although almost all of CAI's revenue since its inception came from contracts with the USAID, the company reconfigured itself from a nonprofit to a for-profit entity. The lead owner of CAI, Maria Charito Kruvant, preferred this move in order to make "a little money" from these publicly funded contracts. It also fit her disposition. Around the time of the Iraq invasion, she sat on corporate and banking boards in Washington and had become known as "a visible and respected member of the D.C. business community." This for-profit, education development company had an attractive profile for Bremer and others in the Bush administration who sought ways to outsource the responsibilities of the US occupation government in Iraq.[6]

After several of months on the ground, CAI and its agency sponsor began to receive mixed reports about its performance. One article glowed about how "more than 2,300 schools have been rehabilitated by USAID, millions of new textbooks have been printed and distributed, and teachers' salaries are far higher than under the former regime." Another came to a very different conclusion, describing their efforts as "poor, sloppy" and mired with a "lack of follow-through, and a lack of perseverance and persistence." Mixed reviews and controversy continued to plague the company's efforts over the course of its work in Iraq that spanned two contracts, three years, and came with a price tag of over $100 million in US government funds.[7]

* * *

USAID issued its first contract to CAI the same month the United States began bombing Baghdad. The $62.6 million contract gave the private company control over Iraq's educational policy, practices, and school rebuilding. The United States called it the Revitalization of Iraqi Schools and Stabilization of Education (RISE) project. They were charged with the task of rebuilding a system that had a long and storied history. The first modern Iraqi educational system had been organized along Western lines during the first quarter of the twentieth with the establishment of Al al-Bayt University, followed by the founding of schools of engineering, law, education, and medicine brought together under the umbrella of the University of Baghdad by midcentury, and a rapidly expanding network of schools in the 1960s and 1970s fueled by increasing oil prices. Despite the politicization of the school and university system by Saddam Hussein and the Ba'athist regime, Iraq in 1990 boasted having a strong, secular educational system with overall literacy rates reaching 90 percent. This trend came to a crashing halt with US- and UK-supported embargos that contributed to an estimated five hundred thousand deaths of Iraqi children during the final decade of the twentieth century and a literacy rate that had dropped to 58 percent by time of the US invasion of Iraq. When CAI arrived, their immediate task was to open approximately twenty-five thousand schools for millions of Iraqi students by the start of the school year in October 2004.[8]

According to a British report, CAI charged USAID a fee of over $4 million to subcontract "at least half" of the projects they'd been assigned to do in the first year alone, such as conduct an Iraqi schools needs assessment (assigned to American University) and recruit Iraqi teachers (assigned to the American Islamic Congress). They sought to "plug expertise gaps" by handing educational policy formation to the Research Triangle Institute, school reconstruction to Bechtel, and the creation of "student kits" including pencils, erasers, and notebooks printed with the USAID logo on them to manufacturing plants in China. Although a lack of transparency from CAI and USAID obscured the actual work performed by CAI employees, reports suggested that their fieldwork consisted of conducting one survey and distributing grants. The survey studied student-teacher ratios that existed in the Iraqi school system. They wanted this census data to inform the work being conducted by their subcontractors. In their efforts distributing grants, they used funds to establish parent-teacher associations and hire a local Iraqi firm to produce school furniture and materials.[9]

The most critical elements of Iraqi school "revitalization" and "stabilization" came not from CAI, but from such organizations as UNESCO, UNICEF, and the World Bank. UNESCO saw the critical dearth of textbooks and printed almost nine million math and science texts for Iraq's school system. UNICEF covered the rest of the curriculum by contributing over forty million textbooks in all other subject areas. The World Bank gave $99 million for textbooks and school rebuilding. By April 2004, CAI had removed most of its international staff from Baghdad for security reasons. Nevertheless, USAID awarded another contract to the company.[10]

The second contract, worth a total of $48.9 million, covered the period from July 2004 to June 2006. CAI charged an estimated $3 million fixed fee for signing the agreement. They doubled their security cost estimates and ultimately charged over $6 million for protection. They also claimed more than $10 million for "profit" and administrative costs. This left approximately 50 percent for actual work in their field. Their assignment was to offer "technical assistance" to the Ministry of Education in Iraq and to promote the privatization and decentralization of the country's schools through "public-private partnerships." By then, the US CPA occupation government had transferred authority to a transitional Iraqi government and, along with it, a Ministry of Education that enjoyed a higher level of autonomy. In one of its first moves, the ministry conducted a report that contradicted the glowing estimates reported in the popular press about the advances made by US companies like CAI and others in the "revitalization" and "stabilization" of Iraqi schools. While the United States celebrated having "completely rehabilitated and reconstructed" over fifteen hundred schools, the Iraq school survey offered a far more sanguine picture. Enormous problems persisted as results showed that approximately two-thirds (or seven thousand) of all primary schools either lack functioning sewage systems or had never received one at all. Over a third of primary schools (or four thousand) had roofs that leaked. And well over thirty thousand classrooms had yet to be constructed to meet demand.[11]

While providing the Education Ministry with "technical assistance" and neglecting the vast majority of Iraqi schools that fell further into disrepair, the new contract directed CAI to establish eighty-four model schools, train secondary school teachers, and distribute supplies and grants. It also gave them the resources to design educational television programming and distribute additional funds to local communities.[12]

After three years of work and over $100 million in expenses, US inspectors conducted an extensive investigation into CAI's work. They discovered that the company had failed to complete even half of its objectives and to follow basic documentation procedures for major accomplishments the company claimed and celebrated. From the start, CAI was paid to complete eighty-two "outputs." By 2005, they had reduced their objectives to fifty-five. When inspectors on the ground conducted their final audit in 2007, complete with interviews and site visits, they found that only seven of the sixteen highest cost outputs had been completed. CAI reported having succeeded in flying a few dozen Ministry of Education officials to Amman, Jordan, for lectures on such topics as "What is a Team?," but had not reached the targeted number of officials. The company succeeded in purchasing eighty-four computer laboratories, another eighty-four science labs, and high-end educational records management servers, but had never delivered any of this equipment to schools or regional offices. It spent millions of dollars developing 13 five-minute television programs intended for preschoolers, but did not collaborate on programming content with ministry officials and the series was rejected and never aired.[13]

Even in the area CAI claimed the highest degree of expertise, inspectors noted that the company had missed the mark. CAI had agreed to provide training to fifty thousand teachers and administrators. They targeted forty-two thousand secondary teachers, eleven hundred master trainers, three thousand administrators, twenty-four hundred model teachers, and eighty four model school administrators. They intended to train these school officials in such subject areas as "English, science, math, and computers as well as general pedagogy." Some of these students were to receive their training in Jordan. Others were to take professional development courses in a "teacher-training center" in south central Iraq. In both cases and throughout the period of training, CAI agreed to document how much students learned in these training sessions. To that end, they received funding to "develop [an] instrument to assess the impact of training in each component" and to "administer pre- and post-tests." Nidhal Kidham, an Iraqi educator and adviser to CAI described the process, however, as a sham. "It doesn't matter who comes, where they come from," she was told, "it's not properly planned—just count so we have 44,000." Just before leaving Iraq, CAI claimed to have taught a mere seventeen thousand, but failed to provide documentation and impact assessments to verify completion and quality of work funded by the contracts.[14]

When pressed for further documentation to explain these failures, a representative for the agency replied that it "questions the utility of this type of review."[15]

* * *

When it came to higher education, the CPA handed the Iraqi university system over to Andrew P. N. Erdmann, a recently minted Harvard PhD. This recent graduate had never previously been to Iraq, had no academic training or background in the Middle East, and had no experience in administration and governance in higher education. What's more, he considered his own academic work on American foreign policy "a failure" and decided to get out of academia altogether. Ready to take any job, "anything," even "load bags of grain," Erdmann got a lucky break and joined the US occupation as a staff member to Colin Powell. When the occupation needed someone to head up Iraq's Ministry of Higher Education and

Research, they turned to Erdmann. Although he served as "senior advisor" to the ministry, he became the de facto interim minister.[16]

Erdmann began his tenure by dismissing all of the university presidents across the country. The former regime had appointed these officials and he believed it would be necessary to get a fresh start. After wrangling with the US occupation about how to replace the university presidents, he received approval from Bremer to hold open elections by the faculty in mid-May 2003. These were some of the first instances of democracy in the country. Iraqi professors took charge of the nominations, voting, and ballot counting. One student who observed the process broke down in tears, declaring that "[t]his is an answer to my prayers...We prayed for this, to see this." What the faculty and student body didn't know was that the US occupation reserved the right to veto any results they found disagreeable. They also didn't know that the United States was out of options, not knowing which candidates might be most sympathetic to US interests. Had there been clear front-runners from the US perspective, things might have proceeded differently.[17]

Erdmann and his team established four objectives for Iraqi higher education, none of which had been designed and developed in collaboration with Iraqi officials. Erdmann called for de-Ba'athification of faculty and staff, reorganization of university governance, reintegrating the university system with the world community, and "normalizing" the Iraq scientific community. The purging of Ba'athist faculty and staff had the same effect that denazification of university personnel had on occupied Germany. It created a severe shortage of qualified professors. Erdmann received papers from desperate faculty members on the streets of Baghdad, papers stating that they fully recanted their previous Ba'athist affiliations, but he refused to see them and stated that Bremer alone could waive the policy. With the dismissal of all university presidents, Erdmann created the opportunity for a complete reorganization of Iraq's universities. His goal centered on making the universities more autonomous. He wanted to make them independent and free from political influence. To that end, he floated the idea of abolishing the ministry altogether, but opted for promoting less drastic measures such as creating independent trustees for each campus. In terms of reintegrating the universities into the world community and normalizing the country's scientific community, Erdmann wanted to see an increase in exchange programs. He wanted greater involvement of Western faculties teaching and conducting research in Iraq and he wanted Iraqi faculty doing the same at Western institutions.[18]

Recognizing an expertise deficit in the US occupation's handling of Iraq's higher education, a team of scholars of Middle Eastern history drawn from universities in the United States, Canada, and France assembled the Iraq Observatory (IO). The IO had as its goal an independent review of the US occupation's reform of higher education. Their report, based on a nine-day visit to the country, was written independent of the CPA and US influence.

The IO report summarized the looting and destruction of Iraqi universities and blamed a lack of interest on the part of the US occupation—with its 168,000 troops—to prevent this from happening. It recorded the lack of basic university facilities—chairs, desks, tables, chalk—and noted that the great, indiscriminant purging of faculty and personnel "lies at the heart of academic discontent." Many dismissed professors continued teaching as "volunteers" without salary. IO representatives called for a revision to the de-Ba'athification policies, as well as a serious investment in basic university needs, library holdings, and security.[19]

The IO reserved its harshest comments for Erdmann and the CPA's higher education reform policies. They described his appointment as a "wasted opportunity" and that Iraq could have benefited from "someone expert in how universities can and should be run, who understands better the history and culture of the region." According to dozens of interviews with local academics, intellectuals, administrators, and NGO officials, Erdmann "does not seem to command the respect of the few Iraqi academics and intellectuals with whom we spoke who have met him." Iraqis perceived that the US agenda was less about the development of a system of higher education as a pillar of civil society and more about counterterrorism and nonproliferation. The heart of the reform policies, according to the IO, was about using these institutions to give "pro-American propaganda" through "Public Diplomacy" and "monitoring the research agenda for Iraqi nuclear engineers, biologists and chemists capable of aiding in the production of 'Weapons of Mass Destruction.'" Rather than rebuilding their facilities and establishing long-term exchanges, Erdmann's interests was in "keeping impoverished Iraqi scientists from selling their expertise to terrorists or governments hostile to the U.S."[20]

Erdmann's tenure came to a close with the appointment of John Agresto as senior advisor to the Ministry of Higher Education and

Scientific Research during the period when the CPA handed partial control of Iraq to the transitional government. To the chagrin of IO officials, Agresto, like Erdmann, had "no training in Middle Eastern society or culture and no experience in the region." He had strong connections with conservative elements in the Bush administration, however, having served as a Ronald Reagan appointee to the National Endowment for the Humanities and collaborated with William Bennet and Lynne Cheney in the 1980s. As former president of St. Johns College of Santa Fe, New Mexico, Agresto credited Arabs for "preserving the core Greek texts of the liberal arts when, here, they had fallen more or less out of memory." Otherwise, he had little official comment on Middle Eastern society, culture, and history. After his brief role as advisor to the CPA, he stated that the occupation had failed in rebuilding Iraqi higher education. One success Agresto highlighted on his return was an institution he helped establish called The American University of Iraq—Sulaimani in the Kurdish-controlled region of the country. "The American brand is much more welcome here," claimed Agresto. "This is probably the last place in the whole world where George Bush could still win an election."[21]

John Dolan, a former faculty member of Agresto's American University of Iraq, described the institution as rife with fraud and violations of US law. Dolan painted the college's administration as shot-through with "raw gangsterism," including payments in cash for trips without receipts or documentation and uncredentialed faculty receiving salaries of $15,000 per month for "history" lessons that involved showing World War II movies to students. Upon arriving at the regional airport, Dolan was greeted with a $5000 cash payment to "help settle in." What's more, university officials warned new faculty that "if you're Jewish—keep it to yourself" and that a recent rape of an ESL teacher was the result of revealing clothing by the victim. What they didn't tell Dolan was that his political views would ultimately cost him his job. After signing a two-year contract with Dolan, Agresto found an article Dolan had written in opposition to the Iraq War. Dolan received an immediate dismissal.[22]

* * *

The fraud that surfaced in education reconstruction appeared even more prominently in the economic reconstruction of Iraq. CPA officials turned the once nationalized resource of oil, the dominant source of revenue for the country, into a free-market bonanza for multinational corporations. Bremer's Order Number 12 and Order Number 39 opened Iraq's national treasure to international market forces without consent of the Iraqi people. US contractor Halliburton won a two-year contract worth over $2 billion that created a monopoly in the reconstruction, maintenance, and control over the oil fields of the country. Halliburton's competitors protested over the way the administration handled these contracts. Sheryl Tappan, a chief negotiator for Bechtel Corporation, stated that the contract "competition was far more corrupt than the secret sole-source award." She argued that the contracts required that all purchases, subcontracts, and materials be made through Halliburton, which allowed them to bill a fee for all reconstruction done in the oil fields of Iraq. Any major oil company interested in doing business in Iraq would ultimately have to go through Halliburton.[23]

US control over the budget and oil reserves limited the ability of Iraqis to fund schools and universities to provide the kind of basic needs—the seven thousand schools without sewage systems, the four thousand with leaking roofs, the thirty thousand classrooms needed, the universities without desks, tables, chalk, and adequate faculty—that audits, observers, and faculty reported as gravely problematic. As a result, Iraq's interim director of general education Majeed Allaq began pushing privatization as the answer to Iraq's educational problems and shortages. "The citizen is realizing," he claimed, "that not everything can be provided by the government."[24]

Not all Iraqis accepted this explanation of events. Between the middle and end of the first decade of the twenty-first century, several trade unions fought sweetheart deals brokered by the US occupation that crippled their ability to provide for basic education and health needs. The Federation of Oil Employees criticized, struck against, and shut down pipelines over contracts the Oil Ministry was negotiating with the United States and multinational corporations that would have included rare "production-sharing agreements." These agreements would have ceded sovereignty over the country's oil to foreign interests. The Electrical Utility Workers Union challenged the mismanagement of billions in power plant reconstruction given to General Electric that resulted in little or no improvement to blackouts in Basra. The electrical union's clashes with police resulted in at least one death and several injured. Longshoremen's unions opposed the privatization of their ports and won the cancellation of overly generous concession to Maersk and Stevedoring Services of America brokered by US officials. Educators protested as well, resulting in the jailing of a regional president of the Iraqi Teachers Union. They too considered unions as an important pillar of democracy in the fight for civil liberties, the preservation of natural resources for the benefit of Iraqis, and a more equitable society. These trade unions—in oil, electricity, port authorities, and education—fought an uphill battle because of the legacy left by the CPA before its dissolution. Bremer and his associates quietly kept on the books Law 150 from the Saddam Hussein regime that they found appealing, a law that banned union organizing. The jailing of union officials, erosion of collective bargaining, and intimidation of union members through the use of US military land and air forces continued through the end of the decade. Contracts signed between the Iraqi government and companies like General Electric, Boeing, American Cargo Transport, and a dozen other firms in 2010 totaled $80 billion in projects. The contracts also prohibited the use of unions in these sectors.[25]

In this way, the US occupation overturned the Iraqi tradition of nationalized oil and nationalized schools and universities in favor of free-market models. It left a legacy that shaped the way business would be conducted in Iraq for the foreseeable future. In doing so, the occupation introduced a complex problem to Iraq. It was a problem left unresolved at home and present throughout the American century.

Chapter Ten
Complex Problem

It took twenty-nine drafts. That's how many times Dwight D. Eisenhower revised and revisited the farewell address he gave a few days before the end of his presidency in 1961. Each version, from first to last, maintained his original intent: a warning to the American public about the "large and permanent military establishment" and "large and permanent arms industry" that, if unchecked, threatened American "liberty and security." His concern by the final draft was even more palpable. "The potential for the disastrous rise of misplaced power exists and will persist," he cautioned. It would take "an alert and knowledgeable citizen" to make sure that the US guards against the "total influence—economic, political, even spiritual"—already felt in "every city, every State house, and every office of the Federal government." This was his warning to the American people about the threat to democracy posed by the military, industrial, and financial complex.[1]

Eisenhower's speech, long considered by critics as either puzzling or prophetic or disingenuous, also suggests more than a hint of buyer's remorse. In 1953 he'd bought into the idea of using covert CIA operations led by Kermit Roosevelt, grandson of Theodore Roosevelt, to topple the first democratically elected government of Iran, something Harry Truman flatly refused to do a few years earlier. After Iran, Eisenhower was sold on the idea of doing the same to one of the most popular, left-leaning governments in Guatemalan history. This kicked off what became the "Eisenhower Doctrine" that promised military and economic aid to allied countries around the world and secured a never-ending commitment of funding to expand the military-industrial complex. To this end, he quadrupled military spending while in office from previous postwar lows. All of this he did in the name of containing communism and supporting dictatorships agreeable to US interests, particularly in the Middle East.[2]

But Eisenhower's final presidential speech didn't focus on the external threat of communism. Rather he looked at the "arms industry" as a more immediate threat to "the very structure of our society" that could consume "our toil, resources and livelihood." As he saw it, the profit-driven complex threatened peace abroad and democracy at home.[3]

The speech came at a midpoint between the opening salvo of the War of 1898 and the War on Terror. It spoke to the twin concerns of humanitarianism and efficiency that evolved and developed in a variety of ways across the American century. In the war with Spain—resulting in the US acquisition of Cuba, the Philippines, and Puerto Rico—humanists like Alexis Frye and David Barrows struggled against the efficiency, extraction-minded policies of people like Leonard Wood and W. Cameron Forbes. In Haiti and the Dominican Republic, economic interests trumped educational efforts, especially when it came to basic accounting principles that eroded the potential for meaningful school development and maintenance. With Germany and Japan, the United States exercised its "supreme" will, producing uneven results in the attempt to balance humanitarian interests with cultural empire building to prevent markets and trade from following a competing communist economic system. And in the case of Afghanistan and Iraq, important decisions related to the economy and education were handed over to the private sector. The push for outsourcing and privatization was sold as a cure to inefficiency and corruption in government and nonprofit contracts.

Eisenhower's speech raises a simple question about how these and future interventions impact "the very structure of our society": Will the United States be dominated by humanitarian and democratic values or will it be dominated by the efficiency-minded military, industry, and finance sectors? The two segments of American life, he believed, did not coexist happily. He feared more than anything at the time that the desires of financial, industrial, and military officials would ultimately dictate not only America's foreign policy, but also its domestic policy. Eisenhower warned that the very future of American democracy depended on the public learning about and being vigilant against the vast forces that, if left unregulated, would subvert the will of the people for its own ends. The complex he spoke of would launch wars for profit, sold in terms of humanitarian crises, but, as Henry Cabot Lodge originally put it, intended to produce "a new field for American enterprise and capital." Eisenhower looked optimistically to education and the "knowledgeable citizen" to protect against the wealth-extracting empire building desired by the few. As Jefferson, DuBois, and Dewey once suggested and as Eisenhower also sought to voice in his farewell address, education is central to the maintenance of a democratic society. These individuals would have used a simple metric for evaluating America's attempt to spread democracy abroad: whether a robust system of democracy promoting education was established. To this, Eisenhower added a new assignment for teachers and schools. The preservation of a democratic society now required preparing future citizens to be skeptical of the claims of the military, industrial, and financial sectors—particularly in the drive for war and its desire to maintain this state in perpetuity.[4]

As the first decade of the twenty-first century came to a close, Eisenhower's test was as relevant as ever. Americans learned that, in many ways, they'd largely failed in either being "alert" or "knowledgeable" about the drive to go to war in Iraq. According to a University of Maryland study completed after the Iraq invasion, over half of the American public believed incorrectly that links among Iraq, Al-Qaeda, and the attacks on the World Trade Center existed. Almost as many continued to believe this long after the initial invasion. Over two-thirds believed Saddam Hussein had personal involvement in the World Trade Center attacks. Even after the United States stopped searching for nonexistent weapons of mass destruction, over 20 percent believed incorrectly that not only had such weapons been found but that they had also been used against US soldiers during the war.

Part of the reason for these gross misperceptions was, of course, the media engine that worked overtime against creating Eisenhower's informed citizen. Over three-fourths of all commentators on news networks in one sample month of news coverage during the first year in Iraq were former or current government and military officials. None of them spoke of the "potential for the disastrous rise of misplaced power" in the hands of a vast military, industrial, and financial complex. Military "experts" sold their expertise as commentators, without revealing their personal stake in war contractor companies like Boeing, Lockheed-Martin, Raytheon, Northrop Grumman, General Dynamics, and others. Television networks failed to disclose the consulting fees these military pundits received from the armaments industry and failed to disclose their own conflict of interest in being wholly owned network subsidiaries of conglomerate corporations that owned the very companies paying these consulting fees. In 2011, as the occupation in Afghanistan began to lose public support, the military went so far as to deploy a $6 million information war against US senators visiting the country. In its quest to expand and extend the Afghan campaign, the army used "Psychological Operations" against them. Psyops were originally developed to manipulate "hostile foreign groups" and exploit their weaknesses. In this case, they used the same tactics to influence elected officials and the direction of war spending. A whistleblower in the case sarcastically dubbed it "Operation Fourth Star," after the three-star general who sought to use army resources in this way to extend his tour of duty for personal gain and self-promotion.[5]

This seemingly new reality, or new "structure of our society," is neither new, as this book has argued, nor necessarily permanent. None of this would have surprised people like Major General Smedley Butler, one of the most decorated US military officials of the early- to mid-twentieth century. He understood the problem from the inside and, as early as 1935, spoke publicly about how commercial forces shaped foreign policy-making decisions: "I helped make Haiti and Cuba a decent place for the National City Bank boys to collect revenues in. I helped in the raping of half a dozen Central American republics for the benefit of Wall Street." "The record of racketeering," he continued, "is long."

> I helped purify Nicaragua for the international banking house of Brown Brothers in 1909–1912. I brought light to the Dominican Republic for American sugar interests in 1916. I helped make Honduras "right" for American fruit companies in 1903...Looking back on it, I feel I might have given Al Capone a few hints. The best *he* could do was operate his racket in three city districts. We Marines operated on three *continents*.[6]

While Butler described military-corporate occupations abroad, an obscure contemporary of his—Alabama Congressman George Huddleston—sized up more directly what these interventions might mean for Americans back home, in much the same way as Eisenhower's final speech. Huddleston believed there were domestic implications for what the United States does on foreign soil. "We can not exist as an imperialism abroad and a democracy at home," he asserted on the floor of Congress, and

> we can not exist as a tyrant in foreign countries and a free people in the United States. We can not hold securely upon our liberties here and take them away from people that live in other parts of the world—poor or ignorant or whatever they may be, the consequences will come back to us—the recoil will fall on us.[7]

While all of this wasn't news for the Butlers, Huddlestons, and Eisenhowers of the twentieth century, what's always new are the opportunities to reconsider the place of humanitarian needs over the wants of those who benefit from efficiency, wealth extraction, and empire building. According to Eisenhower, the United States needed to tame, leash, and regulate the corporate titans that now own the major outlets of news and information as well as the companies that make the most destructive products in the world. That's what he likely meant when he warned against leaving these institutions "unchecked." He also looked to education to help the public become more skeptical about the drive toward war and thwart the overwhelming interests of the military, industrial, and financial classes in American society. Butler, meanwhile, would have wanted more. To fully rebalance American society in favor of humanitarian priorities, he argued, the incentives that have driven the desire for war throughout the American century must be removed. The most important solution he offered to this seemingly intractable problem was to eliminate profit from the war industry. To make war unprofitable is to inevitably reduce the potential for future conflict and destruction.

But the warnings of Eisenhower, Butler, and many others across the American century have been largely drowned out by clamor for continued US interventionism from the War of 1898 to the War on Terror. What these US military and civilian occupations put in sharp relief is the significant relationship between capital and education in American attempts to promote democracy abroad and the implications this has for the structure of society at home.

Acknowledgments

The idea for this book began to take shape after many conversations I had with friends and colleagues about the wars in Afghanistan and Iraq. These were conversations held across the country at universities and conferences as well as coffee shops and local taverns. Some conversations centered on the idea that greed and a desire for scarce resources was the real reason for intervening in these countries. Others viewed the real mission as spreading democracy abroad and overthrowing cruel dictatorships and cabals. Along the way, I encountered a striking diversity of opinion and this diversity fueled my desire to turn what was a personal interest into a program of research. As the drumbeat for war grew louder, I immersed myself in the scholarship on American expansionism to gain some perspective on what was commonly touted as the "new reality" of American empire-building. As a historian of education, I wanted to read a single volume study on the way America has handled both intervention and education abroad. What I found instead was an extensive body of published, unpublished, and archival sources on individual occupations, each with its own fascinating but disconnected history. Nowhere could I find a study that brought all of them—since the War of 1898—together. I wrote *Empire and Education* because I couldn't wait to read such a study and I owe a great debt of gratitude to the many scholars whose research made this book possible. The bibliography serves not only as a starting place for further reading, but also as an acknowledgments section of its own.

Closer to home, I also owe a great debt to a number individuals and institutions who not only made this book possible but also a pleasure to write and research. As noted in the front matter, this book is dedicated to William F. Mills and his energy and enthusiasm for inquiring into all things historical, political, and cultural. We exchanged reading lists over coffee several years ago and a few key works on his list inspired me to write *Empire and Education* in a way that would bring to life the many colorful figures and personalities I encountered in the literature. Mills passed away before this book reached the publisher, but his influence is present in every copy. Thomas G. Dyer is an academic force of nature who inspires those around him to do great work. I've had the good fortune of calling him a colleague and friend. Many of my works, including *Empire and Education*, are far better for having crossed his desk.

Lauren Smalley read every chapter just as they came out of the oven. Sometimes the chapters came out too soon and I'm grateful she gave them a try and identified sections that needed more time before they were done. Donald Warren also read every chapter and had precisely the kind of insights and review comments that scholars can only hope to receive. After he shared an earlier version of this book with a doctoral seminar at Indiana University, I heard from his students as well. Thanks go to Jeremy Jernigan and Abigail Gundlach Graham for sending their copyedits and thoughtful reviews of the manuscript from Bloomington.

I owe an institutional debt to my alma mater, Harvard University, mostly for providing the kind of grants and fellowships that made it possible to start thinking about empire and education while still working on my first book. It's also home to two terrific scholars—Julie Reuben and Kate Elgin—who offered encouragement and advice at critical stages of the publishing process. I thank them for giving generously of their time and taking a genuine interest in this study. A further institutional debt of gratitude is to Winthrop University. I'm fortunate to have landed at an institution that recognizes the value of faculty scholarship and how it benefits students and the community. Not all institutions of Winthrop's size strive to maintain a balance between teaching, research, and service. I'm grateful to Jonatha Vare, in particular, for supporting my research interests and accommodating my teaching schedule needs. Without her leadership and logistical support, I would not have been able to complete the research for this book. The interlibrary loan staff at Dacus Library has assisted in tracking down published and unpublished works critical to the completion of this study. They came through when I most needed their assistance. Others at Winthrop who offered critical support and feedback include Susan Green, Laura Parks, and Cam Heiliger.

Palgrave's Burke Gerstenschlager, Kaylan Connally, and Katie Haigler all put in the countless hours required to make publication possible. They, and their associates at Newgen, graciously answered my many questions along the way. A final note of appreciation goes to the Canadian journal *Historical Studies in Education*. Sections of chapter four first appeared as "Education during the American Occupation of Haiti, 1915–1934" in their fall 2010 issue. I want to thank the journal for permission to reprint the contents of the article and for the feedback received through their editorial and peer-review process.

Notes

Preface

1. Lodge to Taft, November 22, 1900, cited in Glenn A. May, *Social Engineering in the Philippines: The Aims, Execution, and Impact of American Colonial Policy, 1900–1913* (Westport: Greenwood Press, 1980), 152.
2. This study draws from and builds on the wave of "empire" studies that appeared following the events of September 11, 2001, and the US invasion of Iraq. For a sampling of this literature, see the following: Stephen Howe, *Empire: A Very Short Introduction* (Oxford: Oxford University Press, 2002); Niall Ferguson, *Colossus: The Price of America's Empire* (New York: Penguin Press, 2004); Jeffrey Ostler, *The Plains Sioux and U.S. Colonialism from Lewis and Clark to Wounded Knee* (New York: Cambridge University Press, 2004); Charles S. Maier, *Among Empires: American Ascendancy and its Predecessors* (Cambridge, Mass.: Harvard University Press, 2006); Michael Hunt, *The American Ascendancy: How the United States Gained and Wielded Global Dominance* (Chapel Hill: University of North Carolina Press, 2007); Walter T. K. Nugent, *Habits of Empire: A History of American Expansion* (New York: Alfred A. Knopf, 2008); Julian Go, *American Empire and the Politics of Meaning: Elite Political Cultures in the Philippines and Puerto Rico during U.S. Colonialism* (Durham: Duke University Press, 2008); Pekka Hamalainen, *The Comanche Empire* (New Haven: Yale University Press, 2008); Alfred W. McCoy and Francisco A Scarano, eds., *Colonial Crucible: Empire in the Making of the Modern American State* (Madison: University of Wisconsin Press, 2009).
3. Lodge to Taft, November 22, 1900, cited in May, *Social Engineering in the Philippines*, 152; Steven Kinzer, *Overthrow: America's Century of Regime Change from Hawaii to Iraq* (New York: Times Books, 2006), 47. On the role of education in the expansion of the British empire, see John Willinsky, *Learning to Divide the World: Education at Empire's End* (Minneapolis: University of Minnesota Press, 1998). This work offers a broad discussion of museums, science, literature, and other practices and disciplines enlisted in the service of imperial expansion.
4. Jefferson, cited in Saul K. Padover, *Thomas Jefferson on Democracy* (New York: Appleton-Century Company, 1939), 89; see also Jennings Wagoner, *Thomas Jefferson and Education* (Chapel Hill: University of North Carolina Press, 2005); Carl Kaestle, *Pillars of the Republic: Common Schools and American Society, 1780–1860* (New York: Hill and Wang, 1983); James Anderson, *Education of Blacks in the South, 1860–1935* (Chapel Hill: University of North Carolina Press); Robert Westbrook, *John Dewey and American Democracy* (Ithaca: Cornell University Press, 1991); Louis Menand, *The Metaphysical Club: A Story of Ideas in America* (New York: Farrar, Straus and Giroux, 2002).

5. For a concise survey of these kinds of interventions, see Kinzer, *Overthrow*.
6. See, e.g., Steven J. Diner, *A Very Different Age: Americans of the Progressive Era* (New York: Hill and Wang, 1998).

1 After the *Maine*

1. "Frye's Fist," *Boston Daily Globe*, July 3, 1900. The literature on education during the US occupation in Cuba is thin. Edward Douglass Fitchen's "Alexis Everett Frye and the Organization of Cuban Education, 1899–1901" (PhD diss., University of California, Santa Barbara, 1970), hereafter cited as *EDF*, is perhaps the best work on the topic. Other relevant works by Fitchen include the following: "The Cuban Teachers and Harvard, 1900: A Unique Experiment in Inter-American Cultural Exchange," *Horizontes* 26 (1973), 61–71; and "Alexis E. Frye and Cuban Education, 1898–1902," *Revista Interamericana* 2 (1972), 123–149. See also Carlos Rodriguez-Fraticelli, "Education, Politics, and Imperialism: The Reorganization of the Cuban Public Elementary School System during the First American Occupation, 1899–1902" (PhD diss., University of California, San Diego, 1984), hereafter cited as *CRF*; Jack McCallum, *Leonard Wood: Rough Rider, Surgeon, Architect of American Imperialism* (New York: New York University Press, 2005); Erwin H. Epstein, "The Peril of Paternalism: The Imposition of Education on Cuba by the United States," *American Journal of Education* 96 (November 1987), 1–23; James H. Hitchman, *Leonard Wood and Cuban Independence, 1898–1902* (The Hague: Nijhoff, 1971). For starters on the broader historiography of Cuba and the War of 1898, see Louis A. Perez, Jr.'s *Cuba: Between Reform and Revolution* (New York: Oxford University Press, 2006); and *The War of 1898: The United States and Cuba in History and Historiography* (Chapel Hill: UNC Press, 1998); and Richard Gott, *Cuba: A New History* (New Haven: Yale University Press, 2004).
2. "Frye's Fist," *Boston Daily Globe*, July 3, 1900; see also, *EDF*, 179–180.
3. Leonard Wood to Elihu Root, January 8, 1901, and Leonard Wood to Charles W. Eliot, August 6, 1900, cited in *CRF*, 228, 252, 256; on Wood's interventionist and imperialist views, see McCallum, *Leonard Wood*, 188–191.
4. Wood to Eliot, May 2, 1900, cited in *EDF*, 163; Alexis Frye's "Introduction from Harvard University to the Teachers of Cuba," cited in *EDF*, 163.
5. See Philip S. Foner, *A History of Cuba and Its Relations with the United States* (2 vols, New York: International Publishers, 1963); for a long view of US interventions abroad, see Steven Kinzer, *Overthrow: America's Century of Regime Change from Hawaii to Iraq* (New York: Times Books, 2007); see also Michael Hunt, *The American Ascendancy: How the United States Gained and Wielded Global Dominance* (Chapel Hill: University of North Carolina Press, 2007) for a discussion of the "nineteenth-century foundations" of the United States' expansionist efforts.
6. See John Offner, *An Unwanted War: The Diplomacy of the United States and Spain Over Cuba, 1895–1898* (Chapel Hill: University of North Carolina Press, 1999).
7. Textile Record, March 1898; *Boot and Shoe Recorder*, March 30, 1898, cited in Daniel Schirmer, *Republic or Empire: American Resistance to the Philippines War* (Cambridge: Schenkman Publishing Co., 1972), 52; Lodge on military imperial expansion, cited in Julius Pratt, *Expansionist of 1898: The Acquisition of Hawaii and the Spanish Islands* (Gloucester, MA: Peter Smith Co., 1959), 207; see also *CRF*, 14; Evan Thomas, *The War Lovers: Roosevelt, Lodge, Hearst, and the Rush to Empire, 1898* (New York: Little, Brown and Company, 2010); Alfred W. McCoy and

Francisco A Scarano, eds., *Colonial Crucible: Empire in the Making of the Modern American State* (Madison: University of Wisconsin Press, 2009).
8. For the Teller Amendment, see Benjamin Beede, *The War of 1898 and U.S. Interventions, 1898–1934: An Encyclopedia* (New York: Garland Press, 1994), 538.
9. John Brooke, *Civil Report of Major General John R. Brooke, U. S. Army, Military Governor Island of Cuba* (Havana, 1899).
10. "Report of Brigadier-General William Ludlow," in John Brooke, *Annual Report of Major General John R. Brooke* (Havana, 1899), 32; *EDF*, 40; McCallum, *Leonard Wood*, 111–146.
11. Discussion of the Lanuza law can be found in Alexis Frye's "First Annual Report of the Superintendent of Schools of Cuba for the Year Ending June 30, 1900," cited in *EDF*, 68–78; see also *CRF*, 83–90.
12. William T. Harris, "An Educational Policy for Our New Possessions," *Educational Review* 18 (September 1899), 108–109.
13. William T. Harris, "An Educational Policy for Our New Possessions," *Educational Review* 18 (September 1899), 114–115. For background on Root's expansionist views, see Warren Zimmerman, *First Great Triumph: How Five Americans Made Their Country a World Power* (New York: Farrar, Straus, and Giroux, 2002), 123–148, 233–267; Joyce M. Gayden, "The Latin American Policy of Elihu Root, 1899–1909" (MA thesis, University of South Carolina, 1954).
14. Frye to Root, September 18, 1899, Records of the Military Government of Cuba, Record Group 140, Decimal File 5947, National Archives, cited in *CRF*, 117; see also *EDF*, 62–67.
15. *CRF*, 116–119; *EDF*, 64–67, 89–90.
16. *CRF*, 116–119; *EDF*, 64–67, 89–90.
17. "Dos Fechas Luctuosas," *Escuela Moderna*, April 15, 1899, cited in *CRF*, 80; "Una Preuba de Desconfianza," *La Lucha*, October 24, 1899, cited in *CRF*, 134; "Junta Municipal de Educacion," *La Discusion*, October 19, 1899; "El Plan de Instruccion Publica," *La Discusion*, October 20, 1899; *CRF*, 133.
18. "Notas Rapidas," *La Lucha*, November 4, 1899, cited in *CRF*, 137; "Nobramiento Descertado," *La Discusion*, November 6, 1899, cited in *CRF*, 138; "Instruccion Publica," *El Diario de la Marina*, October 30, 1899, cited in *CRF*, 136.
19. Eliot to Frye, September 7, 1899, cited in *EDF*, 63; "Oh! La Filantropia!," *El Cubano*, December 21, 1899, cited in *EDF*, 123; "El Plan de Educaccion," *La Patria*, December 15, 1899, cited in *CRF*, 156.
20. Alexis E. Frye, *Elements of Geography* (Boston: Ginn and Co, 1898); "Bids for Supplying the Schools," *Havana Journal*, December 2, 1899, cited in *EDF*, 112–113; Carlos Genova de Zayas, *Apuntes Sobre la Fundacion de la Escuela Cubana* (Havana, 1958), 48, 125, cited in *CRF*, 173; Alexis E. Frye, "First Annual Report of the Superintendent of Schools of Cuba for the Year Ending June 30, 1900," Records of the Military Government of Cuba, Record Group 140, Decimal File 4963, National Archives, cited in *EDF*, 95, 141; "Los Libros de Texto," *La Lucha*, November 1, 1899, cited in *CRF*, 146; "Education for Cuba," *Havana Herald*, October 19, 1899, cited in *CRF*, 132.
21. See "Early Educational Reforms of Alexis Everett Frye," in *EDF*, 79–103.
22. Frye, "First Annual Report," cited in *EDF*, 108–109.
23. Frye's academic freedom clause stated "Libertad absoluta a todo maestro para que emplee su propio meted de ensenanza." Cited in "El Manual Para los Maestros," *La Patria*, March 3, 1900, cited in *EDF*, 124; "Cronica," *Esuela Moderna*, February 28, 1900, cited in *CRF*, 173.

24. Data on school openings and attendance in *EDF*, 142–144, and *CRF*, 178.
25. Budget data analyzed and discussed in *CRF*, 182, and *EDF*, 144–152.
26. Reorganization and Wood-Frye politics in *CRF*, 186–189.
27. "Arrangements for the Harvard Summer School," in *EDF*, 153–178.
28. Frye cited in *EDF*, 155; see also *EDF*, 155–160, and *CRF*, 204.
29. "Cuban Teachers in the United States," *American Monthly Review of Reviews* 22 (July 1900), cited in *CRF*, 209–210.
30. Wood to Root, June 13, 1900, and Wood to Root, June 18, 1899, cited in *CRF*, 216; see also *EDF*, 170–178.
31. "The Cuban Teachers at Harvard University," in *EDF*, 179–201.
32. Julia Martinez, "The Cuban Teachers at Cambridge," *The Independent* 52 (August 1900), cited in *EDF*, 185.
33. David F. Healy, *The United States in Cuba, 1898–1902: Generals, Politicians, and the Search for Policy* (Madison: University of Wisconsin Press, 1963), 163.
34. "Himno de Baymo. Al Pueblo Cuban," *Diario de la Marina*, December 17, 1900, cited in *CRF*, 254–255; George Eugene Bryson, "Affidavit," December 31, 1903, cited in *EDF*, 260; *CRF*, 252–256.
35. "La Renuncia de Mr. Frye," *La Discusion*, January 10, 1901, and "Un Amigo de los Cubanos," *La Discusion*, January 10, 1901, cited in *CRF*, 256.
36. Hanna cited in *CRF*, 285; see also "Implementing Hanna's School Law," *CRF*, 248–275.
37. Wood to McKinley, October 28, 1901, cited in *CRF*, 278; "The Patriotic League" (1900), cited in *CRF*, 289; Eliot to Root, September 19, 1900, cited in *CRF*, 290.
38. Kinzer, *Overthrow*, 90.
39. See, Louis A. Perez, Jr.'s *Cuba: Between Reform and Revolution* (New York: Oxford University Press, 2006); Richard Gott, *Cuba: A New History* (New Haven: Yale University Press, 2004).

2 Benevolent Education

1. McKinley quoted in Steven Kinzer, *Overthrow: America's Century of Regime Change from Hawaii to Iraq* (New York: Henry Holt and Company 2006), 47; on McKinley's "imperial impulse," see Michael Hunt, *The American Ascendancy: How the United States Gained and Wielded Global Dominance* (Chapel Hill: University of North Carolina Press, 2007), 46–51. See also James C. Bradford, ed., *Crucible of Empire: The Spanish American War and Its Aftermath* (Annapolis: Naval Institute Press, 1993); Julian Go, *American Empire and the Politics of Meaning: Elite Political Cultures in the Philippines and Puerto Rico during U.S. Colonialism* (Durham: Duke University Press, 2008); Alfred W. McCoy and Francisco A Scarano, eds., *Colonial Crucible: Empire in the Making of the Modern American State* (Madison: University of Wisconsin Press, 2009); on Spanish-period parishes, see Peter C. Smith, "Crisis Mortality in the Nineteenth Century Philippines: Data from Parish Records," *The Journal of Asian Studies* 38 (November 1978), 53.

    The literature on the Philippines, both published and unpublished, is vast and well-developed. For a sampling of classic, recent, and education-related works, see the following: Stuart Creighton Miller, *"Benevolent Assimilation": The American Conquest of the Philippines, 1899–1903* (New Haven: Yale University Press, 1982); Stanley Karnow, *In Our Image: America's Empire in the Philippines* (New York: Ballantine Books, 1989); H. W. Brands, *Bound to Empire: The United States and the Philippines* (New York: Oxford University Press, 1992); Julian Go and Anne

L. Foster, eds., *The American Colonial State in the Philippines: Global Perspectives* (Durham: Duke University Press, 2003); Paul A. Kramer, *The Blood of Government: Race, Empire, the United States & the Philippines* (Chapel Hill: University of North Carolina Press, 2006); John Morgan Gates, *Schoolbooks and Krags: The United States Army in the Philippines, 1898–1902* (Westport: Greenwood Press, 1973); Kenton J. Clymer, "Humanitarian Imperialism: David Prescott Barrows and the White Man's Burden in the Philippines," *Pacific Historical Review* 49 (1980), 29–50; Jane A. Margold, "Egalitarian Ideals and Exclusionary Practices: U.S. Pedagogy in the Colonial Philippines," *Journal of Historical Sociology* 8 (1995), 375–394; Jeffrey Ayala Milligan, "Democratization or Neocolonialism? The Education of Muslims under U.S. Military Occupation, 1903–20," *History of Education* 33 (July 2004), 451–467; Anne Paulet, "To Change the World: The Use of American Indian Education in the Philippines," *History of Education Quarterly* 47 (May 2007), 173–202; Judith Raftery, "Textbook Wars: Governor-General James Francis Smith and the Protestant-Catholic Conflict in Public Education in the Philippines, 1904–1907," *History of Education Quarterly* 38 (Summer 1998), 143–164; Glenn Anthony May, *Social Engineering in the Philippines: The Aims, Execution, and Impact of American Colonial Policy, 1900–1913* (Westport: Greenwood Press, 1980), hereafter cited as *GAM*.
2. McKinley in Kinzer, *Overthrow*, 47.
3. Paul A. Kramer, "Race-Making And Colonial Violence in the U.S. Empire: The Philippine-American War as Race War," *Diplomatic History* 30 (2006), 169–210; Paul A. Kramer, *The Blood of Government: Race, Empire, the United States & the Philippines* (Chapel Hill: University of North Carolina Press, 2006); Glenn Anthony May, "The Business of Education in Colonial Philippines, 1909–1930," in Alfred W. McCoy and Francisco A Scarano, eds., *Colonial Crucible: Empire in the Making of the Modern American State* (Madison: University of Wisconsin Press, 2009), 151–162.
4. Taft cited in *GAM*, 10, 14; Forbes cited in *GAM*, 113, 116; see also Oscar M. Alfonso, "Taft's Early Views on the Filipinos," *Solidarity* 4 (June 1969), 52–58; David Henry, *Taft, Holmes, and the 1920s Court: An Appraisal* (Madison: Fairleigh Dickinson University Press, 1998); Henry F. Pringle, *The Life and Times of William Howard Taft* (2 vols, Hamden: n.p., 1939).
5. Todd cited in Fredrick W. Nash, "Education in the Philippines," *Educational Review* 22 (October 1901), 218; see also, *GAM*, 79, 83.
6. *GAM*, 79–81.
7. Fredrick W. Eddy, "Planning for Filipino Schools," *New York Times* (August 5, 1900).
8. Atkinson cited in *GAM*, 84.
9. Eddy, "Planning for Filipino Schools," *New York Times* (August 5, 1900).
10. *GAM*, 95.
11. Ibid., 88–89, 92.
12. Ibid., 87, 93.
13. See Kenton J. Clymer, "Humanitarian Imperialism: David Prescott Barrows and the White Man's Burden in the Philippines," *Pacific Historical Review* 49 (1980), 29–50.
14. *GAM*, 98.
15. Clymer, "Humanitarian Imperialism," 512–513.
16. Ibid., 504.
17. David Barrows, "The Prospect for Education in the Philippines," *The Philippine Teacher* 1 (December 1904), 7; see also Barrows, "What May Be Expected from

Philippine Education?" *Journal of Race Development* 1 (October 1910), 156–168; *GAM*, 101.
18. *GAM*, 105.
19. Barrows to James LeRoy, June 29, 1908, cited in ibid., 110.
20. Forbes to Mrs. Edward Cunningham, May 31, 1909, cited in *GAM*, 113, 116.
21. *GAM*, 116–117; see also Frank R. White, "Our School System—Some Comparisons," *Philippine Education* 5 (January 1909), 13.
22. *GAM*, 118–120. See also "Outline for the Teachers of Manners and Right Conduct," Circular No. 143 (1910), cited in ibid., 119.
23. *La Vanguardia*, September 28, 1911, cited in *GAM*, 122.
24. *GAM*, 124–126.
25. The lead Filipino critic was Manuel Quezon, a lawyer and representative in the Philippine Assembly. Later, Quezon became the second president of the country after the end of US occupation.
26. Philippine commissioners cited in *GAM*, 133, 135, 138.
27. Quezon cited in *GAM*, 173.
28. Ibid., 170.
29. Taft to Lodge, October 17, 1900, cited in *GAM*, 142.
30. May, "The Business of Education," 151; Maria Guillen Acierto, "American Influence in Shaping Philippine Secondary Education: An Historical Perspective, 1898–1978" (EdD diss., Loyola University of Chicago, 1980), 170, 195.

3 Culture and Citizenship

1. Long cited in Warren Zimmerman, *First Great Triumph: How Five Americans Made their Country a World Power* (New York: Farrar, Straus, and Giroux, 2002), 243; Roosevelt and Lodge cited in Stephen Kinzer, *Overthrow: America's Century of Regime Change from Hawaii to Iraq* (New York: Henry Holt and Company, 2006), 44; see also Stanley Karnow, *In Our Image: America's Empire in the Philippines* (New York: Galantine Books, 1989), 11; Walter Nugent, *Habits of Empire: A History of American Expansion* (New York: Knopf, 2008), 265–266; H. W. Brands, *Bound to Empire: The United States and the Philippines* (New York: Oxford University Press, 1992), 22–23.

    Relevant works on Puerto Rico's political, economic, and educational history include the following: Cesar J. Ayala and Rafael Bernabe, *Puerto Rico in the American Century: A History since 1898* (Chapel Hill: UNC Press, 2007); Raymond Carr, *Puerto Rico: A Colonial Experiment* (New York: NYU Press, 1984); Julian Go, *American Empire and the Politics of Meaning: Elite Political Cultures in the Philippines and Puerto Rico during U.S. Colonialism* (Durham: Duke University Press, 2008); James L. Dietz, *Economic History of Puerto Rico: Institutional Change and Capitalist Development* (Princeton: Princeton University Press, 1986), hereafter cited as *JLD*; Jose-Manuel Navarro, *Creating Tropical Yankees: Social Science Textbooks and U.S. Ideological Control in Puerto Rico* (New York: Routledge, 2002), hereafter cited as *JMN*; Juan Jose Osuna, *A History of Education in Puerto Rico* (New York: Arno Press, 1975), hereafter cited as *JJO*; Aida Negron De Montilla, *Americanization in Puerto Rico and the Public School System, 1900–1930* (Barcelona: University of Puerto Rico, 1975), hereafter cited as *ANDM*.
2. Miles's letters cited in *ANDM*, 2–3; Robert Wooster, *Nelson A. Miles and the Twilight of the Frontier Army* (Lincoln: University of Nebraska Press, 1993), describes the mixed and strained relationship between Roosevelt and Miles, summed up in Roosevelt's nickname for the general: the "brave peacock" (273); see also Jeffery

Ostler's *The Plains Sioux and U.S. Colonialism from Lewis and Clark to Wounded Knee* (New York: Cambridge University Press, 2004) that describes the broad contours and controversies of US westward expansionism and Miles's military campaigns in Native American territory within this history.
3. San Juan Theater resolution of October 30, 1898, cited in *ANDM*, 6; Spanish colonial government cited in *JJO*, 65; see also *JMN*, 3–29.
4. Puerto Rican petition calling for end to US occupation, cited in *ANDM*, 16.
5. Guy's "Circular" (January 19, 1899) cited in *ANDM*, 10; "Laws Governing Public Instruction" (May 1899) cited in *JJO*, 131.
6. Victor S. Clark cited in George W. Davis, *Report on Civil Affairs of Porto Rico, 1899* (Washington, DC: GPO, 1900), 180; see also *ANDM*, 12–14; for more on Clark, see Victor S. Clark, *Porto Rico and Its Problems* (New York: Arno Press, 1975); *What is Money?* (Boston: Houghton Mifflin Company, 1934); and *History of Manufactures in the United States* (New York: McGraw-Hill, 1929).
7. Victor S. Clark, *Teachers' Manual for the Public Schools of Puerto Rico* (New York: Silver, Durdett & Company, 1900). Public outcry over pay disparities and discrimination can be found in local papers, including the *Puerto Rico Herald*, *La Democracia*, and *La Educacion Moderna*; see *ANDM*, 54–56.
8. Victor S. Clark cited in George W. Davis, *Report on Civil Affairs of Porto Rico, 1899* (Washington, DC: GPO, 1900), 179–180; *ANDM*, 14.
9. *Report of the United States Insular Commission to the Secretary of War Upon Investigations Made into the Civil Affairs of the Island of Porto Rico, with Recommendations* (Washington, DC: GPO, 1899) cited in *JMN*, 33, 35.
10. *JMN*, 37.
11. *ANDM*, 15, 23.
12. Brumbaugh cited in *ANDM*, 37, 39, 51.
13. Ibid., 29, 30.
14. Ibid., 32, 33; and *JMN*, 60; *Puerto Rico Herald*, July 27, 1901, cited in *ANDM*, 55; school and attendance statistics cited in *ANDM*, 59.
15. Lindsay cited in *ANDM*, 62, 69.
16. *JMN*, 70, 83; *ANDM*, 72, 93.
17. *ANDM*, 95, 96; *JMN*, 86.
18. *ANDM*, 100, 114; *La Educacion Moderna*, August 26, 1900, cited in *ANDM*, 105.
19. *ANDM*, 117, 127; *JMN*, 95, 98.
20. *La Educacion*, January 15, 1913; *La Democracia*, January 12, 1915; and *La Democracia*, March 9, 1915; newspapers cited in *ANDM*, 134, 140, 141; see also "Commissioner Edward M. Bainter, 1912–1915," *ANDM*, 131–149.
21. *Porto Rico Progress*, March 31, 1915, cited in *ANDM*, 147.
22. *Porto Rico Progress*, July 28, 1915; *La Democracia*, August 27, 1915; Bainter cited in *La Democracia*, October 21, 1915; newspapers cited in *ANDM*, 150, 152.
23. *ANDM*, 155, 157.
24. Ibid., 170; Young Turks cited in *La Democracia*, January 20, 1919; Miller on the "enemy flag" and Puerto Ricans responding to his "abusive power" in *La Correspondencia*, June 17, 1921 and June 20, 1921; newspapers cited in *ANDM*, 171, 172;
25. *ANDM*, 172, 164, 166.
26. This and the following discussion based on *JLD*, 79–134.
27. *JMN*, 39;
28. *JLD*, 89, 109.
29. Ibid., 116–119
30. Ibid., 109, 126, 91.

4 Hampton Creole

1. Bryan quoted in Hans Schmidt, *The United States Occupation of Haiti, 1915–1934* (rev. ed., New Brunswick: Rutgers University Press, 1995), 48. The story of America's first occupation of Haiti has been told many times. Scholars have closely examined the social, political, economic, and military dimensions of this intervention. The central literature on Haiti is as follows: Mary A. Renda's *Taking Haiti: Military Occupation and the Culture of U.S. Imperialism* (Chapel Hill: University of North Carolina Press, 2001); Magdaline W. Shannon, *Jean Price-Mars, the Haitian Elite and the American Occupation, 1915–1935* (New York: St. Martin's Press, 1996); Brenda Gayle Plummer, *Haiti and the Great Powers, 1902–1915* (Baton Rouge: Louisiana State University Press, 1988); Robert M. Spector, *W. Cameron Forbes and the Hoover Commissions to Haiti (1930)* (Lanham: University Press of America, 1985); David Healy, *Gunboat Diplomacy in the Wilson Era: The U.S. Navy in Haiti, 1915–1916* (Madison: University of Wisconsin Press, 1976); Arthur C. Millspaugh, *Haiti under American Control, 1915–1930* (rev. ed., Westport: Negro University Press, 1970); Emily Greene Balch, ed., *Occupied Haiti* (rev. ed., New York: Negro Universities Press, 1969); Dana G. Munro, *Intervention and Dollar Diplomacy in the Caribbean, 1900–1921* (Princeton: Princeton University Press, 1964); John A. Vernon, "Racial Gamesmanship and the U.S. Occupation of Haiti: An Illustrative Episode," *Alabama Historical Quarterly* 40 (1978), 144–161; Richard Millett and G. Dale Gaddy, "Administering the Protectorates: The U.S. Occupation of Haiti and the Dominican Republic," *Revista Interamericana* 6 (1976), 383–402.

    Schmidt's *Occupation of Haiti, 1915–1934* (hereafter cited as *HS*) and Renda's *Taking Haiti* remain two of the most comprehensive works on the topic. Despite these and other excellent histories, there have been very few sustained analyses of education during the occupation. Much of the work in this area is atomized and fragmented. Of late, Leon D. Pamphile's *Clash of Cultures: America's Educational Strategies in Occupied Haiti, 1915–1934* (Lanham: University Press of America, 2008) is the only book-length work that explicitly aims at filling the historiographical gap.

2. On Bryan's relationship to the banking industry, see Matthew Simon, "The Hot Money Movement and the Private Exchange Pool Proposal of 1896," *Journal of Economic History* 20 (1960), 31–50; Paola E. Coletta, "William Jennings Bryan and Currency and Banking Reform," *Nebraska History* 45 (1964), 31–57; Farnham's relationship with Bryan recounted in Munro, *Intervention*, 332ff.

3. Navy Department, "Plan for Landing and Occupying the City of Port-au-Prince [1914]," cited in *HS*, 64; Farnham's executive and political roles described in Plummer, *Haiti and the Great Powers*, 169–171; and Schmidt's "Haiti before the Intervention" and "Decision to Intervene," in *HS*, 10–63. The decision to remove the Haitian government's gold was also likely motivated by Haiti's refusal to complete payments on the National Railway of Haiti (headed by Farnham). The 108 miles of railway completed lay in three disconnected sections over nonmountainous area. Haiti refused to pay the maximum agreed upon amount of $33,000 per mile, citing lack of completion. For further discussion on the National Railway project, see Healy, *Gunboat Diplomacy*, 29–34, 54–58.

4. Secretary of State Robert Lansing quoted in *HS*, 67; on earlier US interventions in Haiti, see *HS*, 31. Banking and railroad interests had approximately four million dollars invested in Haiti with concessions to cultivate 3,240 square miles of land

(15 miles each direction from the railroad of 108 miles). See Plummer, *Haiti and the Great Powers*, 156.
5. Munro, *Intervention*, 368–371; *HS*, 118. Franklin Delano Roosevelt stated in a campaign speech that "I wrote Haiti's constitution myself, and if I do say it, I think it is a pretty good constitution." FDR quoted in James McCrocklin, *Garde D'Haiti, 1915–1934: Twenty Years of Organization and Training by the United States Marine Corps* (Annapolis: United States Naval Institute, 1956), 74.
6. Harding quoted in *HS*, 118. See also, Spector, *Hoover Commissions*, 39.
7. Pamphile, *Clash of Cultures*, 24–26; Munro, *Intervention*, 365–384.
8. Farnham quoted in Pamphile, *Clash of Cultures*, 96. At the start of the occupation, education ranked near the bottom on the list of priorities. Ongoing rebellion, sanitation issues, infrastructure, and unemployment consumed much of the early work of US officials who took over leadership roles in Haiti. Only as stability increased and resistance waned did the US military begin to take seriously the role of education in supporting American interests.
9. Russell quoted in Pamphile, *Clash of Cultures*, 42; Russell quoted in Millspaugh, *American Control*, 110. Russell took charge of the American military occupation in Haiti from 1918 to 1930. He had the added distinction of being Haiti's "high commissioner" from 1922 to 1929. During the first few years, he supported "corvee" or the policy of forced labor for Haitians for infrastructure projects.
10. Spector, *Hoover Commissions*, 19; Pamphile, *Clash of Cultures*, 54, 70, 72, 106. Russell viewed uneducated Haitians as "more or less of an animal, who will do whatever he is told." Quoted in *HS*, 125.
11. Pamphile, *Clash of Cultures*, 92–93.
12. *HS*, 182–185; Pamphile, *Clash of Cultures*, 75–77.
13. Pamphile, *Clash of Cultures*, 76.
14. *HS*, 177–178, 180–182, 185; Pamphile, *Clash of Cultures*, 76–78; United States, *Congressional Record* 72 (December 18, 1929), 916; Balch, ed., *Occupied Haiti*, 32, 82–84.
15. According to the Hoover Commissions (1930), the National School System consisted of 217 urban primary, 384 rural primary, 6 secondary, and 1 superior (University of Port-au-Prince) schools, or a total of 608 institutions. See Spector, *Hoover Commissions*, 161, 164; Balcher, *Occupied Haiti*, 85; Russell and Freeman cited in Pamphile, *Clash of Cultures*, 79, 81, 106.
16. The Service Technique received 4,550,257.20 Gourdes; the National Schools, 2,053,664.29 Gourdes. See *Review of Finances—Republic of Haiti, 1924–1930* and *Annual Report of the Service Technique, 1929–1930*, cited in Pamphile, *Clash of Cultures*, 106.
17. The Service Technique had 11,430 students; the National Schools, 95,696. Numbers are estimates provided by the US military occupation government. See "Bulletin Officiel du Departement de l'Instruction Publique" (October–November 1928) and *Annual Report of the Service Technique, 1929–1930* cited in Pamphile, *Clash of Cultures*, 106.
18. Russell never believed in power-sharing with the Haitians. "The absurdity of dual control, or of two nations administering the affairs of a country" he asserted, "is too obvious to need comment." Quoted in *HS*, 124.
19. Spector, *Hoover Commissions*, 161–164; Pamphile, *Clash of Cultures*, 106.
20. For a discussion on Haiti's preoccupation history of education, see Pamphile, *Clash of Cultures*, 1–21.
21. Ibid., 91.

22. Ibid., 107–111; *US Congressional Record* 72 (December 18, 1929), 914.
23. Spector, *Hoover Commissions*, 164; Pamphile, *Clash of Cultures*, 118. What's more, reports indicated that few Haitians ever attended secondary schools. Statistics indicated that out of every 1,000 Haitians, a mere 2.8 had schooling beyond the elementary level. In the United States, out of every 1,000 African Americans, there were almost 10 (9.8) who had reached the secondary level. Spector, *Hoover Commissions*, 166.
24. This and the following discussion about student protests are based on *HS*, 196–206; and Pamphile, "Student Strike Triggers National Crisis over American Educational Policy," in *Clash of Cultures*, 124–153.
25. Pamphile, *Clash of Cultures*, 124–134.
26. Schmidt states that Russell also imposed martial law and a curfew. See *HS*, 198; Pamphile, *Clash of Cultures*, 124–134.
27. Pamphile, *Clash of Cultures*, 124–134.
28. The most comprehensive treatment of the commissions can be found in Spector, *Hoover Commissions*.
29. On Forbes's background and term in the Philippines, see Glenn May, *Social Engineering in the Philippines: The Aims, Execution, and Impact of American Colonial Policy, 1900–1913* (Westport: Greenwood Press, 1980), 21, 113. Forbes was also known for working for British, Belgian, and French stockholders of the Brazilian Railway Company from 1914 to 1920 as sole receiver of the operation valued at three hundred million dollars with 38 corporations in five South American countries. In his later years, Forbes vacationed in Honduras where he was a director of the United Fruit Company.
30. Spector, *Hoover Commissions*, 144–145; Vernon, "Racial Gamesmanship," 149; Pamphile, *Clash of Cultures*, 137.
31. For more on Moton, see William H. Hughes, *Robert Russa Moton of Hampton and Tuskegee* (Chapel Hill: University of North Carolina Press, 1956).
32. Vernon, "Racial Gamesmanship," 150.
33. Ibid., 152, 157; Pamphile, *Clash of Cultures*, 140.
34. Pamphile, *Clash of Cultures*, 140, 142; Spector, *Hoover Commissions*, 161–164; Moton was hardly the only one with strong words about the occupation's mishandling of education in Haiti. See also Balch, ed., *Occupied Haiti*, 93–108.
35. Moton cited in Spector, *Hoover Commissions*, 157.
36. Pamphile, *Clash of Cultures*, 147, 149.
37. United States, *Congressional Record* 72 (December 8, 1929), 912.
38. Ibid., 910, 911; *HS*, 214.
39. Ibid., 911.

5   By Executive Order

1. The story of America's first occupation of the Dominican Republic has received the most extensive treatment in Bruce Calder's *Impact of Intervention: The Dominican Republic during the U.S. Occupation of 1916–1924* (rev. ed., Princeton: Markus Wiener, 2006). Education occupies a very small portion (approximately ten pages) of his overall analysis. Other literature on the Dominican Republic during US occupation is as follows: Thomas Snowden, *Santo Domingo, Its Past and Its Present* (Santo Domingo City: n.p., 1920); Melvin M. Knight, *The Americans in Santo Domingo* (New York: Vanguard Press, 1928); Sumner Welles, *Naboth's Vineyard: The Dominican Republic, 1844–1924* (2 vols, New York: Payson and Clarke, 1928); Howard J. Wiarda, *The Dominican Republic: Nation in Transition*

(New York: Praeger 1969); Richard Millett and G. Dale Gaddy, "Administering the Protectorates: The U.S. Occupation of Haiti and the Dominican Republic," *Revista Interamericana* 6 (1976), 383–402; Stephen M. Fuller and Graham A Cosmas, *Marines in the Dominican Republic, 1916–1924* (Washington, DC: US Marine Corps., 1973); Ian Bell, *The Dominican Republic* (Boulder: Westview Press, 1981); Richard Lee Turtis, *Foundations of Despotism: Peasants, the Trujillo Regime, and Modernity in Dominican History* (Stanford: Stanford University Press, 2003); Frank Moya Pons, *The Dominican Republic: A National History* (rev. ed., Princeton: Markus Wiener Publishers, 2010).
2. Knight's *Americans in Santo Domingo* offers the most compelling, comprehensive, and still relevant economic history of the US occupation.
3. Knight, *Americans in Santo Domingo*, 16–21, 30–39; Calder, *Impact of Intervention*, 1–7.
4. Calder's revised preface to *Impact of Intervention* outlines a 12-part process he's distilled from the "common pattern" of US relations with Latin America. The process is as follows: (1) US displeasure toward a Latin American country; (2) US threats issued to the same; (3) US provocation and confrontation with the same; (4) claims of threats to US interest in the Latin American country; (5) US destabilization efforts; (6) pretext found for invasion; (7) establishment of an occupation military government or a puppet regime; (8) domestic resistance; (9) guerrilla warfare; (10) human rights violations on both sides; (11) bad publicity over human rights violations; and (12) US withdrawal.
5. Millet and Gaddy, "Administering the Protectorates," 392–399.
6. Ibid.; on the legacy of military dictatorship imparted by the US occupation, see Turtis, *Foundations of Despotism*.
7. *Annual Report of the Military Government of Santo Domingo, from date of Proclamation, November 29, 1916 to June 30, 1917* (Records of the State Department Relating to Internal Affairs of the Dominican Republic, 1910–1929, National Archives, Record Group 59, Decimal File 839 [hereafter cited as, USNA RG 59, DF 839]), 12. Julian Go's *American Empire and the Politics of Meaning: Elite Political Cultures in the Philippines and Puerto Rico during U.S. Colonialism* (Durham: Duke University Press, 2008) describes the drive for legitimacy as the attempt by occupation officials to ensure efficient rule by organizing "colonialism according to perceived local demands local demands and interests" (34).
8. Military Government of Santo Domingo, *Executive Order No. 25* (USNA RG 59, DF 839); *Annual Report of the Military Government of Santo Domingo, from date of Proclamation, November 29, 1916 to June 30, 1917* (USNA RG 59, DF 839), 12. Knapp's decision to form a Dominican education commission can be understood in terms of Go's "tutelary colonialism." That Knapp viewed the commission as a rhetorical ornament does not preclude the possibility that he valued the "political education" or "school of politics" this work gave the elite Dominicans who were involved. For an introduction to Go's discussion on this kind of tutelary colonialism, see *American Empire*, 49–53.
9. *Quarterly Report of the Military Government of Santo Domingo, from July 1, 1917 to September 30, 1917* (USNA RG 59, DF 839), 4. Knapp stated that "the report of the Commission on Education has not yet been submitted, but the main features of it, as applied to present conditions, have been decided upon" (4). *Coleccion de Ordenes de la Secretaria de Estado de Justicia e Instruccion Publica* (Santo Domino: Imp. y Linotipo J.R. Vda Garcia, 1919) lists all 23 education-related executive orders issued before the commission report was submitted. The orders prescribed a curriculum and system of educational governance for all levels of instruction.

10. Secretary of Justice and Public Education, *Executive Order No. 11*, in *Coleccion de Ordenes*, 18; *Quarterly Report of the Military Government of Santo Domingo, from July 1, 1917 to September 30, 1917* (USNA RG 59, DF 839), 4.
11. "Brigadier General Rufus H. Lane, USMC (Deceased)," Biographical File, US Marine Corps History Division, Quantico, VA; Jack Shulimson, "Daniel Pratt Mannix and the Establishment of the Marine Corps School of Application, 1889–1894," *The Journal of Military History* 55 (October 1991), 484; Calder, *Impact of Intervention*, 36–37; Secretary of Justice and Public Education, *Executive Order No. 4*, in *Coleccion de Ordenes*, 9–10; Secretary of Justice and Public Education, *Executive Order No. 13*, in *Coleccion de Ordenes*, 21–24; Military Government of Santo Domingo, *Executive Order No. 145* (USNA RG 59, DF 839).
12. *Quarterly Report of the Military Government of Santo Domingo, from January 1, 1918 to March 31, 1918* (USNA RG 59, DF 839), 3; Military Government of Santo Domingo, *Executive Order No. 145* (USNA RG 59, DF 839); *Gaceta Oficial* (April 17, 1918), 3.
13. Military Government of Santo Domingo, *Executive Order No. 114* (USNA RG 59, DF 839).
14. *Annual Report of the Military Government of Santo Domingo, from date of Proclamation, November 29, 1916 to June 30, 1917* (USNA RG 59, DF 839); Calder, *Impact of Intervention*, 34–35; Snowden, *Santo Domingo*, 31–32; on the "caudillo" political culture in the Dominican Republic, see Calder's discussion in *Impact of Intervention*, 116–120. Dominicans took matters into their own hands under the Snowden administration through the formation of "Popular Societies of Education" during Rear Admiral Thomas Snowden's administration.
15. *Quarterly Report of the Military Government of Santo Domingo, from July 1, 1918 to September 30, 1918* (USNA RG 59, DF 839), 4; *Quarterly Report of the Military Government of Santo Domingo, from July 1, 1920 to Sept 30, 1920* (USNA RG 59, DF 839), 31; Snowden, *Santo Domingo*, 33–34.
16. Edward Douglass Fitchen, "Alexis E. Frye and Cuban Education, 1898–1902," *Revista Interamericana* 2 (1972), 123–149; Glenn Anthony May, *Social Engineering in the Philippines: The Aims, Execution, and Impact of American Colonial Policy, 1900–1913* (Westport: Greenwood Press, 1980); Aida Negron De Montilla, *Americanization in Puerto Rico and the Public School System, 1900–1930* (Rio Pierdras: University of Puerto Rico, 1975); Leon D. Pamphile, *Clash of Cultures: America's Educational Strategies in Occupied Haiti, 1915–1934* (Lanham: University Press of America, 2008). Jonathan Zimmerman, *Innocents Abroad: American Teachers in the American Century* (Cambridge: Harvard University Press, 2006); *Quarterly Report of the Military Government of Santo Domingo, from January 1, 1918 to March 31, 1918* (USNA RG 59, DF 839), 3.
17. *Quarterly Report of the Military Government of Santo Domingo, from January 1, 1918 to March 31, 1918* (USNA RG 59, DF 839), 3.
18. Ibid.
19. Military Government of Santo Domingo, *Executive Order No. 145* (USNA RG 59, DF 839).
20. Ibid.; my translation from *Gaceta Oficial* (April 17, 1918), 5–6.
21. Military Government of Santo Domingo, *Executive Order No. 145* (USNA RG 59, DF 839); see *Gaceta Oficial* (April 17, 1918), 26–40; *Quarterly Report of the Military Government of Santo Domingo, from January 1, 1918 to March 31, 1918* (USNA RG 59, DF 839), 3; for a description of the push for technical education in Haiti, see

Leon D. Pamphile's *Clash of Cultures: America's Educational Strategies in Occupied Haiti, 1915–1934* (Lanham: University Press of America, 2008).

Military Government of Santo Domingo, *Executive Order No. 145* (USNA RG 59, DF 839); my translation from *Gaceta Oficial* (April 17, 1918), 7–26, 41. Much like the Commission on Education, the Consejo Nacional de Educacion could also be understood as an example of what Go's *American Empire* describes as "tutelary colonialism" because of the political education the Consejo offered Dominican elites.

22. Military Government of Santo Domingo, *Executive Order No. 145* (USNA RG 59, DF 839); see *Gaceta Oficial* (April 17, 1918), 7–11.
23. *Annual Report of the Military Government of Santo Domingo, from date of Proclamation, November 29, 1916 to June 30, 1917* (USNA RG 59, DF 839), 8–10; see also, Knight, *Americans in Santo Domingo*, 37–39; Snowden, *Santo Domingo*, 7–12.
24. Knight, *Americans in Santo Domingo*, 129–143.
25. Calder, *Impact of Intervention*, 72–75.
26. Ibid., 75–77; Knight, *Americans in Santo Domingo*, 102–105.
27. Calder, *Impact of Intervention*, 110–113.
28. *Quarterly Report of the Military Government of Santo Domingo, from October 1, 1918 to December 31, 1918* (USNA RG 59, DF 839), 8; *Quarterly Report of the Military Government of Santo Domingo, from October 1, 1920 to December 31, 1920* (USNA RG 59, DF 839), 39–40.
29. *Quarterly Report of the Military Government of Santo Domingo for the Period Ending March 31, 1921* (USNA RG 59, DF 839), 36–38.
30. *Quarterly Report of the Military Government of Santo Domingo, from April 1, 1921 to June 30, 1921* (USNA RG 59, DF 839), 36–37; *Quarterly Report of the Military Government of Santo Domingo, from January 1, 1923 to March 31, 1923* (USNA RG 59, DF 839), 10–11.
31. See *Quarterly Reports* on Public Works projects from 1921 to 1924; Calder, *Impact of Intervention*, 50–52.
32. *Quarterly Report of the Military Government of Santo Domingo, from July 1, 1919 to September 30, 1919* (USNA RG 59, DF 839), 24–30; *Quarterly Report of the Military Government of Santo Domingo, from April 1, 1920 to June 30, 1920* (USNA RG 59, DF 839), 26–27. *Quarterly Report of the Military Government of Santo Domingo, from October 1, 1920 to December 31, 1920* (USNA RG 59, DF 839), 37–38.
33. *Quarterly Report of the Military Government of Santo Domingo for the Period Ending March 31, 1921* (USNA RG 59, DF 839), 36–38; *Quarterly Report of the Military Government of Santo Domingo, from April 1, 1921 to June 30, 1921* (USNA RG 59, DF 839), 36–37; *Quarterly Report of the Military Government of Santo Domingo, from July 1, 1921 to September 30, 1921* (USNA RG 59, DF 839), 49; *Quarterly Report of the Military Government of Santo Domingo, from October 1, 1921 to December 31, 1921* (USNA RG 59, DF 839), 23, 55–57.
34. *Quarterly Report of the Military Government of Santo Domingo, from October 1, 1921 to December 31, 1921* (USNA RG 59, DF 839), 56, 55.
35. Ibid., 56–57.
36. *Annual Report of the Military Government of Santo Domingo, from date of Proclamation, November 29, 1916 to June 30, 1917* (USNA RG 59, DF 839); the Occupation Proclamation presented in full in Snowden, *Santo Domingo*, 65–67.
37. Calder, *Impact of Intervention*, 105.
38. Snowden, *Santo Domingo*, 5–9.

39. James Anderson, *The Education of Blacks in the South, 1860–1935* (Chapel Hill: University of North Carolina Press, 1988); more recent examples of Anderson's notion of double taxation discussed in the following: Julian Savage Carter, "Cultural Capital and African American Agency: The Economic Struggle for Effective Education for African Americans in Franklin, Tennessee, 1890–1967," *The Journal of African American History* 87 (2002), 206–235; Kara Miles Turner, "'Getting It Straight': Southern Black School Patrons and the Struggle for Equal Education in the Pre- and Post-Civil Rights Eras," *The Journal of Negro Education* 72 (Spring 2003), 217–229.
40. Knight, *Americans in Santo Domingo*, 126–128; Calder, *Impact of Intervention*, 39–40.

6 Greatest Generation

1. Harry Truman cited in Masako Shibata, *Japan and Germany under the U.S. Occupation: A Comparative Analysis of the Post-War Education Reform* (Lanham: Lexington Books, 2005), 60; the literature on occupied Japan includes the following: Toshino Nishi, *Unconditional Democracy: Education and Politics in Occupied Japan, 1945–1952* (Stanford: Hoover Institution, 1982); Joseph Trainor, *Educational Reform in Occupied Japan: Trainor's Memoir* (Tokyo: Meiji University Press, 1983); Robert Wolfe, ed., *Americans as Proconsuls: United States Military Government in Germany and Japan, 1944–1952* (Carbondale: Southern Illinois University Press, 1984); Gary Hoichi Tsuchimochi, *Educational Reform in Postwar Japan: The 1946 U.S. Education Mission* (Tokyo: University of Tokyo Press, 1993); Bernd Martin, *Japan and Germany in the Modern World* (Oxford: Berghahn Books, 1995); Ray A. Moore and Donald L. Robinson, *Partners for Democracy: Crafting the New Japanese State Under MacArthur* (Oxford: Oxford University Press, 2002); Eiji Takemae, *The Allied Occupation of Japan* (New York: Continuum, 2002); Hans Martin Kramer, "Reforms of their Own: The Japanese Resistance to Changes in Higher Education Administration under the U.S. American Occupation, 1945–1952," *Paedagogica Historica* 43 (June 2007), 327–345; Kentaro Ohkura and Masako Shibata, "Demystifying the Divine State and Rewriting Identity in the U.S. Occupation of Japan," in Noah W. Sobe, *American Post-Conflict Educational Reform: From the Spanish-American War to Iraq* (New York: Palgrave, 2009), 129–145; Ruriko Kumano, "Anticommunism and Academic Freedom: Walter C. Eells and the 'Red Purge' in Occupied Japan," *History of Education Quarterly* 50 (November 2010), 513–537; Masako Shibata's *Japan and Germany* has been particularly useful and is hereafter cited as *MS*.
2. *MS*, 8.
3. Ibid., 73.
4. Ibid., 65.
5. Kramer, "Reforms of their Own," 327. The US occupation's economic reforms had mostly to do with steering Japan away from communist ideas and organization. Thus, the occupation opposed unions, encouraged a "red purge" from schools and universities (e.g., dismissal of suspected communist sympathizers), and land reform. MacArthur's "Rural Land Reform" directive of December 9, 1945, forced absentee landowners to gift their land to laborers working the land. "The redistribution," MacArthur argued, "formed a strong barrier against any introductions of communism in rural Japan. Every farmer in the country was now a capitalist in his own right" (Nishi, *Unconditional Democracy*, 79).
6. *MS*, 67.

7. Ibid., 19–20, 66–67, 80–82; Ohkura and Shibata, "Demystifying the Divine State," 132–135.
8. *MS*, 67; Ohkura and Shibata, "Demystifying the Divine State," 135.
9. *MS*, 68.
10. Ibid., 78, 79, 83; Nishi, *Unconditional Democracy*, 205–206.
11. *MS*, 85–87; Kramer, "Reforms of their Own," 332, 329. The critical challenge facing all parties—supporters, critics, occupation officials, and school board members—was the cost of these reforms, including school renovation, free secondary programs, and the creation and maintenance of self-governing boards. The US occupation passed on 70 percent of the cost for these reforms to local governments. As a result of the great burden placed on local communities, some administrators resigned or committed suicide because of their inability to implement the drastic, sweeping changes.
12. *MS*, 87–94; Kramer, "Reforms of their Own," 330–331. Japanese institutions also supported the broadening of university studies and the establishment of general, broad, humanistic requirements for students of all specialties and programs of study. Occupation officials used a study commissioned by James Bryant Conant, then president of Harvard, as a guide for incorporating "General Education in a Free Society" into the Japanese college curriculum.
13. *MS*, 87–94.
14. Kramer, "Reforms of their Own," 336; Kumano, "Anticommunism," 515, 517; see also Nishi, *Unconditional Democracy*, 258–267.
15. Kramer, "Reforms of their Own," 336–337.
16. Ibid., 337–338; Nishi, *Unconditional Democracy*, 219–222.
17. Kramer, "Reforms of their Own," 339–340.
18. Ibid., 338–339, 344.
19. Ibid., 340, 342; Kumano, "Anticommunism," 521; Nishi, *Unconditional Democracy*, 224–226.
20. Kramer, "Reforms of their Own," 343.
21. Kumano, "Anticommunism," 515, 516, 520.
22. Ibid., 521.
23. Ibid., 533, 523, 532, 535–536.
24. Ibid., 532; Hunt, *American Ascendancy*, 174–175.

7   Zero Hour

1. FDR cited in James Tent, *Mission on the Rhine: Reeducation and Denazification in American Occupied Germany* (Chicago: University of Chicago Press, 1982), 30; the literature on Germany includes the following: Harold Zink, *The United States in Germany: 1944–1955* (Westport: Greenwood Press, 1957); Henry J. Kellermann, *Cultural Relations as an Instrument of U.S. Foreign Policy: The Educational Exchange Program between the United States and Germany, 1945–1954* (Washington: GPO, 1978); Charles D. Biebel, "American Efforts for Educational Reform in Occupied Germany, 1945–1955—a Reassessment," *History of Education Quarterly* 22 (Fall 1982), 277–287; Robert Wolfe, ed., *Americans as Proconsuls: United States Military Government in Germany and Japan, 1944–1952* (Carbondale: Southern Illinois University Press, 1984); Gregory P. Wegner, "Germany's Past Contested: The Soviet-American Conflict in Berlin over History Curriculum Reform, 1945–1948," *History of Education Quarterly* 30 (Spring 1990), 1–16; Bernd Martin, *Japan and Germany in the Modern World* (Oxford: Berghahn Books, 1995); Val Rust, "The

German Image of American Education through the Weimar Period," *Paedagogica Historica* 33 (1997), 25–44; Stefan Paulus, "The Americanisation of Europe after 1945?: The Case of the German Universities," *European Review of History* 9 (2002), 241–253; Masako Shibata, *Japan and Germany under the U.S. Occupation: A Comparative Analysis of the Post-War Education Reform* (Lanham: Lexington Books, 2005); Charles Dorn and Brian Puaca, "The Appeal to the German Mind: Educational Reconstruction in the American Zone of Occupation, 1944–1949," in ed. Noah W. Sobe, *American Post-Conflict Educational Reform: From the Spanish-American War to Iraq* (New York: Palgrave, 2009), 105–128; Brian Puaca, *Learning Democracy: Education Reform in West Germany, 1945–1965* (New York: Berghahn Books, 2009). Tent's *Mission on the Rhine* has been particularly helpful and is hereafter cited as *JT*. Puaca's *Learning Democracy* hereafter cited as *BP*.
2. *JT*, 13–17.
3. See "Planning for Reeducation," in ibid., 13–39.
4. The following occupation governors led the American zone's military government from 1945 to 1949: Dwight D. Eisenhower (May–November 1945), George S. Patton (November 1945), Joseph T. McNarney (November 1945–January 1947), Lucius Clay (January 1947–May 1949), and Clarence Huebner (May–September 1949).
5. Early growth of ERA discussed in *JT*, 44–50.
6. Ibid., 6–8; Dorn and Puaca, "Appeal to the German Mind," 117; *BP*, 18–22.
7. *JT*, 23–24; *BP*, 24–25.
8. *JT*, 23–24; John W. Taylor, "Youth Welfare in Germany: A Study of Governmental Action Relative to Care of the Normal German Youth" (PhD diss., Columbia University, 1936).
9. *JT*, 50–69; *BP*, 32–39.
10. *JT*, 50–69; Dorn and Puaca, "Appeal to the German Mind," 115.
11. See "A Second Purge," in *JT*, 74–109.
12. *JT*, 23, 22, 17–18. For Tillich's sociocultural analysis of German life that fed into his postwar views, see *The Religious Situation* (New York: Henry Holt, 1932) and *The Protestant Era* (Chicago: University of Chicago Press, 1948).
13. *JT*, 42–43; *BP*, 27–31.
14. *JT*, 112–123; Dorn and Puaca, "Appeal to the German Mind," 118–120.
15. *JT*, 116; *Report of the United States Education Mission to Germany* (Washington: GPO, 1946).
16. *JT*, 118, 119.
17. Ibid., 124; see also, George F. Zook, *Japan and Germany: Problems in Reeducation* (New York: Carnegie Endowment for International Peace, 1947).
18. *JT*, 24.
19. Ibid., 134–135, 141–152.
20. Ibid., 142.
21. Ibid., 145–147.
22. Ibid., 174–175; *BP*, 22.
23. Ibid., 8.
24. *BP* argues alternatively that the seeds of change toward a US-style "democratization of classroom practice" (8) were planted during this time. These seeds came to fruition over the next two decades and included the development of new texts, the expansion of student government, and substantive reforms in teacher training.
25. *JT*, 195, 167–200.
26. Ibid., 200–238.

27. Ibid., 241, 238–250; Wegner, "Germany's Past Contested," 7–10.
28. *JT*, 241.
29. See Michael J. Sullivan, *American Adventurism Abroad: Invasions, Interventions, and Regime Changes since World War II* (Hoboken: Wiley-Blackwell, 2007).

8 In Perpetuity

1. Barton Gellman, "'I Saw Bodies Falling Out—Oh, God, Jumping, Falling,'" *Washington Post* (September 12, 2001); Gene Weingarten, "Getting Bush's Goat: A Primer on Priorities," *Washington Post* (July 18, 2004); *The 9/11 Commission Report: Final Report of the National Commission on Terrorist Attacks Upon the United States* (New York: W.W. Norton, 2004); Philip Delves Broughton, "'The Rest of the World Hears You,'" *The Daily Telegraph* [London] (September 15, 2001).
2. "Bin Laden Says He Wasn't Behind the Attacks," CNN (September 16, 2001); David Rohde, "A Nation Challenged: The Opposition; Afghan Rebels Courted by U.S. and Russia to Defy Taliban," *New York Times* (September 25, 2001); Hayat Alvi, "Reconstruction in Post-Taliban Afghanistan: Women and Education," *RFR/DRF* 30 (2003), 24.
3. Caroline B. Fleming, "Islamic Fundamentalism and the Education of Women in Afghanistan," *William and Mary Journal of Women and Law* 597 (Spring 2005), 607–609; Roozbeh Shirazi, "Islamic Education in Afghanistan: Revisiting the United States' Role," *CR: The New Centennial Review* 8 (2008), 215–216, 218–219.
4. Fleming, "Islamic Fundamentalism," 598–600, 609–611; "Afghanistan's Education Dilemma," *The Economist* (March 25, 2002); "Literacy," in Peter R. Blood, ed., *Afghanistan: A Country Study* (Washington: GPO for the Library of Congress, 2001); John F. Burns, "For Women in Kabul, This Test is Welcome," *New York Times* (February 10, 2002); Jennifer Seymour Whitaker, "Don't Betray the Women," *Washington Post* (November 15, 2001).
5. Norimitsu Onishi, "Medical Schools Show First Signs of Healing from Taliban Abuse," *New York Times* (January 15, 2002); Shirazi, "Islamic Education," 226; Craig Davis, "'A' is for Allah, 'J' is for Jihad," *World Policy Journal* (Spring 2002), 92–93.
6. Shirazi, "Islamic Education," 211; for a discussion of the Cold War emotions fueling the tensions between the United States and the USSR after the Soviet invasion of Afghanistan, see Michael H. Hunt, *The American Ascendancy: How the United States Gained and Wielded Global Dominance* (Chapel Hill: University of North Carolina Press, 2007), 249–250.
7. Alvi, "Reconstruction," 18–21; Ahmed Rashid, *Taliban: Militant Islam, Oil and Fundamentalism in Central Asia* (New Haven: Yale University Press, 2000), 166, 179; William Maley, *The Afghanistan Wars* (New York: Palgrave, 2002), 245; "Taliban's Unlikely Story," *Al-Ahram Weekly* (October 17, 1996); Irene I. Gendzier, "Invisible by Design: U.S. Policy in the Middle East," *Diplomatic History* 26 (Fall 2002), 608; Fleming, "Islamic Fundamentalism," 611–612; Susan Dominus, "Shabana is Late for School," *New York Times* (September 29, 2002).
8. "A Nation Challenged: Bush Says America Sees a 'Greater Hope,'" *New York Times* (April 18, 2002).
9. "U.S. First Lady Laura Bush Promises More Support to Afghan Education," *BBC Monitoring South Asia* (June 8, 2008); Steven Edwards, "Afghan Women Mark Freedom from Tyranny: International Women's Day: First Lady Laura Bush Recites How U.S. Aids War Victims," *National Post* (Canada) (March 9, 2002); John Brummet,

"DOD, State, and USAID Obligated $17.7 Billion to about 7000 Contractors and Other Entities for Afghanistan Reconstruction during Fiscal Years 2007–2009," Office of the Inspector General for Afghanistan Reconstruction, SIGAR Audit-11–4 Contractor Performance and Oversight (October 2010).
10. "Louis Berger Group," Center for Public Integrity, http://projects.publicintegrity.org/wow/bio.aspx?act=pro&ddlC=35; Fariba Nawa, "Deconstruction the Reconstruction," CorpWatch, http://www.corpwatch.org/article.php?id=14076.
11. Of the $300 million, $81 million went to school and clinic reconstruction. See, USAID Office of Inspector General, "Audit of USAID/Afghanistan's School and Health Clinic Reconstruction Activities," Audit Report No. 5–306–06–008-P (August 18, 2006), 2; between 2007 and 2009, Louis Berger continued to receive the highest proportion of grants from USAID (37 percent) with a budget of $732 million. See Brummet, "DOD, State, and USAID," 13, 32.
12. USAID Office of Inspector General, "Audit of USAID/Afghanistan's School and Health Clinic Reconstruction Activities," Audit Report No. 5–306–06–008-P (August 18, 2006), 2; Nawa, "Deconstruction the Reconstruction."
13. USAID Office of Inspector General, "Audit of USAID/Afghanistan's School and Health Clinic Reconstruction Activities," Audit Report No. 5–306–06–008-P (August 18, 2006), 4; David Voreacos, "Louis Berger Group Chairman Derish Wolff Subject of U.S. Probe," *Bloomberg Business Week* (August 14, 2010); Richard Korman, "U.S. Settles Case Against Berger Group for $69 Mil," *Engineering News-Record* (November 5, 2010); Sananda Sahoo, "Lack of Oversight for USAID Contractors in Afghanistan is Not a New Story," *InterPress Service* (February 16, 2010); "Scheme to Defraud Government on Reconstruction Contracts Leads to Criminal Charges and Civil Penalties for Louis Berger Group, Inc.," US Department of Justice Press Release, November 5, 2010 (Retrieved from: http://www.justice.gov/usao/md/).
14. "NGOs Discuss Reconstruction of Afghanistan Ahead of Tokyo Donor Conference," *BBC Monitoring International Reports* (January 20, 2002); Alvi, "Reconstruction," 27; "Afghanistan's Education Dilemma," *The Economist* (March 25, 2002); "China to Increase Economic, Education Contributions to Afghanistan," *BBC Monitoring International Reports* (August 28, 2010); "Afghanistan—Education for Peace: Article by Minister of State Cornelia Pieper in Frankfurter Allegemeine Zeitung," *States News Service* (March 15, 2010).
15. "Afghanistan: Education," *Economic Intelligence Unit: Country ViewsWire* (August 24, 2007); World Bank, *Afghanistan: National Reconstruction and Poverty Reduction* (Washington, DC: Macro Graphics, March 2005), 33; "Progress and Challenges for Education in Afghanistan," *States News Service* (January 11, 2011); "Afghan MP Hails Taliban's Reported Change on Girls' Schooling," *BBC Monitoring International Reports* (January 14, 2011).
16. "Taleban No Longer Opposing Education in Some Parts of Afghanistan," *BBC Monitoring International Reports* (December 15, 2010); "Afghan Official Complains of Poor Schooling Conditions in North," *BBC Monitoring International Reports* (December 17, 2008); UNICEF, "Afghanistan," http://www.unicef.org/infobycountry/afghanistan_statistics.html; Walter Pincus, "In Building Afghan Army, It's Back to Basics," *Washington Post* (September 29, 2009); for a discussion about the difference between "simple traditional literacy" versus "functional literacy" in relation to education in Afghanistan, see Sadmani Fakir, Mohammad Golam, and Sakil Malik, "Literacy: A Path out of Extremism in Afghanistan?" *Reading Today* (October 2007), 20.

17. "Report Finds Girls' Schools in Afghanistan Face Highest Risk of Violence: Suggests Steps for Preventing Attacks," *US Newswire* (November 23, 2009); Dana Burde, "It Takes a Village to Raise a School," *New York Times* (September 17, 2010); Abdul Waheed Wafa, "Afghan Parliament Rejects Budget Over Teacher Raises," *New York Times* (May 22, 2006); Carlotta Gall, "Laura Bush Carries Pet Causes to Afghans," *New York Times* (March 31, 2005). Afghan Education Minister Mohammad Hanif Atmar thanked the work of such organizations as Oxfam, but disagreed with them that textbooks, rather than salaries and other budgetary concerns, were still a priority five years after US intervention. See "Afghan Education Ministry Says Not Suffering Book Shortage," *BBC Monitoring International Reports* (November 29, 2006); Oxfam International, "Free, Quality Education for Every Afghan Child," Oxfam Briefing Paper (November 2006), 1–32; for a discussion of other misaligned priorities, see Hayat Alvi-Aziz, "A Progress Report on Women's Education in Post-Taliban Afghanistan," *International Journal of Lifelong Education* 27 (2008), 169–178; and Stephanie Guimbert, Keiko Miwa, and Duc Thanh Nguyen, "Back to School in Afghanistan: Detriments to School Enrollment," *International Journal of Educational Development* 28 (2008), 419–434.
18. "U.S. First Lady Laura Bush Promises More Support to Afghan Education," BBC Monitoring South Asia (June 8, 2008); "Tuition & Fees," American University of Afghanistan, http://www.auaf.edu.af/admissions/tuition-fees; Mark Memmott, "Afghans Can See Progress since Fall of Taliban," *USA Today* (July 7, 2003); N. C. Aizenman, "First Lady Applauds Afghans: On Brief Visit, Bush Focuses on Women," *Washington Post* (March 31, 2005).
19. "Over 1,000 Afghan Servicemen Complete Training at Military Academy," *BBC Monitoring South Asia* (May 15, 2010); Michael Hoffman, "Largest Class Enters Afghan Military Academy," *Army Times* (October 17, 2010); Sarah Brown, "Cornerstone Laid for Afghan Defense University," Afghanistan International Security and Assistance Force (retrieved April 27, 2012), http://www.isaf.nato.int/article/news/cornerstone-laid-for-afghan-defense-university.html.
20. "At What Cost? Contingency Contracting In Iraq and Afghanistan," Report to the United States Congress (June 10, 2009), 1–72; see "Forward," in "At What Risk? Correcting Over-Reliance on Contractors in Contingency Operations," Report to the United States Congress (February 24, 2011); Gendzier, "Invisible by Design," 593–618; "Pakistan Article Lists Factors Working Against NATO Victory in Afghanistan," *BBC Monitoring South Asia* (January 12, 2011); "Meet the Press," NBC (January 2, 2011); "U.S. First Lady Laura Bush Promises More Support to Afghan Education," *BBC Monitoring South Asia* (June 8, 2008).
21. Marisa Taylor and Warren P. Strobel, "U.S. Contractor Accused of Fraud Still Winning Big Afghan Projects," *McClatchy Newspapers* (September 19, 2010); "Pakistan Article Lists Factors Working Against NATO Victory in Afghanistan," *BBC Monitoring South Asia* (January 12, 2011); Marisa Taylor, "U.S. Gave Firm Low Rating for Afghan Work—And More Business," *McClatchy Newspapers* (February 14, 2011).
22. Greg Mortenson and David Oliver Relin, *Three Cups of Tea: One Man's Mission to Promote Peace… One School at a Time* (New York: Penguin, 2007), 150.
23. Carlotta Gall, "Afghan Students Are Back, But Not the Old Textbooks," *New York Times* (December 27, 2004).
24. Linda J. Bilmes and Joseph E. Stiglitz, *The Three Trillion Dollar War: The True Cost of the Iraq Conflict* (New York: W.W. Norton, 2008).

9 Private Matter

1. Sources that address the topic of education in Iraq include the following: Pratrap Chatterjee, *Iraq, Inc.: A Profitable Occupation* (New York: Seven Stories Press, 2004); Larry Diamond, *Squandered Victory: The American Occupation and the Bungled Effort to Bring Democracy to Iraq* (New York: Times Books, 2005); Eric Herring, *Iraq in Fragments: The Occupation and Its Legacy* (Ithaca: Cornell University Press, 2006); Patrick Cockburn, *The Occupation: War and Resistance in Iraq* (New York: Verso, 2007); Dahr Jamail, *Beyond the Green Zone: Dispatches from an Unembedded Journalist in Occupied Iraq* (Chicago: Haymarket Books, 2007); John Agresto, *Mugged by Reality: The Liberation of Iraq and the Failure of Good Intentions* (New York: Encounter Books, 2007); Ali A. Allawi, *The Occupation of Iraq: Winning the War, Losing the Peace* (New Haven: Yale University Press, 2008); James Dobbin, *Occupying Iraq: A History of the Coalition Provisional Authority* (Santa Monica: Rand, 2009); Joy Gordon, *Invisible War: The United States and the Iraq Sanctions* (Cambridge: Harvard University Press, 2010); Steven Carlton-Ford and Morten G. Ender, *Handbook of War and Society: Iraq and Afghanistan* (New York: Routledge, 2011); Christian Parenti, "Fables of Reconstruction," *The Nation* (August 30/September 6, 2004), 16–19.

    See also Center for Public Integrity, "Windfalls of War: Creative Associates International, Inc." (Unpublished document, Washington, DC); Mary Ann Zehr, "Schools Open in Iraq, After Two Week Delay," *Education Week* 24 (October 13, 2004); "Iraq Gets Approval to Control Destiny of School System," *Education Week* (April 4, 2004); "Creative Associates Gets New Iraq Contract," *Education Week* (July 14, 2004); "World Bank Joins School Rebuilding Campaign," *Education Week* (April 14, 2004); Valerie J. Brown, "Reconstructing the Environment in Iraq," *Environmental Health Perspectives* 112 (June 2004); Robin Fields, "Iraq Ministry of Education Withholds Approval for Private Assyrian School," *The Los Angeles Times* (February 9, 2005); David Morris, "Criticism Grows of No-Bid Work for Iraq Reconstruction," *CongressDaily* (April 16, 2004); "Foreign Affairs: Iraq by the Numbers," *Atlantic Monthly* (July/August 2004); John Prados, *Hoodwinked: The Documents that Reveal How Bush Sold Us a War* (New York: The New Press, 2004); Michael Smerconish, "A Rush to War?," *The Philadelphia Inquirer* (February 20, 2011). Significant insights into life in occupied Iraq from a soldier's perspective offered in the following: Paul Rieckhoff, *Chasing Ghosts: Failures and Facades in Iraq: A Soldier's Perspective* (New York: NAL Caliber, 2007); Kayla Williams, *Love My Rifle More than You: Young and Female in the U.S. Army* (New York: W.W. Norton, 2006).

2. Cullen Murphy and Todd S. Purdum, "Farewell to All That: An Oral History of the Bush White House," *Vanity Fair* (February 2009). See Rieckhoff's *Chasing Ghosts* for a soldier's account of the disorganization and lack of preparedness on the ground in occupied Iraq.

3. Jaqueline Ismael, Tareq Y. Ishmael, and Raymond William Baker, "Iraq and Human Development: Culture, Education, and the Globalization of Hope," *Arab Studies Quarterly* 26 (2004), 49–66; Brian Whitaker, "Free to Do Bad Things," *The Guardian*, April 12, 2003.

4. *Emergency Supplemental Appropriations for Iraq and Afghanistan Security and Reconstruction*, 108th Cong., 1st Sess., *Congressional Record* 149 (October 15, 2003), S12579–S12599.

5. In his *Wall Street Journal* op-ed of June 20, 2003, Bremer announced his intentions of conducting a "wholesale reallocation of resources and people from state control to

private enterprise" in Iraq; Morris, "Criticism Grows of No-Bid Work," 3; Assistant Inspector General Bruce N. Crandlemire to Wendy Chamberlin and Timothy T. Beans, June 6, 2003, Office of the Inspector General, "USAID's Compliance with Federal Regulations in Awarding the Iraq Education Sector Contract," USAID (Memorandum, 03–001), 3, 8, 4; Timothy T. Beans and Wendy Chamberlin to Everett Mosely, Henry L. Barrett, and Bruce N. Crandlemire, June 23, 2003, Management Bureau, Office of Procurement, "USAID Compliance with Federal Regulations in Awarding the Iraq Education Contract: IG Review No. EDG-C-00–03–00011–00," USAID (Unnumbered Memorandum), 7, 2; on crony capitalism, see Chatterjee, *Iraq, Inc.*; and Allison Stranger, *One Nation under Contract: The Outsourcing of American Power and the Future of Foreign Policy* (New Haven: Yale University Press, 2009); on Bremer and free-market ideology, see Michael Schwartz, *War without End: The Iraq War in Context* (Chicago: Haymarket Books, 2008), 38.

6. Kenneth J. Saltman, "Creative Associates International: Corporate Education and 'Democracy Promotion' in Iraq," *The Review of Education, Pedagogy, and Cultural Studies* 28 (2006), 35, 37, 40–42. Carter Dougherty, "Building Democracies, Free Market for a Small Profit: D.C. Executive Combines Business Consultancy with Community Ideals," *Washington Times* (May 14, 2001); Center for Public Integrity, "Windfalls of War: Creative Associates International" (Unpublished Document, Washington, DC).

7. "Foreign Affairs: Iraq by the Numbers," *Atlantic Monthly* (July/August 2004), 60; Zehr, "Schools Open in Iraq," 6–7.

8. US Agency for International Development, "Creative Associates," Award/Contract No. EDG-C-00–03–00011–00 (March, 26, 2003) (signed April 11, 2003); Office of Inspector General, "Audit of USAID/Iraq's Basic Education Activities [Audit Report No. E-267–06–001-P]" (December 20, 2005), 2; see also Christine Aziz, "Engulfed in a Tyrant's Wake," *Times Higher Education Supplement* 1294 (1997), 10; Ismael et al., "Iraq and Human Development," 56–57; Delwin A. Roy, "The Educational System of Iraq," *Middle Eastern Studies* 29 (1993), 167–197; Office of Inspector General, "Follow-up Audit of USAID/Iraq's Education Activities [Audit Report No. E-267–07–003-P]" (February 4, 2007), 1–11; Dennis J. Halliday, *The Impact of the UN Sanctions on the People of Iraq* (Berkeley: University of California Press, 1999); Christina Asquith, "Turning the Page on Iraq's History," *Christian Science Monitor* (November 4, 2003); Agustin V. De Santisteban, "Sanctions, War, Occupation and the De-Development of Education in Iraq," *International Review of Education* 51 (2005), 60–63; on the politicization of Iraq's texts under the Ba'athist regime, see Jonathan Zimmerman, "Iraq's Textbooks—and Ours," *Washington Post* (July 13, 2003).

9. Stephen Phillips, "Post-War Contracts Attacked," *The Times Educational Supplement* (April 4, 2003); US Agency for International Development, "Creative Associates"; Center for Public Integrity, "Windfalls of War: Creative Associates International, Inc." (Unpublished Document, Washington, DC).

10. Kenneth J. Saltman, "Corporate Education and 'Democracy Promotion Overseas: The Case of Creative Associates International in Iraq, 2003–4," in Noah Sobe, ed., *American Post-Conflict Educational Reform: From the Spanish-American War to Iraq* (New York: Palgrave, 2009), 240–241.

11. Inspector General, "Audit of USAID/Iraq's Basic Education Activities," 3; Inspector General, "Follow-up," 2; "Foreign Affairs: Iraq by the Numbers," *Atlantic Monthly* (July/August 2004), 60; Zehr, "Schools Open in Iraq," 6–7.

12. Inspector General, "Audit of USAID/Iraq's Basic Education Activities," 1–22.
13. Ibid., 1, 4; Inspector General, "Follow-up," 7, 11.
14. Inspector General, "Audit of USAID/Iraq's Basic Education Activities," 7; Mary Zehr, "U.S. Withdraws from Education Reform in Iraq," *Education Week* 26 (August 25, 2006), 3; Inspector General, "Follow-up," 11.
15. Inspector General, "Follow-up," 10.
16. George Packer, *Assassins' Gate: America in Iraq* (New York: Farrar, Straus, and Giroux, 2005), 103–104.
17. Ibid., 188.
18. Ismael et al., "Iraq and Human Development," 57–59.
19. Keith Watenpaugh, Edouard Méténier, Jens Hanssen, and Hala Fattah, "Opening the Doors: Intellectual Life and Academic Conditions in Post-War Baghdad: A Report of the Iraqi Observatory" (Unpublished Report, July 15, 2003), 7.
20. Watenpaugh et. al., "Opening the Doors," 26–27, 29.
21. Agresto cited in Sam Dagher, "Prospects Abound Among the Kurds," *New York Times* (July 14, 2010); Keith Watenpaugh, "'Opening the Doors' One Year Later: Reflections on the Iraq War and the Middle East Studies Community," *Middle East Studies Association Bulletin* (June 2004), 8–10.
22. John Dolan, "I Was a Professor at the Horribly Corrupt American University of Iraq… Until the Neocons Fired Me," AlterNet (October 8, 2010), http://www.alternet.org/world/148443/I_was_a_professor_at_the_horribly_corrupt_american_university_of_iraq…_until_the_neocons_fired_me?page=entire.
23. John Ehrenberg, J. Patrice McSherry, Jose Ramon Sanchez, and Caroleen Marji Sayej, eds., *The Iraq Papers* (Oxford: Oxford University Press, 2010), 1977–198; Sheryl Tappan, *Shock and Awe in Fort Worth: How the U.S. Army Rigged the 'Free and Open Competition' to Replace Halliburton's Sole Source Oil Field in Iraq* (San Mateo: CA, Pourquoi Press, 2004), 18; Jim Landers, "Author Says Pentagon Favored Halliburton Houston Firm Joins Corps of Engineers in Defending Contracts," *Dallas Morning News* (September 11, 2004).
24. Robin Fields, "Iraq Ministry of Education Withholds Approval for Private Assyrian School" *Los Angeles Times* (February 9, 2005).
25. David Bacon, "Unionbusting, Iraqi-Style," *Middle East Online* (October 10, 2010); Saba Jerges, "Iraqi Oil Workers Postpone May 10 Strike, Deliver Ultimatum on Pay, Profit-Sharing," *Platts Oilgram News* (May 11, 2007); Danny Fortson, "Oil Giants are Itching to Invade Iraq: The Big Players Have Been Shut Out Since Nationalisation in 1972, Now They See Their chance to Get In," *The Sunday Times* [London] (December 28, 2008).

10 Complex Problem

1. Jim Newton, "Ike's Speech," *The New Yorker* (December 20, 2010).
2. Steven Kinzer, *All the Shah's Men: An American Coup and the Roots of Middle East Terror* (Hoboken: Wiley, 2008); Salim Yaqub, *Containing Arab Nationalism: The Eisenhower Doctrine and the Middle East* (Chapel Hill: University of North Carolina Press, 2004); Stephen G. Rabe, *Eisenhower and Latin America: The Foreign Policy of Anticommunism* (Chapel Hill: University of North Carolina Press, 1988); William D. Hartung, "Eisenhower's Warning: The Military-Industrial Complex Forty Years Later," *World Policy Journal* (Spring 2001), 39–44.
3. Dwight D. Eisenhower, "Farewell Address" (1961), http://www.eisenhower.archives.gov/all_about_ike/Speeches/Farewell_Address.pdf.

4. Ibid.; Lodge to Taft, November 22, 1900, cited in Glenn A. May, *Social Engineering in the Philippines: The Aims, Execution, and Impact of American Colonial Policy, 1900–1913* (Westport: Greenwood Press, 1980), 152.
5. Steven Kull, Clay Ramsay, and Evan Lewis, "Misperceptions, the Media, and the Iraq War," PIPA/Knowledge Networks: The American Public on International Issues [University of Maryland] (October 2, 2003), 1–21, http://www.worldpublicopinion.org/pipa/pdf/oct03/IraqMedia_Oct03_rpt.pdf; according to soldier Kayla Williams in *Love my Rifle More than You*, the idea of an Iraqi chemical attack against US troops was ludicrous: "Laughing hysterically. Why? That's hard to explain. But there's something so blatantly bizarre about this situation. So manifestly hallucinatory. We don't feel threatened. We know we are not the target of a chemical attack. Just a cosmic joke" (96); Jon Whiten, "If News From Iraq Is Bad, It's Coming From U.S. Officials," Fairness & Accuracy in Reporting, http://www.fair.org/index.php?page=1167; "The Times and Iraq," *New York Times* (May 26, 2004); David Barstow, "Behind TV Analysts, Pentagon's Hidden Hand," *New York Times* (April 20, 2008); Michael Hastings, "Another Runaway General: Army Deploys Psy-Ops on U.S. Senators," *Rolling Stone* (February 23, 2011).
6. Butler cited in Niall Ferguson, *Colossus: The Price of America's Empire* (New York: Penguin, 2005), 58–59, emphasis in the original; see also Hans Schmidt, *Maverick Marine: General Smedley D. Butler and the Contradictions of American Military History* (Lexington: University Press of Kentucky, 1998), 74–95, 231.
7. United States, *Congressional Record* 72 (December 8, 1929), 923.

Bibliography

Periodicals

Al-Ahram Weekly
Alternet
Army Times
Atlantic Monthly
Bloomberg Business Week
Boston Daily Globe
Christian Science Monitor
CongressDaily
The Daily Telegraph (London)
Dallas Morning News
Economic Intelligence Unit: Country ViewsWire
The Economist
Education Week
Engineering News-Record
Gaceta Oficial (Dominican Republic)
The Guardian (London)
InterPress Service
Los Angeles Times
McClatchy Newspapers
Middle East Online
National Post (Canada)
New York Times
The New Yorker
Platts Oilgram News
Rolling Stone
States News Service
The Sunday Times (London)
Times Higher Educational Supplement (London)
US Newswire
Vanity Fair
Washington Post
Washington Times (London)

Published and Unpublished Works

The 9/11 Commission Report: Final Report of the National Commission on Terrorist Attacks upon the United States (New York: W.W. Norton, 2004).

Acierto, Maria Guillen. "American Influence in Shaping Philippine Secondary Education: An Historical Perspective, 1898–1978" (EdD diss., Loyola University of Chicago, 1980).
Agresto, John. *Mugged by Reality: The Liberation of Iraq and the Failure of Good Intentions* (New York: Encounter Books, 2007).
Alfonso, Oscar M. "Taft's Early Views on the Filipinos." *Solidarity* 4 (June 1969), 52–58.
Allawi, Ali A. *The Occupation of Iraq: Winning the War, Losing the Peace* (New Haven: Yale University Press, 2008).
Alvi, Hayat. "A Progress Report on Women's Education in Post-Taliban Afghanistan." *International Journal of Lifelong Education* 27 (2008), 169–178.
Alvi-Azia, Hayat. "Reconstruction in Post-Taliban Afghanistan: Women and Education." *RFR/DRF* 30 (2003), 13–37.
Anderson, James. *Education of Blacks in the South, 1860–1935* (Chapel Hill: University of North Carolina Press).
Ayala, Cesar J., and Rafael Bernabe. *Puerto Rico in the American Century: A History since 1898* (Chapel Hill: UNC Press, 2007).
Balch, Emily Greene, ed. *Occupied Haiti* (rev. ed., New York: Negro Universities Press, 1969).
Barrows, David. "What May Be Expected from Philippine Education?" *Journal of Race Development* 1 (October 1910), 156–168.
Beede, Benjamin. *The War of 1898 and U.S. Interventions, 1898–1934: An Encyclopedia* (New York: Garland Press, 1994).
Bell, Ian. *The Dominican Republic* (Boulder: Westview Press, 1981).
Biebel, Charles D. "American Efforts for Educational Reform in Occupied Germany, 1945–1955—a Reassessment." *History of Education Quarterly* 22 (Fall 1982), 277–287.
Bilmes, Linda J., and Joseph E. Stiglitz. *The Three Trillion Dollar War: The True Cost of the Iraq Conflict* (New York: W.W. Norton, 2008).
Blood, Peter R., ed. *Afghanistan: A Country Study* (Washington: GPO for the Library of Congress, 2001).
Bradford, James C., ed. *Crucible of Empire: The Spanish American War and Its Aftermath* (Annapolis: Naval Institute Press, 1993).
Brands, H. W. *Bound to Empire: The United States and the Philippines* (New York: Oxford University Press, 1992).
Brook, John. *Annual Report of Major General John R. Brook* (Havana: n.p., 1899).
———. *Civil Report of Major General John R. Brooke, U. S. Army, Military Governor Island of Cuba* (Havana: n.p., 1899).
Brown, Valerie J. "Reconstructing the Environment in Iraq." *Environmental Health Perspectives* 112 (June 2004), A464.
Brummet, John. "DOD, State, and USAID Obligated $17.7 Billion to about 7000 Contractors and Other Entities for Afghanistan Reconstruction during Fiscal Years 2007–2009," Office of the Inspector General for Afghanistan Reconstruction, SIGAR Audit-11-4 Contractor Performance and Oversight (October 27, 2010), 1–45.
Calder, Bruce. *Impact of Intervention: The Dominican Republic during the U.S. Occupation of 1916–1924* (rev. ed., Princeton: Markus Wiener, 2006).
Carlton-Ford, Steven, and Morten G. Ender. *Handbook of War and Society: Iraq and Afghanistan* (New York: Routledge, 2011).
Carr, Raymond. *Puerto Rico: A Colonial Experiment* (New York: NYU Press, 1984).

Carter, Julian Savage. "Cultural Capital and African American Agency: The Economic Struggle for Effective Education for African Americans in Franklin, Tennessee, 1890–1967." *The Journal of African American History* 87 (2002), 206–235.

Chatterjee, Pratrap. *Iraq, Inc.: A Profitable Occupation* (New York: Seven Stories Press, 2004).

Clark, Victor S. *History of Manufactures in the United States* (New York: McGraw-Hill, 1929).

———. *Porto Rico and Its Problems* (New York: Arno Press, 1975).

———. *Teachers' Manual for the Public Schools of Puerto Rico* (New York: Silver, Durdett & Company, 1900).

———. *What is Money?* (Boston: Houghton Mifflin Company, 1934).

Clymer, Kenton J. "Humanitarian Imperialism: David Prescott Barrows and the White Man's Burden in the Philippines." *Pacific Historical Review* 49 (1980), 29–50.

Cockburn, Patrick. *The Occupation: War and Resistance in Iraq* (New York: Verso, 2007).

Coleccion de Ordenes de la Secretaria de Estado de Justicia e Instruccion Publica (Santo Domino: Imp. y Linotipo J.R. Vda Garcia, 1919).

Coletta, Paola E. "William Jennings Bryan and Currency and Banking Reform." *Nebraska History* 45 (1964), 31–57.

Davis, Craig. "'A' is for Allah, 'J' is for Jihad." *World Policy Journal* (Spring 2002), 90–94.

Davis, George W. *Report on Civil Affairs of Porto Rico, 1899* (Washington, DC: GPO, 1900).

De Montilla, Aida Negron. *Americanization in Puerto Rico and the Public School System, 1900–1930* (Barcelona: University of Puerto Rico, 1975).

De Santisteban, Agustin V. "Sanctions, War, Occupation and the De-Development of Education in Iraq." *International Review of Education* 51 (2005), 59–71.

Diamond, Larry. *Squandered Victory: The American Occupation and the Bungled Effort to Bring Democracy to Iraq* (New York: Times Books, 2005).

Dietz, James L. *Economic History of Puerto Rico: Institutional Change and Capitalist Development* (Princeton: Princeton University Press, 1986).

Diner, Steven J. A *Very Different Age: Americans of the Progressive Era* (New York: Hill and Wang, 1998).

Dobbin, James. *Occupying Iraq: A History of the Coalition Provisional Authority* (Santa Monica: Rand, 2009).

Ehrenberg, John, J. Patrice McSherry, Jose Ramon Sanchez, and Caroleen Marji Sayej, eds. *The Iraq Papers* (Oxford: Oxford University Press, 2010).

Eisenhower, Dwight D. "Farewell Address" (1961), http://www.eisenhower.archives.gov/all_about_ike/Speeches/Farewell_Address.pdf.

Epstein, Erwin H. "The Peril of Paternalism: The Imposition of Education on Cuba by the United States." *American Journal of Education* 96 (November 1987), 1–23.

Fakir, Sadmani Mohammad Golam, and Sakil Malik. "Literacy: A Path Out of Extremism in Afghanistan?" *Reading Today* (October/November 2007), 20.

Ferguson, Niall. *Colossus: The Price of America's Empire* (New York: Penguin, 2005).

Fitchen, Edward D. "Alexis E. Frye and Cuban Education, 1898–1902." *Revista Interamericana* 2 (1972), 123–149.

———. "Alexis Everett Frye and the Organization of Cuban Education, 1899–1901" (PhD diss., University of California, Santa Barbara, 1970).

———. "The Cuban Teachers and Harvard, 1900: A Unique Experiment in Inter-American Cultural Exchange." *Horizontes* 26 (1973), 61–71.

Fleming, Caroline B. "'Even in Dreams, They are Coming': Islamic Fundamentalism and the Education of Women in Afghanistan." *William and Mary Journal of Women and Law* 597 (Spring 2005), 597–617.

Foner, Philip S. *A History of Cuba and Its Relations with the United States* (2 vols, New York: International Publishers, 1963).

Frye, Alexis E. *Elements of Geography* (Boston: Ginn and Co, 1898).

Fuller, Stephen M., and Graham A Cosmas. *Marines in the Dominican Republic, 1916–1924* (Washington, DC: U.S. Marine Corps., 1973).

Gates, John Morgan. *Schoolbooks and Krags: The United States Army in the Philippines, 1898–1902* (Westport: Greenwood Press, 1973).

Gayden, Joyce M. "The Latin American Policy of Elihu Root, 1899–1909" (MA thesis, University of South Carolina, 1954).

Gendzier, Irene I. "Invisible by Design: U.S. Policy in the Middle East." *Diplomatic History* 26 (Fall 2002), 593–618.

Go, Julian. *American Empire and the Politics of Meaning: Elite Political Cultures in the Philippines and Puerto Rico during U.S. Colonialism* (Durham: Duke University Press, 2008).

Go, Julian, and Anne L. Foster, eds. *The American Colonial State in the Philippines: Global Perspectives* (Durham: Duke University Press, 2003).

Gordon, Joy. *Invisible War: The United States and the Iraq Sanctions* (Cambridge: Harvard University Press, 2010).

Gott, Richard. *Cuba: A New History* (New Haven: Yale University Press, 2004).

Guimbert, Stephanie, Keiko Miwa, and Duc Thanh Nguyen. "Back to School in Afghanistan: Detriments to School Enrollment." *International Journal of Educational Development* 28 (2008), 419–434.

Halliday, Dennis J. *The Impact of the UN Sanctions on the People of Iraq* (Berkeley: University of California Press, 1999).

Hamalainen, Pekka. *The Comanche Empire* (New Haven: Yale University Press, 2008).

Harris, William T. "An Educational Policy for Our New Possessions." *Educational Review* 18 (September 1899), 105–118.

Hartung, William D. "Eisenhower's Warning: The Military-Industrial Complex Forty Years Later." *World Policy Journal* (Spring 2001), 39–44.

Healy, David F. *Gunboat Diplomacy in the Wilson Era: The U.S. Navy in Haiti, 1915–1916* (Madison: University of Wisconsin Press, 1976).

———. *The United States in Cuba, 1898–1902: Generals, Politicians, and the Search for Policy* (Madison: University of Wisconsin Press, 1963).

Henry, David. *Taft, Holmes, and the 1920s Court: An Appraisal* (Madison: Fairleigh Dickinson University Press, 1998).

Herring, Eric. *Iraq in Fragments: The Occupation and Its Legacy* (Ithaca: Cornell University Press, 2006).

Hitchman, James H. *Leonard Wood and Cuban Independence, 1898–1902* (The Hague: Nijhoff, 1971).

Hughes, William H. *Robert Russa Moton of Hampton and Tuskegee* (Chapel Hill: University of North Carolina Press, 1956).

Hunt, Michael H. *The American Ascendancy: How the United States Gained and Wielded Global Dominance* (Chapel Hill: University of North Carolina Press, 2007).

Ismael, Jaqueline, Tareq Y. Ishmael, and Raymond William Baker. "Iraq and Human Development: Culture, Education, and the Globalization of Hope." *Arab Studies Quarterly* 26 (2004), 49–66.

Issa, Jinan H., and Hazri Jamil. "Overview of the Education System in Contemporary Iraq." *European Journal of Social Sciences* 14 (2010), 360–368.

Jamail, Dahr. *Beyond the Green Zone: Dispatches from an Unembedded Journalist in Occupied Iraq* (Chicago: Haymarket Books, 2007).

Kaestle, Carl. *Pillars of the Republic: Common Schools and American Society, 1780–1860* (New York: Hill and Wang, 1983).

Karnow, Stanley. *In Our Image: America's Empire in the Philippines* (New York: Ballantine Books, 1989).

Kellermann, Henry J. *Cultural Relations as an Instrument of U.S. Foreign Policy: The Educational Exchange Program between the United States and Germany, 1945–1954* (Washington: GPO, 1978).

Kinzer, Steven. *All the Shah's Men: An American Coup and the Roots of Middle East Terror* (Hoboken: Wiley, 2008).

———. *Overthrow: America's Century of Regime Change from Hawaii to Iraq* (New York: Times Books, 2006).

Knight, Melvin M. *The Americans in Santo Domingo* (New York: Vanguard Press, 1928).

Kramer, Hans Martin. "Reforms of their Own: The Japanese Resistance to Changes in Higher Education Administration under the U.S. American Occupation, 1945–1952." *Paedagogica Historica* 43 (June 2007), 327–345.

Kramer, Paul A. *The Blood of Government: Race, Empire, the United States & the Philippines* (Chapel Hill: University of North Carolina Press, 2006).

———. "Race-Making and Colonial Violence in the U.S. Empire: The Philippine-American War as Race War." *Diplomatic History* 30 (2006), 169–210.

Kull, Steven, Clay Ramsay, and Evan Lewis. "Misperceptions, the Media, and the Iraq War." PIPA/Knowledge Networks: The American Public on International Issues [University of Maryland] (October 2, 2003), 1–21, http://www.worldpublicopinion.org/pipa/pdf/oct03/IraqMedia_Oct03_rpt.pdf.

Kumano, Ruriko. "Anticommunism and Academic Freedom: Walter C. Eells and the 'Red Purge' in Occupied Japan." *History of Education Quarterly* 50 (November 2010), 513–537.

Maley, William. *The Afghanistan Wars* (New York: Palgrave, 2002).

Margold, Jane A. "Egalitarian Ideals and Exclusionary Practices: U.S. Pedagogy in the Colonial Philippines." *Journal of Historical Sociology* 8 (1995), 375–394.

Martin, Bernd. *Japan and Germany in the Modern World* (Oxford: Berghahn Books, 1995).

May, Glenn A. *Social Engineering in the Philippines: The Aims, Execution, and Impact of American Colonial Policy, 1900–1913* (Westport: Greenwood Press, 1980).

McCallum, Jack. *Leonard Wood: Rough Rider, Surgeon, Architect of American Imperialism* (New York: New York University Press, 2005).

McCoy, Alfred W., and Francisco A. Scarano, eds. *Colonial Crucible: Empire in the Making of the Modern American State* (Madison: University of Wisconsin Press, 2009).

McCrocklin, James. *Garde D' Haiti, 1915–1934: Twenty Years of Organization and Training by the United States Marine Corps* (Annapolis: United States Naval Institute, 1956).

Menand, Louis, *The Metaphysical Club: A Story of Ideas in America* (New York: Farrar, Straus and Giroux, 2002).

Miller, Stuart Creighton. *"Benevolent Assimilation": The American Conquest of the Philippines, 1899–1903* (New Haven: Yale University Press, 1982).

Millett, Richard, and G. Dale Gaddy. "Administering the Protectorates: The U.S. Occupation of Haiti and the Dominican Republic." *Revista Interamericana* 6 (1976), 383–402.

Milligan, Jeffrey Ayala. "Democratization or Neocolonialism? The Education of Muslims under U.S. Military Occupation, 1903–20." *History of Education* 33 (July 2004), 451–467.

Millspaugh, Arthur C. *Haiti under American Control, 1915–1930* (rev. ed., Westport: Negro University Press, 1970).

Moore, Ray A., and Donald L. Robinson. *Partners for Democracy: Crafting the New Japanese State Under MacArthur* (Oxford: Oxford University Press, 2002).

Mortenson, Greg, and David Oliver Relin. *Three Cups of Tea: One Man's Mission to Promote Peace... One School at a Time* (New York: Penguin, 2007).

Munro, Dana G. *Intervention and Dollar Diplomacy in the Caribbean, 1900–1921* (Princeton: Princeton University Press, 1964).

Nash, Fredrick W. "Education in the Philippines." *Educational Review* 22 (October 1901), 217–227.

Navarro, Jose-Manuel. *Creating Tropical Yankees: Social Science Textbooks and U.S. Ideological Control in Puerto Rico* (New York: Routledge, 2002).

Newton, Jim. "Ike's Speech," *The New Yorker* (December 20, 2010).

Nishi, Toshino. *Unconditional Democracy: Education and Politics in Occupied Japan, 1945–1952* (Stanford: Hoover Institution, 1982).

Nugent, Walter. *Habits of Empire: A History of American Expansion* (New York: Knopf, 2008).

Office of Inspector General. "Audit of USAID/Iraq's Basic Education Activities [Audit Report No. E-267–06–001-P]," USAID, Washington, DC (December 20, 2005), 1–22.

———. "Follow-up Audit of USAID/Iraq's Education Activities [Audit Report No. E-267–07–003-P]," USAID, Washington, DC (February 4, 2007), 1–11.

———, USAID. "USAID's Compliance with Federal Regulations in Awarding the Iraq Education Sector Contract," USAID, Washington DC (Memorandum, 03–001) (June 6, 2003).

Office of Procurement, USAID. "USAID Compliance with Federal Regulations in Awarding the Iraq Education Contract: IG Review No. EDG-C-00–03–00011–00," USAID, Washington, DC (June 23, 2003) Unnumbered Memorandum.

Offner, John. *An Unwanted War: The Diplomacy of the United States and Spain over Cuba, 1895–1898* (Chapel Hill: University of North Carolina Press, 1999).

Ostler, Jeffrey. *The Plains Sioux and U.S. Colonialism from Lewis and Clark to Wounded Knee* (New York: Cambridge University Press, 2004).

Osuna, Juan Jose. *A History of Education in Puerto Rico* (New York: Arno Press, 1975).

Oxfam International. "Free, Quality Education for Every Afghan Child," Oxfam Briefing Paper (November 2006), 1–32.

Packer, George. *Assassins' Gate: America in Iraq* (New York: Farrar, Straus, and Giroux, 2005).

Padover, Saul K. *Thomas Jefferson on Democracy* (New York: Appleton-Century Company, 1939).

Pamphile, Leon D. *Clash of Cultures: America's Educational Strategies in Occupied Haiti, 1915–1934* (Lanham: University Press of America, 2008).

Parenti, Christian. "Fables of Reconstruction," *The Nation* (August 30/September 6, 2004), 16–19.

Paulet, Anne. "To Change the World: The Use of American Indian Education in the Philippines." *History of Education Quarterly* 47 (May 2007), 173–202.

Paulus, Stefan. "The Americanisation of Europe after 1945?: The Case of the German Universities." *European Review of History* 9 (2002), 241–253.

Perez, Jr., Louis A. *Cuba: Between Reform and Revolution* (New York: Oxford University Press, 2006).
———. *The War of 1898: The United States and Cuba in History and Historiography* (Chapel Hill: UNC Press, 1998).
Plummer, Brenda Gayle. *Haiti and the Great Powers, 1902–1915* (Baton Rouge: Louisiana State University Press, 1988).
Pons, Frank Moya. *The Dominican Republic: A National History* (rev. ed., Princeton: Markus Wiener Publishers, 2010).
Prados, John. *Hoodwinked: The Documents that Reveal How Bush Sold Us a War* (New York: The New Press, 2004).
Pratt, Julius. *Expansionist of 1898: The Acquisition of Hawaii and the Spanish Islands* (Gloucester, MA: Peter Smith Co., 1959).
Pringle, Henry F. *The Life and Times of William Howard Taft* (2 vols, Hamden: n.p., 1939).
Puaca, Brian. *Learning Democracy: Education Reform in West Germany, 1945–1965* (New York: Berghahn Books, 2009).
Quarterly Reports of the Military Government of Santo Domingo, National Archives.
Rabe, Stephen G. *Eisenhower and Latin America: The Foreign Policy of Anticommunism* (Chapel Hill: University of North Carolina Press, 1988).
Raftery, Judith. "Textbook Wars: Governor-General James Francis Smith and the Protestant-Catholic Conflict in Public Education in the Philippines, 1904–1907." *History of Education Quarterly* 38 (Summer 1998), 143–164.
Rashid, Ahmed. *Taliban: Militant Islam, Oil and Fundamentalism in Central Asia* (New Haven: Yale University Press, 2000).
Records of the Military Government of Cuba, National Archives, Washington, DC.
Renda, Mary A. *Taking Haiti: Military Occupation and the Culture of U.S. Imperialism* (Chapel Hill: University of North Carolina Press, 2001).
Report of the United States Education Mission to Germany (Washington: GPO, 1946).
Report of the United States Insular Commission to the Secretary of War upon Investigations Made into the Civil Affairs of the Island of Porto Rico, with Recommendations (Washington, DC: GPO, 1899).
Reports of the Military Government of Santo Domingo, Record Group 59, Decimal File 839, National Archives, Washington, DC.
Rieckhoff, Paul. *Chasing Ghosts: Failures and Facades in Iraq: A Soldier's Perspective* (New York: NAL Caliber, 2007).
Rodriguez-Fraticelli, Carlos. "Education, Politics, and Imperialism: The Reorganization of the Cuban Public Elementary School System during the First American Occupation, 1899–1902" (PhD diss., University of California, San Diego, 1984).
Roy, Delwin A. "The Educational System of Iraq." *Middle Eastern Studies* 29 (1993), 167–197.
Rust, Val. "The German Image of American Education through the Weimar Period." *Paedagogica Historica* 33 (1997), 25–44.
Saltman, Kenneth J. "Corporate Education and 'Democracy Promotion Overseas: The Case of Creative Associates International in Iraq, 2003–4," in *American Post-Conflict Educational Reform: From the Spanish-American War to Iraq*, ed. Noah Sobe (New York: Palgrave, 2009), 229–249.
———. "Creative Associates International: Corporate Education and 'Democracy Promotion' in Iraq." *The Review of Education, Pedagogy, and Cultural Studies* 28 (2006), 25–65.
Schirmer, Daniel. *Republic or Empire: American Resistance to the Philippines War* (Cambridge: Schenkman Publishing Co., 1972).

Schmidt, Hans. *Maverick Marine: General Smedley D. Butler and the Contradictions of American Military History* (Lexington: University Press of Kentucky, 1998).

———. *The United States Occupation of Haiti, 1915–1934* (rev. ed., New Brunswick: Rutgers University Press, 1995).

Schwartz, Michael. *War without End: The Iraq War in Context* (Chicago: Haymarket Books, 2008).

Shannon, Magdaline W. *Jean Price-Mars, the Haitian Elite and the American Occupation, 1915–1935* (New York: St. Martin's Press, 1996).

Shibata, Masako. *Japan and Germany under the U.S. Occupation: A Comparative Analysis of the Post-War Education Reform* (Lanham: Lexington Books, 2005).

Shirazi, Roozbeh. "Islamic Education in Afghanistan: Revisiting the United States' Role." *CR: The New Centennial Review* 8 (2008), 211–233.

Shulimson, Jack. "Daniel Pratt Mannix and the Establishment of the Marine Corps School of Application, 1889–1894." *The Journal of Military History* 55 (October 1991), 469–486.

Simon, Matthew. "The Hot Money Movement and the Private Exchange Pool Proposal of 1896." *Journal of Economic History* 20 (1960), 31–50.

Smith, Peter C. "Crisis Mortality in the Nineteenth Century Philippines: Data from Parish Records." *The Journal of Asian Studies* 38 (November 1978), 51–76.

Snowden, Thomas. *Santo Domingo, Its Past and Its Present* (Santo Domingo City: n.p., 1920).

Sobe, Noah W. ed., *American Post-Conflict Educational Reform: From the Spanish-American War to Iraq* (New York: Palgrave, 2009),

Spector, Robert M. *W. Cameron Forbes and the Hoover Commissions to Haiti (1930)* (Lanham: University Press of America, 1985).

Stranger, Allison. *One Nation Under Contract: The Outsourcing of American Power and the Future of Foreign Policy* (New Haven: Yale University Press, 2009).

Sullivan, Michael J. *American Adventurism Abroad: Invasions, Interventions, and Regime Changes since World War II* (Hoboken: Wiley-Blackwell, 2007).

Takemae, Eiji. *The Allied Occupation of Japan* (New York: Continuum, 2002).

Tappan, Sheryl. *Shock and Awe in Fort Worth: How the U.S. Army Rigged the "Free and Open Competition" to Replace Halliburton's Sole Source Oil Field in Iraq* (San Mateo CA: Pourquoi Press, 2004).

Taylor, John W. "Youth Welfare in Germany: A Study of Governmental Action Relative to Care of the Normal German Youth" (PhD diss., Columbia University, 1936).

Tent, James. *Mission on the Rhine: Reeducation and Denazification in American Occupied Germany* (Chicago: University of Chicago Press, 1982).

Thomas, Evan. *The War Lovers: Roosevelt, Lodge, Hearst, and the Rush to Empire, 1898* (New York: Little, Brown and Company, 2010).

Tillich, Paul. *The Protestant Era* (Chicago: University of Chicago Press, 1948).

———. *The Religious Situation* (New York: Henry Holt, 1932).

Trainor, Joseph. *Educational Reform in Occupied Japan: Trainor's Memoir* (Tokyo: Meiji University Press, 1983).

Tsuchimochi, Gary Hoichi. *Educational Reform in Postwar Japan: The 1946 U.S. Education Mission* (Tokyo: University of Tokyo Press, 1993).

Turner, Kara Miles. "'Getting It Straight': Southern Black School Patrons and the Struggle for Equal Education in the Pre- and Post-Civil Rights Eras." *The Journal of Negro Education* 72 (Spring 2003), 217–229.

Turtis, Richard Lee. *Foundations of Despotism: Peasants, the Trujillo Regime, and Modernity in Dominican History* (Stanford: Stanford University Press, 2003).

United States. *Congressional Record.*
USAID. "Creative Associates." Award/Contract No. EDG-C-00-03-00011-00 [signed April 11, 2003], (March, 26, 2003), Sections A1-I19.
USAID Office of Inspector General. "Audit of USAID/Afghanistan's School and Health Clinic Reconstruction Activities." Audit Report No. 5-306-06-008-P (August 18, 2006), 1-16.
Vernon, John A. "Racial Gamesmanship and the U.S. Occupation of Haiti: An Illustrative Episode." *Alabama Historical Quarterly* 40 (1978), 144-161.
Wagoner, Jennings. *Thomas Jefferson and Education* (Chapel Hill: University of North Carolina Press, 2005).
Watenpaugh, Keith. "'Opening the Doors' One Year Later: Reflections on the Iraq War and the Middle East Studies Community." *Middle East Studies Association Bulletin* (June 2004), 16-23.
Watenpaugh, Keith, Edouard Méténierm, Jens Hanssen, and Hala Fattah. "Opening the Doors: Intellectual Life and Academic Conditions in Post-War Baghdad: A Report of the Iraqi Observatory" (Unpublished Report, July 15, 2003), 1-29.
Wegner, Gregory P. "Germany's Past Contested: The Soviet-American Conflict in Berlin over History Curriculum Reform, 1945-1948." *History of Education Quarterly* 30 (Spring 1990), 1-16.
Welles, Sumner. *Naboth's Vineyard: The Dominican Republic, 1844-1924* (2 vols, New York: Payson and Clarke, 1928).
Westbrook, Robert. *John Dewey and American Democracy* (Ithaca: Cornell University Press, 1991).
Whiten, Jon. "If News From Iraq Is Bad, It's Coming From U.S. Officials." Fairness & Accuracy in Reporting, http://www.fair.org/index.php?page=1167.
Wiarda, Howard J. *The Dominican Republic: Nation in Transition* (New York: Praeger 1969).
Williams, Kayla. *Love My Rifle More than You: Young and Female in the U.S. Army* (New York: W.W. Norton, 2006).
Willinsky, John. *Learning to Divide the World: Education at Empire's End* (Minneapolis: University of Minnesota Press, 1998).
Wolfe, Robert, ed., *Americans as Proconsuls: United States Military Government in Germany and Japan, 1944-1952* (Carbondale: Southern Illinois University Press, 1984).
Wooster, Robert. *Nelson A. Miles and the Twilight of the Frontier Army* (Lincoln: University of Nebraska Press, 1993).
World Bank. *Afghanistan: National Reconstruction and Poverty Reduction* (Washington, DC: Macro Graphics, March 2005).
Yaqub, Salim. *Containing Arab Nationalism: The Eisenhower Doctrine and the Middle East* (Chapel Hill: University of North Carolina Press, 2004).
Zimmerman, Jonathan. *Innocents Abroad: American Teachers in the American Century* (Cambridge: Harvard University Press, 2006).
Zimmerman, Warren. *First Great Triumph: How Five Americans Made their Country a World Power* (New York: Farrar, Straus, and Giroux, 2002).
Zink, Harold. *The United States in Germany: 1944-1955* (Westport: Greenwood Press, 1957).
Zook, George F. *Japan and Germany: Problems in Reeducation* (New York: Carnegie Endowment for International Peace, 1947).

Index

Aachen, Germany, 99
Abitur, 101
Academy of Drawing, Painting, and Sculpture of Santo Domingo, 81
Adams, John, 40
Afghanistan, xiv, 112–24, 138–9
  Afghan Socialist Constitution, 115
  Afghanistan Defense University, 122
  Al-Qaeda and Osama bin Laden in, 113
  Balkh Education Department, 121
  Constitution of 1964, 114
  economic interests in, 115–24
  home-based education; 117
  Islamic traditions, 115–16
  Kabul, 115–16, 121–3
  Kabul University, 115–16, 122
  loya jirga, 114, 118
  Ministry of Education, 114, 118, 120
  national army, 117
  National Military Academy of Afghanistan, 122
  Northern Alliance, 113–14
  Soviet Union in, 112, 115–16
  Taliban in, 113–14, 116–17, 120, 122–3
  tents as schools in, 121–2
  U.S. Agency for International Development and, 115, 118–19, 121
  U.S. covert war in, 112, 115–16
  U.S. Universities and, 114–15, 121–2
  women's organizations in, 114–15
Afghanistan Defense University, 122
Agresto, John, 133–4
Al al-Bayt University, 128
Alabama, 65, 140
Alexander, Richard Thomas, 109
Allaq, Majeed, 135
Al-Qaeda, 113, 125, 139
American Cargo Transport, 136
American Colonial Bank, 49
American Educational Association, 6
American expansionism, xiii–xv, 3–4, 14, 16, 33
American Islamic Congress, 129
American Patriotic League, 16
American Sugar Refining Company, 29
American University, 129
American University of Afghanistan, 121
American University of Iraq—Sulaimani, 134
Amman, Jordan, 130
"An Education Policy for Our New Possessions" (Harris), 6
annexation, 2–4, 14, 38, 40–4
anti-Americanism, 68, 105
anti-Communism, 97, 99, 112, 115–16, 137–8
Arias, Desiderio, 68
Asia, xiii, xvi, 19–32, 86, 87–98, 106, 118–20, 125, 129, 138
Asian Development Bank, 120
Atkinson, Fred, 21–5, 31
audits, 119, 127, 130, 135
Azerbaijan, 120

Ba'ath Party of Iraq, 128, 132, 133
Baden-Württemberg, 101, 110–11
Badi system, 116
Baghdad, Iraq, 128–9, 132
Bahrami, Gulalai, 122
Bainter, Edward, 43–5
Bank of Nova Scotia, 49

banking industry, xiii, 48–9, 51–3, 60–1, 67–8, 78, 82, 85, 116, 120, 128–9, 138, 140; *see also* finance industry
Banque Nationale, 51–2
Barahona Company, 79
Barrows, David, 24–7, 31, 138
Bauerle, Theodor, 111
Bavaria, 101–3, 107–10
Bechtel corporation, 129, 135
Bell Telephone Company, 20, 62
Bennet, William, 134
Berlin, Germany, 100, 102, 111–12
bin Laden, Osama, 113
"big stick" policy, xv
Black Ships, 87
Bobadilla, Alfredo A. Nouel, 70
Boeing company, 136, 139
Borno, Louis, 59–63, 66
Boston, MA, 13, 21
Bouchereau, Charles, 60–1
Bremen, Germany, 110
Bremer, L. Paul, 126, 128, 132, 135–6
Brink, Gilbert, 26
Brooke, John, 4–7
Brown Brothers bank, 140
Brumbaugh, Martin, 39–42
Bryan, William Jennings, 51–2
Brzezinski, Zbigniew, 116
Bunker Hill, MA, 13
Burma, 118
burqas, 116
Bush, George W., 113–14, 117, 125–6, 128, 134
Bush, Laura, 117, 121–3
Butler, Smedley, 140–1
Byrd, Robert, 126

cadets, 117, 122
California, 6, 25
Cambodia, 118
Cambridge, MA, 11–13
Canada, 49, 133
Caperton, William, 68
Cap-Hatien, Haiti, 61
Capone, Al, 140
Caribbean, xiii–xiv, 32–3, 49, 52; *see also* Cuba; Dominican Republic; Haiti; Puerto Rico

Carroll, Henry, 37–40, 47
Caspian Sea, 123
Catholicism, 19, 107
caudillo, 73
Cayes, Haiti, 62
Central Aguirre Corporation, 48
Central America, xv, 118, 137, 140
Central Asian Republics, 120
Central Intelligence Agency (CIA), xv, 137
Cheney, Lynne, 134
Chile, xv
China, 19–20, 97, 120, 129
Citigroup, 67
Civil War, U.S., xiv
"civilizing" mission, 6, 16, 19, 26, 31, 54, 114, 133
Clark, Victor Selden, 36–9
Clay, Lucius, 106
Cleveland, Grover, 3
Cold War, 97–8, 111–12, 115–16
Colombia, xv
Columbia International Institute, 105
Columbia University, 29, 36, 102, 105, 109, 114, 124
  Teachers College, Columbia University (TCCU), 114, 124
Columbian Law School (now George Washington University), 71
communism, 96–7, 99, 137–8
compulsory education, xvi, 5, 9, 16, 21–3, 34–6, 40–4, 72–5, 78, 91, 112, 115
Conant, Ernest L., 11
Concord, MA, 13
Confucianism, 90
Contra rebels, 127
contracts, 77, 118, 123, 127–8, 131, 135–6
  no-bid, 127
  production-sharing agreements, 135
Cooperative Housing Foundation International, 119
Corrigan, Truax V., 20
Cotton, Joseph, 63
courses of study, 21, 76
  agricultural education, xiv, 5, 21–2, 24–5, 41, 44, 54–65, 76, 118
  civics, xiv, 9, 16, 25, 56, 76, 90–1, 111
  classical education, 55–9, 101
  curricula, 11, 23, 75–6

English language instruction, 6, 9,
13–16, 21–3, 28, 35–45, 74–5, 91,
121–2, 131
industrial education, xiv, 16, 24–5,
27–9, 31, 41–2, 54–6, 63, 76
liberal arts, xiv, 70, 114, 134
manual education, 16, 24, 28, 44, 56, 76
professional studies, 61, 70–1, 76, 81–3,
104, 131
teacher training, 5–7, 9–12, 15–16,
22–3, 25, 34, 41, 45, 61, 64, 71, 75–7,
81, 93, 105, 109, 114, 120, 131
technical education, xiv, 55–65, 95,
104–5, 121
trade studies, xiv, 21–2, 24–7, 54, 62
traditional education, 54–8, 111, 122
vocational education, 24, 28–9, 55–6,
58, 75–7, 101, 106–7, 120
covert war, 115–16
Creative Associates International (CAI),
126–31
crony capitalism, xvi, 3, 15, 21, 25–31,
47–9, 54–5, 65, 116, 123, 127, 135
Cuba, xiii, xvi–xvii, 1–17, 19, 32, 74, 138,
140
Board of Superintendents, 11, 15
City School Program, 16
Department of Justice and Public
Instruction, 4
economic interest in, 3–4, 6, 16–17
Harvard Summer School and, 11–14
Platt Amendment and, 14–16
Office of Superintendent, 14
Teller Amendment and, 4, 8, 14, 16
Ten Years War, 3
U.S. universities and, 12–13, 15–16
Cumberland, W. W., 65
currency, 24, 118

Damien, Haiti, 60–1
Dari, 120
Davies, Glyn, 116
Davila, Miguel, xv
de la Torre, Carlos, 7
de Messina, Gelix, 34
Democratic Organization of Afghan
Women, 115
democratship, 127

de-Ba'athification, *see* Iraq
denazification, *see* Germany
Dewey, John, xv, 139
Dexter, Edwin, 43–4
Diaz, Arturo, 9
dictatorships, 66, 71, 116, 127, 137
Doblin, Alfred, 104
Dolan, John, 134
dollar diplomacy, xv
Dominican Republic, xvi, 67–86,
138, 140
Dominican Congress, dissolved, 68–9
Dominican Tariff Commission of
1919, 79
Dominican Treaty of 1907, 67–8
economic interests in, 67–8, 78–86
education laws during the U.S.
occupation of, 69–70, 72–80, 83
executive orders, 69, 71, 76–7, 81
Executive Power (poder ejecutivo), 76–8
National Education Council (Consejo
Nacionale de Educacion), 76–7
Patent Law (*Ley de Patentes*), 81–2, 85–6
Popular Societies (Sociedad Populares de
Educacion), 83–6
Property Tax of 1919, 79–82, 84–6
"U.S. Occupation Proclamation of 1916"
(Caperton), 85
U.S. universities and, 71, 79
DuBois, W.E.B., xiv, 139

Ecole Centrale d'Agriculture, 56, 61
Economic Cooperation Organization, 120
Edwards, J. H., 80
Eells, Walter C., 94–8
Eisenhower, Dwight D., 137–41
Electrical Utility Workers Union of Iraq,
135–6
Elements of Geography (Frye), 8
Eliot, Charles W., 6–8, 11–13, 16, 21
embargo, 128
energy industry, 116, 123, 126–8, 134–6
Erdmann, Andrew N. P., 131–4
Escuela Moderna (newspaper), 7, 9–10
Europe, xiii, xiv, xvi, 2–4, 19, 33–5, 37,
52, 58–9, 86, 98–9, 116, 118–20,
123, 125, 129, 132–3, 138;
see also under specific countries

factory model, xv–xvi, 42
faculty, 29, 39, 41–5, 61, 76, 79, 93–8, 104–6, 109, 120–4, 132–5
Fairchild, Fred R., 79
Fajardo Corporation, 48
Falkner, Roland, 39, 42–3
Farnham, Roger L., 51–4, 58, 62
"Farewell Address" (Eisenhower), 137–41
Federation of Oil Employees of Iraq, 135–6
Fillmore, Millard, 87
finance industry, xiii, 3, 15, 25–6, 30, 47–9, 51–6, 59–62, 65, 67–8, 78–9, 82–5, 116, 120, 128–9, 137–41
Fish, Hamilton, 66
Fishman, Paul J., 119
Florida, 113
Foraker Act of 1900, 35, 48
Forbes, W. Cameron, 20, 26–9, 31, 62–5, 138
Fourth of July, 36, 44
France, xiv, 58, 100, 111, 133
Freeman, George F., 55–6, 58–61, 64
free-market capitalism, xiii, xvi, 3, 15, 20–1, 25–31, 47–9, 53–5, 65, 87, 95, 98, 111, 127, 135–6, 138, 141
French colonialism, xiv, 51, 56, 58
Freud, Sigmund, 2
Frier, Julio Ortega, 71, 74, 77
Frye, Alexis Everett, 1–2, 6–16, 138
Fuller, B. H., 69

gangsterism, 134
Garner, Jay, 125–6
General Dynamics corporation, 139
General Electric company, 135–6
George Washington University, *see* Columbian Law School
Germany, xvi, 52, 98–112, 120, 125, 132, 138
  Berlin School Law, 111–12
  denazification in, 100, 102–6, 109–11, 132
  economic interests in, 99–100, 108, 111–12
  General Advisory Committee, 102, 104–7
  German Unified School, 110
  Ministry of Education, 110
  Morgenthau Plan, 100
  National Socialism, 109
  Nazism, 101–5, 109
  Public Health and Welfare Division, 101
  U.S. universities and, 102, 105, 109
  Zook Report on, 106–7
Ghani, Ashraf, 122
Graham, Lindsay, 123
Grant, Ulysses S., 40
Great Britain, xiv, 59, 100, 107, 111–12, 128–9
Great White Fleet, xiv
Greater Hesse, 101, 103, 110
Guatemala, xv, 137
gunboat diplomacy, xv
Guy, Henry V., 35–9, 47
Gymnasium, 101

Haiti, xi, xvi, 51–67, 74, 76, 86, 127, 138, 140
  Bureau of Technical Service of Agriculture and Vocational Education (Service Technique), 55–61, 64–5
  classical education, 58–9
  Commission on Education, 63–6
  Department of Agriculture, 55–6, 64
  Haitian Congress, dissolved, 53–4
  economic interests in, 51–6, 59, 65–6
  Forbes Commission, 62–6
  Haitian Gendarmerie, 66
  Haitian League of the Rights of Man, 60–1
  Hoover Commission, 62–6
  Lyceum, 58
  Ministry of Education, 55, 58
  Moton Commission, 62–6
  National Railway of Haiti, 51
  National School System, 55–60
  U.S. universities and, 55, 63
Halliburton company, 135
Hampton Institute, 24, 41, 63
Hanna, Matthew, 11, 14–16
Harding, Warren, 53
Harris, William T., 5–6
Harrison, William Henry, 3
Harvard University, 1–2, 6, 10–16, 21, 55, 131
Havana, Cuba, 3–5, 15
Hirohito, 88–9
Honduras, 140

Hong Kong, 24
Hoover Commission, 62–6
Huddleston, George, 65–6, 140–1
Hundhammer, Alois, 107–9, 111
Hussein, Saddam, 125–6, 128, 136, 139
Huyke, Juan B., 47

Illinois, 6, 43
immigration, xiv, xvi, 102, 104, 119, 124
Imperial University, 92–3
India, 123
instruction, *see* pedagogy
insurgency, 21, 60–2, 112, 121, 127
International Organization for Migration (Switzerland), 119
International School of Kabul, 121
Iran, xv, 118, 120, 137
Iraq, xvi–xvii, 125–36, 138–9
  Bush, G.W. and, 125–6, 128, 134
  Coalition Provisional Authority (CPA), 126, 130–6
  Creative Associates International, Inc. in, 126–31
  de-Ba'athification, 132–3
  economic interests in, 126–30, 134–6
  Kurdish-controlled region of, 134
  Ministry of Education, 129–31
  Ministry of Higher Education and Research, 131–3
  National Museum of Iraq, 126
  National Security Directive (U.S.) and, 126
  Office of Reconstruction and Humanitarian Assistance (ORHA), 125–6
  Order No. 12, 135
  Order No. 39, 135
  Parent-Teacher Associations, 129
  Revitalization of Iraqi schools and Stabilization of Education (RISE), 128–9
  Saddam Hussein's Law, 150, 136
  transitional government, 126, 134
  Teacher's Union, 136
  university governance, dissolution of, 132
  U.S. Agency for International Development and, 127–9
  U.S. universities and, 129, 133–4

Iraq Observatory, 133
Islamic fundamentalism, 115–16, 125

Jack Frost, 23
Jacmel, Haiti, 61
Japan, xvi, 24, 87–98, 106, 119, 125, 138
  Association of Technical Colleges, 95
  Civil Liberties Directive (1945), 96
  economic interests in, 87, 98, 138
  Eells Typhoon, 94
  Governing Boards, 94–5
  Japanese Communist Party (JCP), 96–7
  Japanese Educational Reform Committee (JERC), 89, 94–5
  Japanese Ministry of Education (JME), 89, 92, 94–6
  Japanese University Accreditation Association, 95
  language instruction in, 91
  MacArthur and, 87–90, 98
  "Outline of Proposed Law Governing Universities" (Eells), 94–7
  religion in, 88–90
  School Board Act of 1948, 92–4
  Sonno-Joi, 88
  U.S. Education Mission to, 92, 98
  U.S. universities and, 88, 94–5
Jefferson, Thomas, xiv, 40, 139
Jim Crow, 63–4
Jimenez, Isidro, 68
Jones Act of 1917, 35, 46–7
Jose De Diego Society, 46

Kabul University, 115–16, 122
Karzai, Hamid, 117, 123
Kazakhstan, 118
Kidham, Nidhal, 131
Kipling, Rudyard, 73
Knapp, Harry, 68–79
Kommandatura, 111
Korea, 97
Koto Gakko, 92
Kotschnig, Walter, 105
Kruvant, Maria Charito, 127
Kuhn, Loeb, and Company, 67
Kyoiku Chokugo, 91

La Democracia (newspaper), 44
La Discusion (newspaper), 8, 15
La Educacion Moderna (newspaper), 43
La Lucha (newspaper), 7–8
La Vega, Dominican Republic, 81
labor, xv–xvii, 6, 16, 20–1, 25, 33, 48, 53, 56, 62, 65, 72–3, 82, 96, 113, 135–6
Lane, Rufus, 71–2, 77, 80
Lanuza, Jose Antonio Gonzales, 4–5, 7
Latin America, 51, 127, *see also under specific countries*
Lee, Harry, 69, 82
Lexington, MA, 13
Liberia, 118
Lieberman, Joseph, 127
Lincoln, Abraham, 23, 40
Lindsay, Samuel McCune, 39, 41–2
literacy, 26, 37–8, 48, 54, 69–71, 115–16, 121, 128–9
loans, 25, 49, 51–2, 59, 65, 67, 78, 82–5; *see also* finance industry
Lockheed-Martin corporation, 139
Lodge, Henry Cabot, xiii–xv, 3, 33, 138
Long, John D., 33
Longfellow, Henry Wadsworth, 40
Loomis, Arthur, 95
Louis Berger Group, 118–19
loya jirga, 114, 118
Ludlow, William, 5

MacArthur, Douglas, 87–90, 98
madrassas, 116
Madrid, Spain, 3
Maersk and Stevedoring of America, 136
Manila, Philippines, 25, 33
Mann, Horace, 40, 58
Marshall, George, 125
Marxism, 111
Massachusetts, xiii, 3, 6, 21, 23, 58
McHarg, J.W., 1
McKinley, William, xiv, 3, 5, 14, 19, 23, 31, 37, 39–40
McKinley's Tariff of 1890, 3
Meiji Era, 87, 90
meritocracy, 88
Middle East, 117, 124, 126, 131, 133–4, 137, *see under specific countries*

Miles, Nelson A., 33–5
Miller, Paul, 43, 45–7
Moca, Dominican Republic, 81
Monroe, Paul, 28–9
Monte Cristy, Dominican Republic, 81
Moore, Blaine F., 23
Morgenthau, Henry, 100
Mortenson, Greg, 123–4
Moton, Robert, 62–5
mujahedeen, 115–16

Nang, Asef, 120
National City Bank of New York (later Citigroup), 49, 51–2, 67, 140
National Endowment for the Humanities, 134
National Military Academy of Afghanistan, 122
nationalism, 2, 12, 68, 81, 90, 101, 105
nationalization, 30, 134, 136
Netherlands, the, 126
New England, xiv, 3
New Jersey, 48, 118
New Platz Normal School, 15
New York, NY, 49, 51–2, 59, 66–7, 78–9
New York Tampa Cigar Company, 48
Nicaragua, xv, 118, 140
Nigeria, 118, 125
Niigata University, 97–8
Northern Alliance of Afghanistan, 113–14
Northrop Grumman corporation, 139
Norway, 118
Nouvelliste (newspaper), 59

Ohio State University, 71, 74
oil industry, 126–8, 134–6; *see also* energy industry
"Open Door" policies, 3
overaccumulation of wealth, xiii, 47

Pacific, xiv, xvii, 19–20, 33, 74
pacification, 2–4, 21, 83
Pakistan, 120
Panama, xv
Parker, Francis W., 6
Pashto, 120
patriotism, 16, 39, 42, 46
Paulman, Christian, 110

INDEX / 185

pedagogy, xvii, 9–10, 16, 23, 35–8, 41–6, 54–6, 58–9, 70, 74–6, 91–4, 121, 131
Penhan, Mohammad Zaher, 121
Perry, Matthew, 87–8
Philadelphia, PA, 14, 42
Philippines, xiii, xvi, 4, 6, 19–33, 62, 74, 86, 88, 118, 138
   Act 74, 22
   American teachers in, 22–4
   Department of Public Instruction, 21
   economic interests in, 19–20, 23, 27, 29–31
   Forbes, W. Cameron, and, 20, 26–9, 31
   Monroe Commission, 28–9
   Philippine Assembly, 30
   Philippine Commission, 26–7, 31
   U.S. universities and, 21, 25
   Washington, Booker T., and, 24
Platt Amendment, 14–16
Polk, James, 3
Porto Rican-American Tobacco Company of New Jersey, 48
Port-au-Prince, Haiti, 51, 60
Powell, Colin, 125, 131
Price, Hannibal, 61
privatization, 29–30, 51, 75, 112, 121–3, 126–8, 130, 135, 138
progressivism, xvi–xvii
property tax, 79–81
Psychological Operations, 140
public-private partnerships, 130
Puerto Plata, Dominican Republic, 81
Puerto Rico, xiii, xvi, 4, 33–49, 74, 86, 138
   Carroll Commission, 37–40, 47
   Department of Education, 43–5
   economic interests in, 33–7, 47–9
   education laws during the U.S. occupation of, 36, 44
   Falkner Policy, 42–4
   Foraker Act of 1900, 35, 48
   House of Delegates, 44–6
   Jones Act of 1917, 35, 46–7
   Porto Rico Commission, 37–8, 40, 47
   Puerto Rican Teacher's Association, 44–5
   Roosevelt, Theodore, and, 33–4
   U.S. universities and, 36, 39, 41–3, 45
Pullman Strike Riots of 1894, 33

Quezon, Manuel, 30–1

railroads, 20–1, 30, 51, 54, 62, 96
Raytheon Company, 139
Reagan, Ronald, 127, 134
Red Purge, 94–8
Research Triangle Institute, 129
Revolutionary Association of the Women of Afghanistan (RAWA), 114
Robison, Samuel, 69, 82
Roosevelt, Franklin Delano, 52–3, 99
Roosevelt, Kermit, 137
Roosevelt, Theodore, xv, 33–4, 137
Root, Elihu, 6–7, 13–15, 30
Royal Bank of Canada, 49
Rumsfeld, Donald, 125
Russell, John H., 53–62, 64, 66
Russell, William, 68, 80
Russia, *see* Soviet Union

Sam, Vilbrun Guillame, 52, 60
Samana, Dominican Republic, 84
San Domingo Improvement Company, 67–8
San Francisco de Macoris, Dominican Republic, 81
San Juan, Puerto Rico, 34, 42–4, 46
San Juan Central High School, 44, 46
Sandinista National Liberation Front, 127
Santa Fe, New Mexico, 134
Santiago, Cuba, 5
Santiago, Dominican Republic, 70–1, 82
Santo Domingo, Dominican Republic, 70–1, 76–8, 80–2
Santo Domingo: Its Past and Its Present Condition (Snowden), 85
Saudi Arabia, 116
Schramm, Franz, 110
September 11, 2001, attacks, 113, 122
Seybo, Dominican Republic, 84
Shepherd, Margaret Jo, 124
Shigeru, Nanbara, 94
Shuster, W. Morgan, 26
Sitting Bull, 33
Smith, James, 26
Smith College, 105
Snowden, Thomas, 69, 73, 78–83, 85
South Porto Rico Corporation, 48

Soviet Union, 97, 99–100, 111–12, 115–16
Spain, xiii, 2–4, 19, 33–5, 37, 138
Springfield, MA, 21
St. Johns College, 134
St. Louis Exposition of 1904, 42
St. Marc, Haiti, 61
Stanford University, 94, 105
Star Spangled Banner, 44
Stein, Erwin, 110
Sugar Association of Santo Domingo, 80
sugar industry, 3, 27, 29, 48, 56, 79–81, 140
Supreme Commander for the Allied Powers, 87–90, 98
Sweden, 118, 120
Swedish Committee for Afghanistan, 120
Synchronized Predeployment Operational Tracker (SPOT), 119

Taft, William H., xiii, xv, 20–2, 24, 31
Taliban, 113–14, 116–17, 120–3
Tappan, Sheryl, 135
tariffs, 3, 29–30, 48–9, 79–82, 85–7
taxes, xv–xvi, 10–12, 20, 27, 35, 37, 51–2, 68, 71, 79–86, 127
Taylor, John, 102–9
Teller Amendment (1898), 4, 8, 14–16
Tenno (Emperor), 88–91
Texas Agricultural Experiment Station, 55
textbooks, 5–9, 21–4, 34–6, 40–2, 59, 74, 90–2, 105–6, 108, 115–16, 120, 124, 128–9
Thanksgiving, 36
Thomasites, 23, 74
Three Cups of Tea (Mortenson), 123–4
Tillich, Paul, 104
tobacco industry, 27, 48, 82
Todd, Albert, 21
Tokyo, Japan, 94–6, 98, 120
Tokyo Technical University, 95
Tokyo University, 94–5, 98
trade, xiv, 3, 20, 26, 31, 54, 79, 80, 98, 122, 138
Trainor, Joseph, 92
Trans-Afghanistan Pipeline, 123
Treaty of Amity and Commerce (1858), 87
Treaty of Kanagawa (1854), 87
Trujillo, Raphael, 71

Truman, Harry, 87, 100, 137
Turkey, 120
Tuskegee Institute, 24, 41, 63

unions, 92, 96, 106, 135–6
United Nations, 117, 119, 124
    United Nations Children's Fund (UNICEF), 121, 124, 129
    United Nations Educational, Scientific, and Cultural Organization (UNESCO), 129
United Porto Rico/Eastern Sugar Corporation, 48
universal education, 5, 25, 28, 34, 89, 110–12, 117
University of Baghdad, 128
University of Chicago, 25
University of Illinois, 43
University of Leipzig, 21
University of Maryland, 139
University of Nebraska at Omaha, 114–15
University of Pennsylvania, 39, 41–2
University of Puerto Rico, 41
University of Santiago, 70–1
University of Santo Domingo, 70–1, 76–7
University of Wisconsin, 45
University of Wyoming, 114
Unocal oil company, 116
U.S. Agency for International Development (USAID), 115, 118–21, 127–9
U.S. Congress, xiii, 3, 29–30, 33, 65–6, 119, 123, 126–7, 140
U.S. Education Mission to Japan, 91, 92, 98
U.S. military
    Air Force, 136
    Army, 2, 8, 33, 90, 140
    Marines, 3, 51, 61–2, 68, 71, 140
    Navy, xiv–xv, 1–4, 13, 19, 23, 33, 52, 62–4, 71, 74, 80
    see also U.S. military officials: Brooke, John; Butler, Smedley; Caperton, William; Clay, Lucius; Fuller, B.H.; Garner, Jay; Guy, Henry V.; Hanna, Matthew; Knapp, Harry; Lane, Rufus; Lee, Harry; Ludlow, William; Miles, Nelson; Robison, Samuel; Russell,

John H.; Snowden, Thomas; Todd, Albert; Wood, Leonard
U.S. Naval Academy, 71
U.S. State Department, xv, 6, 51–2, 61–5, 67–8, 78, 80–1, 84, 99–106, 116, 119, 125–6
U.S. Treasury Department, 38, 47, 99–101, 125
U.S. War Department, 6, 100–4
U.S.S. Maine (U.S. warship), 3–4, 19
U.S.S. Rochester (U.S. warship), 62–4
U.S.S. Sedgwick (U.S. warship), 1–2, 13
U.S.S. Thomas (U.S. warship), 23, 74
U.S.S.R, *see* Soviet Union

Varabajal, Francisco Henriquez, 68
Virginia Military Institute, 117
Volksschule, 101

Wahhabi Islam, 116
Walker, Scott Anthony, 119
War of 1898, xiii, xvi, 1, 6, 19, 86, 88, 138, 141; *see also* Cuba; Philippines; Puerto Rico
War on Terror, xiii, xvi, 117, 125, 138, 141; *see also* Afghanistan; Iraq
Washington, Booker T., xiv, 24, 63

Washington, D.C., 3, 5–6, 14, 21, 37, 46, 62, 66, 80, 83, 127–8
Washington, George, 23, 36, 40
weapons of mass destruction, 97, 125, 133, 139
Weimar Republic, 101–2, 105
West Virginia, 126
Weyler, Valeriano, 3
White, Frank R., 27–8, 31
White House, xv, 53, 100
"White Man's Burden" (Kipling), 73
Wilson, Woodrow, 45, 51–3, 67
Wolff, Derish M., 119
women's groups, xvi, 96, 114–15
Wood, Leonard, 2, 5, 9–16, 138
Woodard, William, 90
World Bank, 129
World War I, 45, 100
World War II, 86, 88–90, 96, 99–100, 112, 125, 134

Yale University, 79
Young Turks, 46

Zahir Shah, Mohammed, 114
Zelaya, Jose, xv
Zook, George, 106–7

GPSR Compliance

The European Union's (EU) General Product Safety Regulation (GPSR) is a set of rules that requires consumer products to be safe and our obligations to ensure this.

If you have any concerns about our products, you can contact us on

ProductSafety@springernature.com

In case Publisher is established outside the EU, the EU authorized representative is:

Springer Nature Customer Service Center GmbH
Europaplatz 3
69115 Heidelberg, Germany

www.ingramcontent.com/pod-product-compliance
Lightning Source LLC
LaVergne TN
LVHW051916060526
838200LV00004B/169